VISUALLY SPEAKING

VISUALLY SPEAKING

Radio and the Renaissance of Preaching

JOLYON P. MITCHELL

T&T CLARK
EDINBURGH

T&T CLARK LTD
59 GEORGE STREET
EDINBURGH EH2 2LQ
SCOTLAND

www.tandtclark.co.uk

First published 1999

ISBN 0 567 08701 8

British Library Cataloguing-in-Publication Data
A catalogue record for this book is available from the British Library

Typeset by Fakenham Photosetting Limited
Printed and bound in Great Britain by Bell & Bain Ltd, Glasgow

To Clare

Contents

Acknowledgements

I am deeply grateful to many people for helping me write this book. My first thanks are to Professor Duncan Forrester, Professor Kevin Vanhoozer and Dr Michael Northcott for their encouragement, careful reading and constructive criticisms. I am also indebted to Professors David Buttrick, Fred Craddock, John Eldridge, Stewart Hoover, John Killinger, Thomas Long, Alan Main, Walter Ong, and Drs Judith Buchanan, David Cook, David Coulter, Anna King, Ms Catharine Beck, Kit Bowen, David Day and Garrison Keillor for a range of helpful suggestions at different stages of this project. Other broadcasters such as Andrew Barr, David Craig, Tim Dean, Andrew Monaghan, Johnston McKay and Alan Sorenson also offered valuable critical insights. In addition, thanks are due to the faculty of New College, Edinburgh University for providing teaching cover during my sabbatical term.

I am grateful to many people for their willingness to be interviewed, including: Rabbi Lionel Blue, David Coomes, Rt Revd James Jones, Revd John Newbury, Revd Angela Tilby, Canon David Winter, and in America to Fr Nick Barr, Clarence Brown, Pastor Irving Gallimore, Winnifred Garner, J. B. Lineberry, George McClintock, Toby Powers, Pastor Craig E. Soaries, Curtis Stoops, Rt Revd Don Taylor, Dr Gregg Thomas and Mark Ward. Dr Colin Morris and Rt Revd Richard Harries provided valuable written advice.

Thanks also to the archivists and librarians at BBC Caversham, the Bodleian in Oxford, the University Library in Cambridge, the National, the University and New College Libraries in Edinburgh, the WACC Library in London, the

Seminary Library in Princeton, New Jersey, and the Center for the Study of Communication and Culture at St Louis University, Missouri. They provided invaluable help with supplying a wide range of relevant published and unpublished materials. Brief sections in Part I and Part II have been adapted from earlier articles by the author. See especially Mitchell 1996a, 93–101, 1997a, 262–72, 1997b, 3–7, 1998, 51–4 and 1999, 29–34.

Finally, I offer special thanks to Peter Mitchell, Mark Birchall, Angie Inchley, John Pritchard and, most of all, Clare Mitchell for their reading of the manuscript in its various drafts. It is to Clare, who is a natural word artist, that this book is dedicated.

* * *

The author and publishers gratefully acknowledge permission to reproduce extracts from copyright material in this book.

Extracts from *Poetry and the Microphone* by George Orwell (Copyright © George Orwell, 1943) in *The Complete Works of George Orwell* (Secker & Warburg, 1998) are reproduced by kind permission of A. M. Heath & Co. Ltd on behalf of Mark Hamilton as the Literary Executor of the Estate of the Late Sonia Brownell Orwell and Martin Secker and Warburg Ltd.

Extracts from *The Average Man* by Ronald Selby Wright (1942) are reproduced by kind permission of Addison Wesley Longman Ltd, Harlow.

Scripted material from *Thought for Today* is reproduced by kind permission of Angela Tilby and Lionel Blue.

Introduction

What can preachers learn from radio broadcasters, and in particular from religious radio broadcasters? My interest in this question flows from several sources. Producing *Garrison Keillor's Radio Preachers* for BBC Radio 4 reinforced my fascination with the topic. As a radio producer, a preacher and a lecturer in communication and theology, I am intrigued by the ways in which speech radio and preaching interact.

More specifically, when I listened to many of America's radio preachers I was entranced, frustrated, amused, at times even bored. Were these two media, radio and preaching, incompatible? A Southern preacher's roaring into the microphone frequently seemed, at least to a British pair of ears, to be a resounding communication failure. As I became increasingly intrigued by their broadcasting, I expanded my research, interviews and listening in order to provide the basis for part of this book.

At the same time the success of a number of hugely popular movies heightened my sense of frustration at a communication disparity. Films such as *Titanic* and *Braveheart* were apparent communication triumphs. Here was a series of stories that had attracted large and diverse audiences and held many spellbound. The comparison between a 'fifteen-dollar' radio show and a '100 million plus' film is perhaps unfair. Nevertheless, these contrasting experiences, combined with a critical engagement with a number of music videos, TV news and drama programmes, provoked me to reflect on a range of points.

First, in today's communicative environment, where TV, film and increasingly computers appear to rule, what place remains for forms of communication that rely solely on oral discourse? Preaching looked particularly vulnerable. This led me, secondly, to look more closely at the mixed fortunes of speech radio, and especially religious speech radio. In some contexts it had survived and even prospered, whilst in others it was in danger of extinction. Religious radio had weathered, with varying degrees of success, the storm of media explosion. In consequence I asked, thirdly, what was there that preachers could learn from these contrasting experiences in radio?

This brief odyssey pointed to three prime areas for research: radio, homiletics, and the point where they intersect. Once I had identified these fields, the question of how to communicate orally in a society where a whole range of other audio-visual stimuli competes for the audience or congregation's attention took a more defined outline. It became clear that simple, yet imaginative, oral discourse has an important role to play in creating alternative worlds in our audio-visual Babel. This kind of speech is not easily achieved. Attempts to develop it raise the further question of how the meaning of ancient written biblical texts can be translated into contemporary and accessible spoken discourse.

In order to be heard preachers need to take seriously their hearers' communicative situation. The impact of the communication revolutions, or perhaps more accurately the communication evolutions,[1] must be acknowledged. I do not agree with those who argue that the rapid development, expansion and convergence of communication technologies mean that preaching has become an anachronistic form of communication.[2] However, as Stewart Hoover argues:

> Media awareness is no longer a luxury, an affectation or a hobby ... In the future, no one who wishes to develop expertise in the disciplines of teaching, ministry, counselling, or even parenting will be able to consider themselves prepared unless they have also dealt with the development of basic media awareness, consumption, and advocacy skills.[3]

The methods, impact and reception of the communications

media should not and cannot be dismissed by anyone concerned with oral communication in our media rich, but 'disenchanted public sphere'.[4] In our media age, as Donald English writes, 'congregations bring with them the news they have seen on television or heard on radio or read in the newspaper'.[5]

Our communicative context is characterised by both achievement and tragedy. We now have the ability to communicate through huge numbers of pictures and words electronically, instantaneously and globally. But these skills are tempered by our predisposition to communication breakdown, which often contributes to acts of violent revenge. It is hard to write these words without thinking of particular images of tragedy: an empty pram in the middle of rubble in Omagh, Northern Ireland or a rescue worker using bare hands to pull away the debris of the devastated American Embassy in Nairobi, Kenya. Unless we are directly affected by these outrages, such scenes tend to 'date' and rapidly fade from our individual and collective consciousness, only to be replaced, all too often, by a new set of tragic images, such as refugees fleeing Kosovo.

Over the last decade a whole range of writers has wrestled with the question of how to communicate orally in a media saturated environment.[6] Some have argued that preachers now need to learn the language and forms of film and/or television. This case has been promoted from a variety of perspectives. In *The Practice of Preaching*, for example, Paul Scott Wilson encourages preachers to 'create a movie with words'.[7] In *Imagining a Sermon* Thomas Troeger outlines a 'cinemographic technique, which includes leaping through spans of time without the sustained development of a logical argument'.[8] In a more recent text, *Ten Strategies for Preaching in a Multi-Media Culture*, Troeger suggests that preachers might 'write the sermon as a movie script'.[9] David Buttrick, author of *Homiletic*, develops a more 'analogical' style of argumentation. He draws upon a film-making analogy to demonstrate how preachers should make 'moves' in their sermons.[10]

Other writers have turned to television. Timothy Turner suggests that 'preachers should capitalize on TV's strengths and exploit its weaknesses';[11] while Derek Weber argues explicitly, 'preaching must adopt the new language and forms used by television'.[12] David Day, one of the few recent British writers on preaching, goes further and suggests we can learn from television comedians.[13] Some of these, and other scholars who argue for a 'revised rhetoric',[14] will be considered in greater detail in the first part of this book.

These approaches emphasising film and television have much to teach preachers. They do not necessarily offer, however, the complete solution to the problem of communicating orally in a mediated context where not only sight, but also hearing is frequently the recipient of electronic communication. It is possible for such terminology and methodology, when drawn uncritically from the visual media alone, to be misleading and unhelpful.[15] It is crucial to consider oral media as well.

I should stress that I am not suggesting that we ignore the form, the texts or the impact of television and film. Many of the best radio broadcasters agree. Alistair Cooke, for example, in one memorable *Letter from America* contrasts the graphic television coverage of the Vietnam conflict with the heavily censored reports of trench warfare in the First World War. He invites his listeners to imagine seeing a television report from the first day of the Somme offensive in July 1916. We see a reporter in a trench, surrounded by dead bodies, then the camera pans out and we are shown thousands of mutilated corpses on open ground and hundreds more skewered on the barbed wire defences. The correspondent estimates that probably over 50,000 British soldiers had perished in that one day. Cooke asks 'Is it conceivable that if there'd been a population of British viewers to see and hear this sort of thing that they'd simply have shaken their heads and gone off to the railway station to wave their boys off on the troop trains?'[16] Such an approach illustrates not only the power of television to broadcast arresting visual images, but also radio's potential for evoking specific images in the listener's imagination.

Television and film have played a considerable part in shaping today's communicative environment and listeners' expectations. Those concerned with developing preaching and religious radio broadcasting that will connect with congregations and audiences, should not disregard the transformations brought about by television and film. Whilst writers in homiletics are at last beginning to take increasing notice of these two media, they have largely overlooked the significant contribution of radio.[17] I believe that aspects of the theory and practice of radio broadcasting have much to offer preachers.

Radio's 'cultural significance is only beginning to receive wider recognition in academic circles'.[18] Homiletics too has also been viewed as a 'secondary discipline',[19] eclipsed by other theological disciplines.[20] This, however, is changing. Bernard Reymond calls for a re-evaluation of the relationship between homiletics and theology: 'Homiletics is not a peripheral discipline, but a *central*, even *focal*, discipline of theology.'[21] David Buttrick, whilst lamenting an earlier eclipse of homiletics, suggests that all of a sudden homiletics seems to have recovered.[22]

Reymond and Buttrick are addressing the 1990s situation. In the 1950s preaching and the sermon were at the heart of the work of many theologians. For example, Rudolf Bultmann was a regular preacher, who was keen to proclaim a demythologised kerygma which would be accessible for modern listeners. He argues in *Kerygma und Mythos*: 'The preacher in his [sic] sermons must not leave his hearer in any uncertainty as to what he requires them to believe to be true…'[23] For Bultmann preaching was a central concern.

This was also true of the preacher-theologian Karl Barth. 'More than any thinker in the century, Barth linked theology and preaching: He proposed that theology should be "nothing other than sermon preparation".'[24] Barth argued that: 'Preaching is the Word of God which he himself speaks.'[25] Significantly, the actual art of communication and audience reception received little attention from either Bultmann or Barth.

It is unwise, however, to separate content from form or message from technique. They are inextricably linked. For that reason I will consider the interactions between the methods employed by speakers and the content of their proclamation. A form of discourse, however theologically correct, which alienates or bores listeners may undermine or distort the intended message. A preacher who shouts 'angrily' about God's love for humankind may actually communicate a different world-view from the one he or she claims to espouse. A sermon that lacks appropriate images or stories may distance or even disconnect the speaker from the listeners, and risks going unheard.

This book falls into three parts, as we move from exploring issues of form to discussing underlying theological principles. The first part will provide an overview of the homiletical landscape,[26] an insight into the expanding city of radio and a series of brief expeditions into the audio-visual world of music videos. These first chapters will examine some of the challenges to and transformations in preaching and radio. They will also lay the foundations for the detailed case studies that lie at the heart of the book.

The second part of this book will be devoted to considering examples of religious radio discourse. The work of two popular Second World War religious radio broadcasters will be analysed. We will then go forward fifty years to consider the work of two current religious radio broadcasters in the United Kingdom. Next we will move across the Atlantic to analyse the work of a range of American radio preachers.

On the basis of these discussions a theological case for a discourse which engages the listener multi-sensorially will be put forward in the third and final part. In particular, I will assert that there is a need to develop a re-newed or re-formed language that draws less upon abstract theological concepts, and more upon the art of making pictures with words. It will be argued that pictorial and experiential language has the potential to create alternative imaginative worlds for listeners. This 'turn towards the imaginal' finds support from a wide range of writers in homiletics,[27] in what has been described as 'the New Homiletic'.[28] James Wallace, for example, argues that there has been a change in the 'ideal of preaching' from:

> an act of rhetorical excellence to a perception of preaching as an act of imaginative theology. Rhetoric, the art of persuasion, has given way to poesis, the art of making or shaping with words.[29]

One important strand to this book is to attend to the importance 'of making or shaping' pictures with words.

This is closely tied to the importance of engaging the total imagination, which involves not only hearing and sight, but also smell, taste and touch. This is a way of speaking which appeals multi-sensorially to the entire person, not simply to the intellect. It can therefore assist in the translation of written biblical texts into oral forms that will engage listeners successfully. The result is a form of orality that has the potential to contribute to more authentic encounters between speakers and listeners, and so reflect the embodied and transformative communicative process upon which Christianity is founded.

Two particular theological principles emerge. They are the 'embodiment principle' and the 'translation principle', and they provide the theological foundations for the form of preaching being promoted in this book. In a number of recent homiletical texts there has been a strong critique of the translation hermeneutic for preachers. I believe many of these arguments to be flawed. Preachers intent on communicating today cannot help but be involved in some form of translation and embodiment. In the light of this discussion I will therefore conclude with some specific guidelines for preachers.

Notes

1. Traber 1993. He argues provocatively that: 'All genuine revolutions are fundamentally communication revolutions', 30. See also: Weber 1993, 19–20.
2. See Runia 1983. See also: (i) Crowley and Heyer 1995. This text provides a useful range of important articles on the history and development of communication. (ii) Hoover 1982. On the basis of an extensive discussion of the expansion and convergence of various communication technologies, especially television, he argues that 'a revolution is happening, a revolution that will change forever most of what we know and do', 145. (iii) Baldwin, McVoy and Steinfield 1996. This text explores a number of issues relating to the convergence of communication technologies through the development of an integrated broadband system. See especially Chapter 6: 'Convergence of Voice/Video/Data Information'.
3. Hoover 1982, 155.
4. Stevenson 1995. Note the fusing of Weberian and Habermasian terminology.
5. English 1996, 21–2. The preacher, for English, should go beyond the role of observer to interpreter.

6. See, for example, Troeger 1990, especially his 'Theological Reflection on Remote Control', and 'Video Replay in Preacher's Head', 16–23, and Wilson-Kastner 1989.
7. Wilson 1996, 183, 255, 267. This is a recurring theme in this text.
8. Troeger 1990, 48.
9. Troeger 1996, 48–57.
10. I am using this term in the non-technical theological sense to mean that Buttrick draws a likeness between preaching and camera movement. See Buttrick 1987, 55.
11. Turner 1995, 73.
12. Weber 1993, 7.
13. Day 1998, see 65–75.
14. Reymond 1993a, 19–29. See especially the section on 'The Need for a Revised Rhetoric', 26.
15. For example, at times, the vast gulf between the experience of sprawling in a comfy cinema seat on a Saturday night engaged by twenty foot images and sound to match, and wriggling in an uncomfortably hard pew on a Sunday morning, is ignored too easily in these discussions.
16. Alistair Cooke, 'Now Here is the Nightly News', originally transmitted June 1970, from Cooke 1996.
17. The significant exceptions to this observation are to be found in (i) The 1995 Mair Lectures. Johnston McKay, BBC Radio Scotland Head of Religious Radio, occasionally touches on this theme, see McKay 1997. (ii) A three-page article by the former Head of Religious Broadcasting for BBC World Service, Pauline M. Webb, 1988. This is a brief attempt to focus on the challenges facing those who 'aspire to use these [radio and television] modern media as their pulpit', 18. (iii) A short article by the Bishop of Oxford, Richard Harries. See Harries 1984, 24–7.
18. Wilby and Conroy, 1994, 15. For other recent texts on radio see also, Augaitis and Lander 1994, Crisell 1994, Pease and Dennis 1995, Scannell 1996, Biernatzki 1997, Shingler and Wieringa 1998.
19. Reymond 1993b, 30–43, see 38. Reymond argues that dogmaticians and ethics professors consider homiletics as a 'secondary discipline, which comes after other theological disciplines have finished their work', 30.
20. See Buttrick 1996. Buttrick speaks of 'the eclipse of homiletics', 75, and later suggests that: 'all of a sudden, homiletics seems to have recovered', 77.
21. Reymond 1993b, 38.

22. Buttrick 1996, 75.
23. Bultmann 1961 (1948), 15. See also Hilkert 1998, 23–24.
24. Buttrick, 'Introduction' to Barth 1991 (1963), 8.
25. Barth 1991, 44. See also Barth 1975 (1932), especially 56 and 88–99 ('The Word of God preached'). See also Hilkert 1998, 20–23.
26. 'Homiletical landscape' refers in this context to recent significant studies in homiletics that are pertinent to this book. Troeger employs a contrasting metaphor, 'city of homiletical wisdom', to describe significant texts in homiletics. Troeger 1990, 23. See: 'Finding Help in the City of Homiletical Wisdom', 23–6.
27. For the 'turn towards the imaginal' see Wallace 1995, 8. See also Wilson 1988, and Troeger 1990.
28. See Reid 1995, 1–13. 'The paradigm shift in homiletics, known as the New Homiletic, has been occurring during the past two decades primarily in Protestant homiletical theory. The shape of the new paradigm has now been well defined. It represents a radical shift away from the rationalistic and propositional logics of argumentation as the basis of sermon invention and arrangement', 7. One of the central characteristics of the New Homiletic is the 'creation of an affective experience for the audience of a sermon', 7.
29. Ibid., 8.

PART I

Preaching and Radio

CHAPTER 1

Preaching in Crisis

Papa don't preach.
You always taught me right from wrong . . .
Papa don't preach.
I've made up my mind . . .
Papa don't preach.[1]

Madonna's hit song *Papa Don't Preach* shows how the verb 'preach' often now reverberates with negative associations.[2] The words 'preach' and 'preaching' have come to mean 'to give unwelcome or unnecessary moral or religious advice'.[3] People don't want to be preached at. Madonna is by no means a lone voice. The refrain 'don't preach' extends far beyond the world of MTV (Music Television). Some twenty years ago an anonymous editorial in the *Expository Times* made the point that 'we live in an age when preaching is out of favour'. It continued:

> Some today question the effectiveness, even the possibility, of speaking intelligibly to a congregation consisting of persons with widely differing backgrounds, intelligence, education and religious experience. Is not discussion the only satisfactory way of education and communication?[4]

Many people, both inside and outside the church, echo these sentiments and see preaching as an anachronistic and idiosyncratic form of communication, which has no use or relevance for the third millennium. If its critics are to be believed, preaching is undoubtedly in crisis.

The causes and nature of this crisis are difficult to disentangle, but it is important that we try. As Susan White remarks:

> the causes of the current crisis in preaching are extraordinarily complex and ambiguous, deeply rooted in the culture of postmodernity. This culture, like any other, involves firmly embedded attitudes about such things as authority structures, human language and interpersonal relationships. If we aim to restore the power of the preaching office, it is imperative that we understand the problems and possibilities of the context within which we preach.[5]

The precise shape of some of these challenges will be discussed later. They have led to what could be described as a threefold crisis in preaching: a crisis of methodology and a crisis of listening, which in turn have contributed to a crisis of confidence in preaching. These crises strike at the communicative core of preaching. Put in more explicitly Aristotelian rhetorical terms it suggests that the *logos* of preaching, the *ethos* of the preacher and the *pathos* of the congregation have been challenged both individually and corporately.[6]

It would be possible to conclude that these crises have permanently damaged the work of the preacher, and have therefore become a block to effective oral communication. Viewed in this way, it is not surprising that some suggest traditional forms of preaching have *no* future and argue that:

> The pulpit monologue can no longer survive; we must find new forms which involve the congregation in participatory communication and which reach them through films, dance, and musical experiences that supplement, if not abolish, the spoken word.[7]

Preachers can respond to this challenge in a number of ways.[8] For some the simple answer is to follow the advice and not preach, to view the sermon as an outdated and limited form of communication. David Norrington, for example, argues that sermons have little place in today's church: 'Preachers today should be aware of the cultural limitations of their audience.' He asserts that: 'there is no compelling reason to try to reeducate hearers to appreciate a popular method of yesterday'.[9] In this view preaching should be abandoned as an anachronistic and ineffective means of communication. Some pastors, for example, have led their churches away from having regular sermons, replacing them with discussions or participatory drama.[10]

A second, more optimistic option would be simply to highlight the areas where preaching is experiencing a renaissance, and argue that these are successful models worth imitating.[11] But imitation without any understanding of the theological and communicative issues is likely to be at best only a temporary stopgap and at worst a sterile, self-defeating exercise. A third approach, and the one advocated in this book, is 'to preach', but 'to preach differently', taking more notice of our present communicative context and the particular crises that face preachers.

Crisis in Listening

The cinematic techniques employed by the producers of *Papa Don't Preach* illustrate certain characteristics of our communicative environment. The video itself lasts just over five minutes, but crams into this brief time over sixty shots. Compared with some more recent music videos, even this number appears low. Images are juxtaposed with each other in quick succession, telling the simple story of a young girl asserting her romantic independence, her right to have her baby, and a middle-aged father unhappy at first with her flight from the nest. Through flashbacks of an old cine-camera, we see how he remembers her affectionately as a toddler and is now torn by her growing up and her becoming pregnant. He eventually backs down, and the final scene is of a reconciliatory embrace between father and daughter.

This familiar story is brought to life with shots of the New York skyline, the Staten Island ferry, and character close-ups. Interspersed throughout the video are brief shots of Madonna, dressed alluringly, dancing and singing in a small, darkened studio. These add pace and sensuality to the video. In many ways it could be described as a 'typical' music video, especially in the way it attempts to stir the emotions of the audience through the rapid cutting, the juxtaposition of images, and its simple narrative structure. Pat Aufderheide believes that:

> One of music video's distinctive features as a social expression is its open-ended quality, aiming to engulf the viewer in its communication with itself, its fashioning of an alternative world where image is reality.[12]

Papa Don't Preach does fashion an alternative world, a world in which the electronic image appears to be reality. The images themselves give meaning to the lyrics, and offer a 'gloss' on what is meant by the frequently repeated lyric 'Papa don't preach'. Interestingly, this particular video lacks the 'open-ended quality' found in so many other music videos, as the final hug between father and daughter brings a sense of closure. If this form of 'engulfing' video is compared with a preacher's lone voice, a vast chasm between the two communication methodologies becomes apparent, even if they are both attempting, in radically different ways, to create an alternative world.[13] A person brought up on this style of television may have difficulty attending to sermons, which differ so radically from the language of MTV.[14]

While this form of entertainment, the music video, has its own distinctive style, it nevertheless employs many of the standard tools of television, perhaps in a more heightened form.[15] In other words, characteristics of MTV such as rapid cuts, fast camera angle switches, and reliance upon images to tell the story, are also true of other styles of more traditional television. It is as if television speaks the same root language, but expresses itself in different dialects. This basic homogeneity within the language of television adds weight to Leander Keck's observation that it may also have undermined our ability to listen. Television, in his eyes: 'has made it ever more difficult for people to attend carefully to merely verbal communication ... This loss of attentiveness to verbal communication, to oral discourse, has eroded the place of the sermon.'[16] As Keck understands it, the apparent demise of careful listening to oral discourse is but one of the 'grave clothes' constricting today's preacher.[17] Writers on both sides of the Atlantic support the view that audiences now struggle to concentrate as they listen to oral discourse.

Michael Rogness, based at Luther North-western Seminary in St Paul, Minnesota, argues that television 'has produced a passive audience. We are used to listening with half an ear – easily distracted. Translate this to the church, and we have people in the pews who listen for a few minutes, then think about something else.'[18] John Stott, based at All Souls, Langham Place, London, believes that 'preachers have to reckon with a TV-conditioned congregation' and:

> We have a colossal task on our hands if we hope to counteract the baneful tendencies of much modern television. We can no longer assume that people either want to listen to sermons, or indeed are able to listen. When they are accustomed to the swiftly moving images of the screen, how can we expect them to give their attention to one person talking, no frills, no light relief and nothing else to look at?[19]

Each in his own way, Stott and Rogness point to the rivalry between 'the box and the pulpit'.[20] Whilst they avoid explicitly talking about a crisis in preaching, they acknowledge the challenge of image-driven television to the oral medium of preaching.

With television comes the remote channel control 'zapper'. Bernard Reymond, a Swiss Professor of Practical Theology, claims that:

> 'Zapping' has become part of normal behaviour; in front of the TV, the average viewer switches from one channel to another immediately they feel bored; faced with a sermon from the pulpit, they still zapp around in their minds, letting it [sic] wander wherever it will.[21]

The reductionist and fragmentary tendencies of television have, in Reymond's eyes, contributed to a change in listening habits and expectations. These changes have contributed to what could be described as the crisis of attention to preaching.

Stott, Rogness and Reymond make cogent cases. I would sound a note of caution about their arguments, however, as they leave many of their conclusions about the impact of television on listening unsubstantiated. They appear to rely too heavily on what is often described as a hypodermic needle model of communication. This is a 'mechanistic and unsophisticated model of media–audience relationship, which sees the media as "injecting" values, ideas and information into each individual in a passive and atomised audience, thereby producing a direct and unmediated effect'.[22] Their positions presuppose passive audiences who do not actively appropriate meaning from media for themselves. Their approach towards television and listening also reflects other assertions about the detrimental effects of television cited elsewhere in the academy.[23]

In short, certain writers in homiletics argue that television has shortened our attention span. In the literature discussed to date, however, little empirical data is used to support these claims. The danger with such an approach is that it can too easily slide into an over-simplistic 'direct effects' and 'passive audience' understanding of television's influence.[24]

We need to develop a more sophisticated understanding of how audiences use audio-visual forms of communication, and television in particular, and how this usage can cultivate them into particular habits of attending, viewing and listening.[25] Such a twofold approach has the advantage of recognising both the significance of audience use of the media, and that 'exposure to television programmes [and other media] will, over time, have a cumulative influence on viewers' perceptions of the world and their place in it'.[26] My belief is that the cumulative influence of the form and content of the electronic media has not only influenced how congregations now listen, but also provided the resources for active audiences to make meanings for themselves.

I am not arguing that one single video, *Papa Don't Preach*, has directly altered the way in which people listen; nor would I assert that the music video genre of television is solely responsible for changed attention habits. I do, however, want to suggest that repeated exposure to the 'audio-visual tapestry',[27] of which this video is but one example, has a cumulative and gradual influence on how audiences and congregations attend to and construct their own world-views.

Crisis in Confidence

Contrast the production values of the video *Papa Don't Preach* with those employed in producing an average sermon and it is clear that the preacher is often only an amateur in a world of professional communicators. She or he is no longer the only educated voice in the village or town. The preacher is one voice amongst a multitude of others, competing for an audience now presented with a kaleidoscopic choice of rival audio-visual productions.

In one evening of media consumption we can be faced with a range of stories and images that raise questions about the credibility and relevance of a Christian world-view. A Sudanese or Kosovan refugee stares hungrily out at the camera. A Polish Catholic plants a cross outside Auschwitz. An Islamic guide points to the place where thousands of women and children were massacred by eleventh-century 'Christian' crusaders. A dramatic recreation of Charles Darwin's voyages leads into a biologist's lucid defence of the 'selfish gene' theory. A theoretical astrophysicist speaks from his wheelchair of ripples on the edge of the universe, life on other planets and reading the mind of God. Adverts take us to the Garden of Eden with certain deodorants and to hell without a particular lager. A Jewish rabbi and a New Testament scholar debate the historical validity of the Resurrection accounts in the Gospels. The freedom of the individual viewer or listener to choose which voice or story, if any, to listen to is epitomised by Madonna's 'I've made my mind up' line in *Papa Don't Preach.* It is not surprising that we are so often told that single metanarratives are no more.

Increasingly informed and entertained by other sources of communication, congregations are now more likely to test the words of the preacher for credibility and relevance. The way in which Christianity itself has, according to Jürgen Moltmann, 'faced a growing crisis of relevance and credibility' since the Second World War[28] has undoubtedly also contributed to the questioning of the authority, and perhaps also the ethos, of the preacher and therefore of Christian discourse itself.

Such developments have further eroded the authority of the preacher. This is a point that Fred Craddock makes in his frequently cited book, *As One Without Authority* (1979 [1971]). Craddock spoke to what some writers described as an 'anti-authoritarian age'.[29] He emphasised how the questioning of authority had brought 'about a new relationship between speaker and listener'.[30] Just as the daughter asserts her independence from her father's authority in *Papa Don't Preach*, so listeners have asserted their freedom from the traditional authority of preachers. Part of the genius of Craddock's approach is that he appears to have anticipated some of the discussions surrounding postmodernism where it is argued that we now operate with a more 'playful, less authoritative, less authority-bound tone' to our discourse.[31]

Leander Keck draws on the Johannine image of Lazarus, 'bound with bandages and his face wrapped with a cloth', to symbolise the 'plight of the preacher and preaching today'.[32] He suggests that 'one still detects widespread dismay over the state of preaching. Preachers themselves often admit that this element of their vocation is in general disarray...'.[33] Keck's analysis of the crisis in preaching focuses primarily on the appropriate use of the Bible. He begins, however, by arguing that 'many preachers have lost confidence in the importance of preaching'.[34] He too believes that television may be partly to blame for this crisis in confidence.

On such grounds it is too easy to become pessimistic about the future of preaching, and lose confidence in its importance. Some writers are more optimistic. Jay Adams asserts that: 'the present crisis in preaching need not, indeed *must* not, be permitted to continue'.[35] In *Preaching With Purpose: The Urgent Task of Homiletics*, he claims that: 'Men and women (and especially young people) are being turned away from Christ and His church by dull, unarresting, unedifying, and aimless preaching.'[36] This language is uncompromising, and illustrates how much preaching is perceived to be in crisis even from within the church. It also emphasises the need for authentic preaching which is lively, relevant and engaging.

Richard Eslinger also believes that 'Preaching is in crisis'.[37] Whilst the 'way out, toward new effectiveness in preaching is not yet clear', the 'old/topical approach to preaching is critically, if not terminally ill'.[38] Significantly, in *A New Hearing*, he does not argue that preaching itself is 'terminally ill'. Rather it is the 'old conceptual' approach which is suffering sickness, perhaps unto death.[39] It might be more precise, therefore, to alter Eslinger's opening premise so that it reads: preaching is in a crisis in methodology.

Crisis in Method

Some writers in homiletics, therefore, believe that preaching is facing a methodological crisis. This, of course, is closely related to the two crises already considered. We have already noted the claim that frequent exposure to electronic audio-visual stimuli, epitomised by television, has led many people to listen less attentively to sermons[40] and to have less confidence in the act of preaching.[41] This has been described as a crisis in listening and a crisis in confidence. Here we will consider transformations in forms of orality and discourse, and then turn to the suggestion that these transformations have led preaching to a methodological crisis.

In *Eloquence in an Electronic Age* Kathleen Hall Jamieson identifies a significant transformation in orality. She believes that:

> Television has changed public discourse dramatically. Increasingly, eloquence is visual, not verbal. Where once we expected messages laced with impassioned appeals, now we respond positively to a cooler, more conversational art; where once audiences expected to be conquered by an art bent on battle, today's television viewer expects instead an intimate rhetoric of conciliation.[42]

I agree. Eloquence is gradually becoming more conversational. This 'democratisation' of discourse has serious consequences for preachers.[43]

A more colloquial and spontaneous style of orality is now expected. Alyce McKenzie, for example, believes that:

> evidence is growing that our society is shifting from a literate to a postliterate or 'secondary orality culture'.[44] For several centuries we have prized the memorable, formal, respectable qualities of written discourse. Now we are shifting to one that prefers communications that epitomize the colloquial, seemingly spontaneous character of oral communication.[45]

Such changes in public discourse have significant implications for preaching methodology. A sermon that is constructed as a written text may display literary lucidity but may lack the apparent spontaneity or colloquialisms necessary for oral communication.[46] Later in this book we will see that many of the best religious radio broadcasters made or make use of a conversational form of discourse. These broadcasters are very different from the preacher who is constricted by relying on a written text which would be better 'read, silently, by the eye', than 'heard by the ear'.[47] The shift towards a more conversational form of public discourse on television and radio is one factor, therefore, which has contributed to the crisis of methodology in preaching. It is by no means the only factor.

There is an oft repeated critical assertion that preaching is a monologue,[48] in an age more used to dialogue and discussion.[49] A preacher can be caricatured as little more than a talking head murmuring in an empty church, and competing with the vastly more eye-catching methods employed by today's highly skilled television and film producers. Amos Wilder provides an alternative simile: 'The preacher, we are told, is like a man speaking into a dead microphone.'[50] Compare this with a music video and contemplate the differences.

One of the characteristics of music videos such as *Papa Don't Preach* is their lack of explicit 'preaching'. Instead, they sometimes tell a story through images, or more often work in a 'non-narrative form' and 'rely on *mood* and *emotion*', avoiding abstract verbal concepts.[51] The language spoken here is a visual one. Tom Freston, MTV president, said of his own channel that: 'When you get down to it, the only thing we have is image'.[52] He emphasises the power not of the word, but of the image, to 'catch an audience'.

Even in the early 1970s Fred Craddock was arguing that speech and, in particular, words had lost much of their former power.[53] Barbara Brown Taylor reiterated this point in the late 1990s: 'Words keep coming at us through an ever-expanding variety of media – so many words that sometimes it sounds as if we live our lives against a wall of constant noise.'[54] The cacophony of sound that now floods our imaginations limits our openness to words of significance.

Moreover, our modern culture may be 'favoring the eye over the ear'. This 'visually orientated world'[55] may have further undermined the power of words. It is possible that this shift has transformed the function of words. Kathleen Hall Jamieson believes that:

> When visual images can communicate meaning instantaneously to individuals of different languages and faiths around the world, the function of words changes. In such a world, words contextualize pictures and specify desirable or practical courses of ensuing action.[56]

Both Jamieson and Craddock offer useful insights into this transformed cultural setting.[57] Part of the reason for this perceptiveness is not only their reflection on how words have lost some of their original power, but also their serious engagement with the apparent visual turn in communication.[58] The multiplicity of images used in *Papa Don't Preach* reflects the way electronic images are increasingly drawn upon to entertain, to inform and even to educate. This fact has contributed to the crises both in methodology and in listening, which have helped to undermine confidence in preaching.

Conclusion

One response to such an analysis would be for pastors to withdraw from preaching, and concentrate on pastoral care, small discussion groups or liturgical and musical excellence. A more positive response is to argue that our present communicative context raises not only obstacles, but also new opportunities for preachers. If, as Rodney Kennedy argues, 'Christian preaching faces a perpetual crisis',[59] then there are lessons to be learnt from the history of how preaching has adapted to previous transformations in the communicative environment.[60] The advent of the printing press, for example, could have been seen as a direct challenge to preaching.[61] Instead, for reformers, such as Martin Luther, it became a powerful tool for facilitating both the wider dissemination of their sermons and the education of their literate listeners,[62] who could have now read the biblical texts for themselves before hearing the sermon. Similarly, the advent of electronic audio-visual stimuli could be seen as dealing a fatal blow to preaching. The contention of this book is that our changed context does not toll the death-bell for the sermon. Rather, it provides new challenges and opportunities for preachers who are willing to engage critically with our present communicative setting.

Preaching then is facing a series of crises, which raise serious challenges for those seeking to invite their listeners to participate in the Christian story. First, the preacher is faced with the challenge of speaking to an easily distracted audience, many of whom are no longer accustomed to listening to a single speaker for a long period of time. Secondly, when so many other powerful forms of electronic communication are competing for their listeners' imaginations, the preacher can understandably lose confidence in preaching as an effective form of communication. Thirdly, as a communicator probably nurtured in a literary culture, the preacher needs to face the recent transformations in orality, such as those exemplified by the evolving discursive practices employed on television and radio.

Notes

1. Madonna, *Papa Don't Preach* (1986), from *The Immaculate Collection*, Warner Music Vision, 1990.
2. For examples of negative connotations see Nicholas Jones 1995, 2. He relates how in 1992 David Evans, a Conservative MP, told the BBC Radio 4's *World at One* 'that if ministers could not adhere to the "moral standards they are preaching at us every day" then they ought not stay in office'. Or the future Labour Home Secretary Jack Straw, interviewed prior to the 1997 election on *Everyman*, who asserted that he doesn't 'want to preach' on issues of faith or morality within the political arena. Michael Roberts, producer, *Everyman: Vote, Vote, Vote for the Almighty*, London: BBC 1, 27 October 1996. Or Professor Patricia Williams, speaking about her approach in her 1997 Reith Lectures, *A Genealogy of Race – Towards a Theory of Grace*: 'I don't want to preach solutions from on high, but I do believe that to a very great extent we dream our worlds into being.' *The Guardian*, 23 January 1997, G2, 5. Or Dr David Starkey, on Radio 4's *Moral Maze*, 1 May 1997, where the word 'preaching' was used at least six times during a debate on children's sex education. Starkey told 'witness' Colin Hart: 'You want preaching of a particular view!' and 'You are ignoring the fact preaching does not change behaviour!'

3. Garmonsway 1969, 550.
4. Editorial, *Expository Times* 1977, 237–8, see esp. 237.
5. White 1998, 3–4.
6. Kennedy 1980. See also Aristotle 1991, 1 3. 47. 'A speech [situation] consists of three things: a speaker and a subject on which he speaks and someone addressed.' See also Cunningham 1990.
7. Sleeth 1986, 27. It is clear from the entire text that Sleeth does not himself hold this view.
8. Brindley 1996, 2. Brindley outlines three options: (i) ignore the problem, (ii) compromise by turning sermons into 'brief chats', or (iii) enter into a conspiracy of silence between the congregation and the preacher.
9. Norrington 1996, 96.
10. See, for example, Corneck 1995. Corneck, an Anglican vicar in Deptford, London, reflects on the process and rationale of this move away from preaching.
11. Green and Jackman 1995, see especially 11–23.
12. Aufderheide 1986, 57–78.
13. Brueggemann 1995, 313–29. He argues that 'the preacher must show how this counter-text of the gospel is a genuine alternative.' 321.
14. See Schultze *et al.* 1991, Ch. 7, 'Rocking to Images: The Music Television Revolution'. By 1986 'MTV and its imitators reached 43 percent of all American teenagers every week ... By 1989, 47 million American homes received MTV', 179. This has led some Christian communicators to attempt to translate biblical stories into the language of the music video as seen on MTV (Music Television). See, for example, *A Father and Two Sons,* a music video interpretation of Luke 15.11–32, produced by Conduit Communications for the American Bible Society, 1995.
15. The MTV style is a relatively new arrival as a form of TV. Raymond Williams' chapter on 'The forms of television' does not include this development within his section on 'New Forms' of television, 44–77. See Williams 1990 (1975).
16. Keck 1978, 40.
17. Keck also argues that preachers have been affected by the 'general revolt against authority', the 'incongruity between lived experience and orderly presentation of the sermon' and the 'loss of certitude' concerning biblical authority. Ibid., 41–7.
18. Rogness 1994, 29. 'One of the results of passive listening is superficial listening.' See also Weber 1993.
19. Stott 1982, 75. Stott had earlier pessimistically argued that TV has

the tendency to make audiences physically lazy, intellectually uncritical, emotionally insensitive, psychologically confused, and morally disorientated. 70–2.

20. Ibid., 69.
21. Reymond 1993a, 19–29. He believes that 'people are becoming trained by TV to share out their attention in quite new ways'. 24.
22. O'Sullivan, Hartley, Saunders and Fiske 1983, 105. See also Søgaard 1993, 41. Søgaard uses a simple, but helpful, diagram to illustrate the syringe model.
23. See, for example, Postman 1985; or Novak 1982, 335–50. Novak argues that 'television is a molder [sic] of the soul's geography', which speeds up the rhythm of attention, and therefore creates high expectations for audiences. 336ff. See also Vibert 1993, 19. Vibert suggests: 'television provides a threat to serious preaching ... [as] listening capacities are reduced because television has taught us to expect a frequent change in style of presentation – of presenter, scenery, topic – and this is to be accompanied by a rapid succession of visual images. Preaching, it is presumed, is too long and too dull in a TV age.' See also a briefer version of his argument in his 1992 article, 147–58.
24. In fact there is a huge literature on media effects research; recent useful introductory texts include: McQuail 1994 (see especially Chapters 13 and 14); Curran and Gurevitch 1991, especially 'On Understanding and Misunderstanding Media Effects', 235–66; and Lowery and DeFleur 1995.
25. 'Cultivation analysis looks at [television's] messages as an environment within which people live, define themselves and others, and develop and maintain their beliefs and assumptions about reality.' Morgan and Signorielli 1990, 18.
26. Gauntlett 1995, 97.
27. Berry and Asamen 1993, 1. Television is described as an 'audio-visual tapestry on which is being woven a complex and ever-changing national and international set of images that are hung on the small screen for all to see'.
28. Moltmann 1974, 8.
29. Editorial, *Expository Times* 1977. 'We live in an anti-authoritarian age and a society which is aggressively egalitarian. We have come to suspect the "expert". Thus the parson in the pulpit is felt to belong to a by-gone age and to be opposed to values which are held dear by Christians as well as humanists.' 237.
30. Craddock 1979 (1971), 14.
31. See Hebdige 1988, 225–6.

32. Keck 1978, 38 and John 11:44.
33. Ibid, 39.
34. Ibid., 40.
35. Adams 1982, xi.
36. Ibid., xi.
37. Eslinger 1987, 'Preaching is in crisis. This awareness has been with us for some time now, reducing pastoral morale and congregational fervor.' 11.
38. Ibid., 11.
39. Ibid., 11.
40. See Higdon 1995. Higdon argues: 'Competition from television accompanied by a limited attention span has killed long sermons. Many people have the Radio 4 "Today" syndrome – where they have got used to listening to one news item after another, each never lasting more than two minutes, and with the thirty second commercial – these have taken their toll on the sermon.' 5. (Note: Some *Today* features last for 3 or 4 minutes.)
41. Coggan 1987. Coggan's memorable story of a church without a permanent pulpit and a wobbly little stand in its place illustrates how some clergy see no need for a pulpit or a traditional sermon. 24–5. This story also reveals how some preachers have lost confidence in the role of preaching.
42. Jamieson 1988, 44.
43. See Fairclough 1995, on 'democratisation' of media discourse, 148–9.
44. McKenzie here puts into inverted commas Walter Ong's phrase of 'secondary orality culture'. She does not cite Ong, but appears to have been influenced by him in her discussion of 'orality and the recovery of the proverb'. See Chapter 8 of this book.
45. McKenzie 1996, xix.
46. This is a danger identified by many writers in homiletics. See, for example, Jacks 1996; or Hoefler n.d.
47. Jacks 1996, 1.
48. Runia 1983, 9–10. Runia cites R. E. O. White's memorable phrase that a sermon is 'a monstrous monologue by a moron to mutes' from White 1973, 5. Discussed and cited as 'monotonous monologue' in Day 1998, 1.
49. Bond 1991. He argues that the 'height' of the pulpit and 'distance' from the pew represent the gulf between speaker and listener. This gap leaves preachers 'blind, deaf and apathetic, it will soon leave us mute. Burnout is an apt metaphor. The fuel is spent, the fire grows cold. Alone in our preaching, there is no fuel to build a new fire.' 4.

50. Wilder 1971, 1–2.
51. Bob Pittman, chairman MTV, in Schultze *et al.* 1991, 192.
52. Schultze *et al.* 1991, 178.
53. Craddock 1979, 5.
54. Taylor 1998, 13.
55. See Eslinger 1987, 95–132, esp. 98.
56. Jamieson 1988, 126.
57. It is important to recognise that whilst Stott and Runia identify 'contemporary objections' to preaching, they avoid relegating it to the communications dustbin. It is clear from both Stott 1982 and Runia 1983, that whilst they acknowledge a crisis of confidence in aspects of the homiletical method, they have no wish to abandon preaching itself. As apologists for preaching they do portray preaching as embattled; though ultimately both texts read more like a summons to arms than a call to surrender. They are attempting, in different ways, to effect a renewal in confidence in preaching.
58. See Warren 1992, 68. Warren argues: 'with film, television and print technology allowing the cheap reproduction of multi-color graphics, almost all in the post-industrial West are immersed in images. Society is so much awash in them that the prevalence of images is a dominant characteristic of our time.' See also Warren 1997.
59. Kennedy 1993, 1. Kennedy believes that 'the crisis of preaching has been expressed' in a variety of 'ways: ... as secularism vs. supernaturalism, liberalism vs. conservatism, science vs. poetry, concept vs. symbol, rationality vs. irrationality, and secular vs. sacred.' 8. (see his endnote 1).
60. Weber, 1991. See 'The Church's Use of the Media', 8–9. Weber focuses on the significance of the printing press for the Reformation.
61. ibid., 9. See Eisenstein, 1993, especially Chapter 6, 'Western Christendom disrupted: resetting the stage for the Reformation', 148–86.
62. See Matheson 1998. Matheson suggests that: 'Printed sermons are ... a particularly useful example of literature on the edge of a predominantly oral, popular culture.' 20.

CHAPTER 2

Preaching in Transformation

Preaching in our media saturated society is being seriously challenged. We now need to look at a variety of new approaches to the ancient art of preaching[1] that have sought to respond positively to these challenges. This chapter will identify aspects of this audio-visual context and explore the ways in which various writers in homiletics have attempted to relate their approaches to our rapidly evolving communicative environment.

From Single-Camera to Multi-Camera Discourse

Contrast action movies in the 1990s, such as *Jurassic Park, Braveheart* and *Titanic,* with the earliest films, such as *La Sortie des Ouvriers de l'Usine Lumière.* The latter was shot by the Lumière brothers in 1895. They used a stationary camera as workers left the Lumières' factory.[2] The result, breathtaking to viewers over a hundred years ago, is a static backdrop with moving figures on it. The current video and movie industries, exemplified by *Papa Don't Preach* and the 'action adventure' film genre, rely on very different techniques. Tight editing, rapid cuts and computer-created scenes combine with changing camera angles to allow the viewers to gaze at something or to see and hear far more than they ever could without the camera's aid.[3] In other words there has been a dramatic shift in how cameras capture a scene on film. In the earliest days of cinema, a single stationary camera recorded a scene. As the technology developed, film-makers experimented with cameras placed on the back of trains, on cars and even in balloons. Cameras were no longer locked to a single, static location. Today the range of angles or movement available to film-makers and television directors is vast.[4] The advent of computer-created special effects has further extended the directors' range of choices. Consider, for example, the effects in the Star Wars films and *The Matrix.* Viewers have been conditioned to expect motion, speed and variety.

My point here is not simply that preaching is now set in a highly competitive communicative environment, but that a speaker who acts like one of the earliest cameras in his or her discourse and adopts a single, static or fixed point of view may seem slow and turgid to an audience more used to rapid shifts in viewing angles.[5] David Buttrick argues:

> In an earlier era, movie directors worked with a fixed-location camera and moved actors around in front of the lens. Once upon a time the procedure was considered reality, but now when we view old films on late-night TV, they seem stilted and quite unreal. Today directors use a camera on a moving boom so that camera angles change, lenses widen or narrow, distances vary, imitating the actual way we perceive reality ... Twentieth-century consciousness views the world from many different standpoints.[6]

It is significant, however, that Buttrick does not uncritically adopt and translate cinematic techniques in his methodology for movement in sermons. He argues that speakers to large groups, wishing to effect successful moves, need to take time with their transitions:

> Group consciousness simply cannot handle rapid shifts in subject matter. To move along from subject to subject every few sentences would 'freak out' an audience; the effect would be similar to watching a movie film that has been speeded up many times the normal frames per minute. Minds will wander when pace is intense.[7]

Buttrick may draw upon film analogies to support his case, but he does not go so far as to argue that preachers should mimic cinematic devices such as rapid camera movement and swift shifts in point of view in their oral discourse. It is evident from this that he has a clear understanding of the distinction between oral and other audio-visual forms of communication. This can also be seen by the way in which he draws extensively upon the analogy of a photographic camera to consider the 'point-of-view in moves', and how to vary 'focal field, lens depth and focal depth' in preaching.[8]

Buttrick's use of cinematic and photographic analogies in *Homiletic* demonstrates sensitivity to his communicative context. He is aware that listeners are used to a range of electronic communication. Whilst these modern media appear to have influenced the development of some of his homiletical theories, it is clear that he is cautious and critical in the lessons he applies from visual media to oral communication. His reminder of the fundamental differences between preaching and modern media serves as a useful warning to those seeking to glean homiletical lessons from religious radio broadcasting.

David Buttrick is an example of someone who has integrated developments in communication into his homiletical method. A good test of his approach is to reflect on how Buttrick's methodology might work out in practice. Consider, for example, the parable of the good Samaritan (Luke 10:29–37), where the story could be retold from a variety of angles. By persuading the listener to stand by the listening lawyer, walk with the religious professionals and lie in the ditch with the mugged traveller, the preacher can provide provocative insights into this story.[9] Adding a view from the inn might elicit a new response to this familiar parable.[10]

Such shifts from one point of view to another are by no means a new homiletical technique. The danger, however, of being locked into one viewpoint remains. On the basis of Buttrick's argument, this could be described as a single fixed-camera approach, which merely allows the characters to pass across the screen of the imagination, or which simply views the entire story from one perspective. This will also limit the story's power for multi-angle conditioned listeners. A better form could be described as a multi-camera approach. If sensitively handled, this could lead listeners into and through a story and so allow them to experience its movement and its depth.[11]

For Buttrick the power lies not in discovering and making a

single point in three different ways, but rather in enabling listeners to move through the story itself and so encounter its original force afresh. This multi-camera approach appears to have the potential to engage, even empower, listeners who are used to frequent changes of point of view in the cinema or on the small screen. The result may more closely reflect what Mary Boys describes as 'a parabolic form of teaching',[12] which will draw listeners into 'alternative' imaginings.[13] So the listener actually experiences the story first hand.

The methodology advocated by Buttrick, characterised as the move from a single fixed-camera form of preaching to a multi-camera approach to preaching, is robust, especially when it is recognised that both photographic and cinematographic developments have ensured that listeners are now used to viewing from a number of perspectives. Given this evolution of perception, then a form of orality that offers listeners a variety of perspectives is likely to assist in countering the crisis of listening discussed in the previous chapter.

From Proclamatory to Conversational Discourse

For many listeners the single voice attempting to speak authoritatively from the pulpit has lost much of its power. The result is that in our transformed preaching situation, the sermon delivered as a closed monologue will probably fail to connect with listeners. One reason for this crisis of confidence in the efficacy of preaching is identified by Walter Brueggemann: 'Ours is a changed preaching situation', where 'the old modes of church absolutes are no longer trusted'.[14]

This increased suspicion of oral monologues is reflected in today's electronic media. Television, for example, often thrives on conflict and disagreement. At the heart of the music video *Papa Don't Preach* is the conflict between daughter and father. In discussion or news programmes, producers are expected to ensure that opposing views are represented. The goal is not simply to be fair to different sides of the argument but also to provoke dialogue, discussion and even fierce debate.

As a consequence there is a real danger of alienating or at

least distancing listeners by relying on the traditional monological style of preaching.[15] Henry J. Eggold argues in *Preaching is Dialogue* that:

> One of the exciting and hopeful developments in preaching today is the accent on preaching as dialogue. It is an attempt to think of the sermon as a dialogue between preacher and listener instead of as the dreary monologue that it so often is.[16]

Eggold is arguing for a reconceptualisation of preaching as dialogue, rather than a termination of it as a single-voiced communicative practice. He is by no means a lone voice in this understanding of preaching as dialogue.[17] Other writers have moved on from the image of preaching as dialogue to that of preaching as conversation or interaction. David Schlafer suggests that 'preaching is more of a community interaction than an individual monologue'.[18] He develops this point arguing that:

> Preaching is more than speaking *to* a congregation, however sensitively, it is speaking *for* and *with* a congregation as well. Preaching attempts to articulate the concerns, questions, commitments, and celebrations of the whole faith community ... The sermon is not a monologue, but an unfolding conversation of the people of God – a conversation about and with God, and about their struggles to know and be faithful to God.[19]

At the heart of Schlafer's argument for conversational preaching is his strongly stated belief that preachers should listen to a whole range of voices before speaking.[20]

Other writers have also recommended a more dialogical or conversational mode of preaching. Many have drawn upon Fred Craddock's works on preaching mentioned above.[21] Craddock identifies the problem of the monological approach that treats listeners like vessels into which information is to be poured. He proposes that:

> sermons which begin with conclusions and general truths arrived at by the minister in the privacy of a study tend to oppress and treat as less than fully faithful and capable a listening congregation. Today, this is often called the banking method of communicating; that is, the speaker simply makes deposits of information in the mind of the listener.[22]

Craddock is not advocating a balanced, tame or objective style of preaching which lacks passion or vision. Rather he is explaining how he came to prefer an inductive approach to a deductive approach for preaching. He suggests *inductive* movement moves from the 'particulars to the general', and *deductive* moves from 'the general to particulars'.[23] The inductive approach attempts to turn the sermon from a closed monologue into a conversation between 'the congregation and the biblical text'.[24]

In the parable of the Pharisee and Tax Collector (Luke 18:9–14), for example, a deductive approach might begin with the general statement: 'everyone who exalts himself will be humbled, but he who humbles himself will be exalted' (v. 14). The parable would be used as a tool to demonstrate and illustrate this truth. An inductive approach might invite the listeners to reflect on the characters portrayed in this story. How do they act? What do they say? How is it relevant today? These are the questions which the preacher might consider in preparing to preach on this story. In short, Craddock's approach to inductive preaching is an attempt to move the authority from the preacher to the text. Listeners are invited to explore it with the help of the speaker, rather than to have the answers thrust upon them. In such a situation, the skilful use of pictorial language can aid those who want to preach inductively. Some writers have gone further than Craddock's inductive model,[25] and argued that preachers should use an 'interactive'[26] or a 'collaborative'[27] form of preaching. Lucy Rose points to some of the different characteristics of such participative approaches to preaching:

> Conversational sermons are not 'dialogue sermons' or 'interactive sermons', although these forms might lend themselves to conversational preaching. Instead conversational preaching in part grows out of and reflects the ongoing conversations between the preacher and members of the congregation in which the preacher is not the one-in-the-know but an equal colleague in matters of living and believing.[28]

In *Sharing the Word, Interactive Preaching* and *The Roundtable Pulpit*, it is clear that Rose, Bond and McClure (respectively) are keen to move away from the preacher as 'herald' or 'sovereign'[29] approach which often finds its theological support in a Barthian understanding of preaching.[30] They are also struggling with the dilemma that Craddock faced in 1971: 'Since preaching is essentially monological, how best can principles and practices of truly participative dialogue be incorporated?'[31] This is the question that also lies behind Eggold's, Schlafer's and McClure's discussions of preaching as dialogue, conversation and collaboration.

From Visual to Multi-Sensory Discourse

I suggested in the first chapter that the shift in the electronic media towards a more conversational form of discourse was one of the causes of the methodological crisis in preaching. Another cause was the move away from verbal towards visual forms of communication, with audiences being bombarded with a multiplicity of electronic images.[32] In the wake of this tidal wave of images, those who rely upon oral discourse to communicate look beleaguered. The sermon appears to be an anachronism.

A number of writers have attempted to face this crisis in methodology brought about by our image-saturated culture. Richard Eslinger, for example, argues that:

> By (the mixed) virtue of most any congregation's exposure to vast amounts of television programming, images of the culture and world are readily available. Since television advertising depends increasingly on an image-laden format, our culture's images of success, happiness, and popularity are constantly being stockpiled in the congregational consciousness.[33]

This preaching situation, where TV images abound, leads Paul Scott Wilson to argue that: 'What Barth told preachers needs updating: Have the Bible in one hand, the newspaper in the other, and the TV on in the background.' As communication technologies converge, and the Internet becomes increasingly user friendly and world encompassing, perhaps the computer connected to the World Wide Web should also be added to Wilson's list.

So the vision for preaching in culturally appropriate terms and forms has not been abandoned. Indeed, various writers have stressed the importance of structures and language appropriate to our media-saturated age. Let us consider these two areas, sermon structure and preaching language.

Sermon structure

In an interview David Buttrick argued:

> People tend now to think through image systems. Your problem, however, is that a lot of young preachers are trying to preach solely in images; and again, without a logical structure in which these images can form, occur, and mean, they aren't going to do much for you. They are simply going to be images which don't necessarily provoke contemplation. [34]

Buttrick believes that images can provoke thought so long as they function within a structure.[35] Image piled upon image, without obvious meaning, is one of the confusing characteristics of post-modernity. A further danger is identified by Paul Scott Wilson: 'preachers to whom images very readily come will often load their sermons with images'.[36] The risk here is that 'competing images shift the focus to a new scene or example every sentence or two'.[37] The result is that 'rather than the images serving the central idea of the sermon, the central idea is subverted into serving the images'. In short, the images 'take over'.[38] While a picture adds depth and colour, it can so provoke or evoke the listeners' imaginations that the preacher loses their attention, or the image is remembered and the message is forgotten. The unforgettable verbal image has the potential to undermine the structural integrity or plot of a sermon as it may be so powerful that it interrupts the flow of the discourse.

'Plot' is the significant word here. Eugene Lowry's work on *The Homiletical Plot*[39] is useful in this discussion about sermonic structures. He argues that 'plot' is 'the key term for a reshaped image of the sermon. Preaching is storytelling.'[40] This theme also recurs in much recent homiletical literature.[41] Some scholars argue that this move towards narrative in homiletics is partly a result of television, which is mainly narrative in form and is 'shaping the way listeners in the congregation actually' think.[42]

Lowry builds upon the simple cycle of conflict and resolution found in much contemporary television drama.[43] His approach has been associated with what has been described as the 'Copernican Revolution' within homiletics.[44] This is the move away from a spatial building block approach to sermon preparation, towards a sermon as an '*event-in-time*, a narrative art form'.[45] In Lowry's eyes there are parallels between the preacher on the one hand, and the playwright, the novelist and the television writer on the other hand. He does not, however, attempt to mimic the multiple plot development common to most television soap operas. Instead for sermons he espouses a single plot line, something found in other genres of television.[46]

He draws upon specific films and television series to illustrate his argument. By using the 'typical movie plot' of the 1952 Western, *High Noon*,[47] he shows how a plot can begin 'with a felt discrepancy' and move towards 'an unknown resolution'. He contrasts this with a 'television series plot which begins with a felt discrepancy, but then moves towards a known conclusion'.[48] He argues that most sermons tend to follow this second 'kind of plot',[49] where it is clear the star will survive. In spite of this assertion he returns to *High Noon* later in the book in order to explain the 'sudden reversal' stage in the sermonic plot, which he describes as 'disclosing the clue to resolution'.[50] He uses the unexpected reversals in *High Noon* to illustrate the pivotal third stage in his 'homiletical plot',[51] where listeners are given a clue to the denouement of the sermon.

Lowry's groundbreaking work on plotting the sermon structure uses examples from cinema and television to illustrate and support his case. Lowry is clearly open to learning from and even adapting the plotting devices employed by screenwriters for his homiletical endeavour. Like Buttrick, he draws upon but is not controlled or determined by these media. Significantly neither Buttrick nor Lowry appears to consider the plots or structures of radio talks or drama.

Preaching Language

Earlier, I pointed out that a frequent refrain in Paul Scott Wilson's textbook, *The Practice of Preaching*, is the 'need for preachers to make a movie with words',[52] or to become 'movie directors'.[53] Other writers liken the preacher to a photographer. Bryan Chapell, for example, believes that: 'The preacher is much like a photographer, constantly framing one moment, one event, one sequence after another. By doing this, what looks common to the ordinary eye becomes significant.'[54] If the preacher is to become a 'movie director' or 'photographer' with words in the pulpit, then he or she must, according to Charles Rice, learn to experience imaginatively the world of the scriptural text:

> if we have an experience of the text, allow ourselves to be led deeply into its images – in our mind's eye to see its people, places, and things – to experience its language as a new dawning, there is every likelihood that the resulting sermon will in form and content, rely upon and awaken the imagination.[55]

One of the great strengths of using pictorial language and other '*vivid details*'[56] is its ability to create images on the screens of the listeners' imaginations. Fred Buechener speaks evocatively of 'preaching the King who looks like a tramp, the prince of peace who looks like a prince of fools, the lamb of God who looks like something hung up at the butchers'.[57] Such 'vivid language'[58] in preaching has the potential to act like a 'magnet', drawing 'a cluster of reflections and emotions'.[59] A recurring theme in Craddock's work is also the importance of the well-selected verbal image.[60]

One recent significant European text which has briefly considered the place of pictorial language within preaching is Gerd Theissen's *The Sign Language of Faith.*[61] Theissen is uncompromising in his argument for specific 'homiletical imagery': 'images and symbols are not ornaments in a sermon. They are part of its substance. The poverty of imagery is an offence against the task of preaching.'[62] He supports these forceful assertions on a number of levels. First, 'pictorial language is discourse with open referents. Images are not only designations for something that is known but challenges to seek something unknown in the known. They are semantic disruptions which direct our attention to something new.'[63] Part of the power of these 'disruptions' lies in their ability to extend the meaning of the picture, and so lead the listener towards a new vision. Secondly, 'pictorial language is further characterised by a fusion of being and meaning'.[64] In Theissen's understanding, pictorial language simultaneously refers to the picture described and also leads the listener to the meanings beyond the portrayal. Herein lies the fusion of 'being and meaning'. It is almost as if he is arguing that pictorial language can help provoke and answer not only 'Who am I?' but also 'Why am I?' questions. Such questions can be heightened by: 'description of sights, sounds, and sensations that the listeners would take in were they in such a context'; this approach can 'vicariously involve them in that experience'.[65]

Others are keen to go beyond preachers simply engaging the visual imagination. Webb Garrison argues forcefully:

> Words that name colors, shapes, sounds, odors and other tangibles help create backgrounds that evoke moods. Anything that moves you can move your listeners – provided they are brought into firsthand encounter with stimuli that produced the emotion.[66]

This point is extended by those writers who also stress the importance of using vivid multi-sensory language, 'words which you can see, smell, touch, taste, hear and feel'.[67] Patricia Wilson-Kastner who understands 'imagery' in preaching to mean 'more than pictures' supports this view. She uses the word 'imagery' to include 'the whole physical and sensory dimension of the world portrayed in a sermon'.[68] One of the strengths of such multi-sensory language is that it can work on many different levels, feeding different parts of the listeners' imaginations. It is potentially multi-dimensional.[69] If David Buttrick is correct when he asserts 'pulpit language must relate to a new twentieth century consciousness that is simultaneous, perspectival and complex',[70] then the use of such multi-sensory or sensuous language can help answer that need.

Behind many of these calls for the development of pictorial or multi-sensory language is a serious attempt to aid effective oral communication by engaging the listeners' imaginations. This part of the discussion began with a call for preachers to act like movie directors; it ends with an encouragement to develop a discursive and interactive style, which engages all the senses.

Writers in homiletics have once again drawn upon photographic or cinematic models to support their arguments, but the world of radio broadcasting has been left untroubled and unexplored.

Conclusion

There are signs therefore that preachers are facing up to the issues raised by the threefold crisis outlined in Chapter 1, and even experiencing a resurgence of confidence. It seems that the 'papas', and 'mamas', of homiletics are beginning to ignore Madonna's refrain: 'don't preach'. As an immediate face-to-face experience which depends primarily on verbal communication, preaching stands out as a rare species in the electronic media-saturated society of mass communication. When compared to other forms of communication habitually used today, preaching is an uncommon, but not unique, set piece of public speech. This strangeness may be a strength in a context where electronically mediated communication appears to dominate. Nevertheless, even if preaching is '*sui generis*'[71] preachers cannot afford to ignore our audio-visual context, nor should they succumb to its more seductive images.

Preaching has reached a transitional moment where both the theory and practice need to adapt to an environment where many listeners are becoming used to interactive and audio-visually based means of communication. Preachers who wish to be effective today cannot yearn for or mimic styles from the so-called golden age of pulpit princes, nor can they continue without making any concessions to the more dialogical forms of public discourse that listeners are increasingly accustomed to hearing.

Clearly a process of adaptation and learning is taking place. Film and television, for example, are regularly cited and drawn upon by those seeking to overcome the difficulty of making oral communication effective today. It is plain to see, however, that one medium which has many close connections with preaching has largely been ignored. Radio, and the crisis and transformations it has undergone, will therefore be the focus of the next two chapters.

Notes

1. For a clear exposition of recent movements within homiletics see Eslinger 1987.
2. Lumière Brothers film *Sortie d'Usine* (1895), in BFI, *Early Cinema, Primitives and Pioneers.*
3. There is an extensive literature discussing issues of spectatorship, gaze and moving pictures. See, for example, Denzin 1995: '. . . the motionless gaze of the picture was replaced by the moving picture of the cinema. This allowed the viewer to engage the subject of the gaze in real life detail; in the detail which accompanies movement through time and space.' 26.
4. This ability is taken to comic extremes in Peter Weir's film *The Truman Show,* 1998, in which hundreds of hidden cameras are used to turn one person's life into a global soap opera.
5. Buttrick 1987, 'Preaching that talks objectively about everything, as if from a third-person observational position, will not only seem archaic but may have an aura of unreality.' 56.
6. Ibid., 55. See also Buttrick's chapters in Sweet 1993, 316, and Eslinger 1994.
7. Buttrick 1987, 25.
8. Ibid., 55–68 and especially 63.
9. See Funk 1982, 55–65. Funk suggests that this parable should be interpreted from the perspective of the victim (the 'fellow in the ditch') and not the good Samaritan. See McDonald's article 1996, 21–37. McDonald explores how the 'placing of the auditors' may change the meaning of the parable. 29.
10. Eslinger 1995, 145. 'Shifts in character point of view, as with the parable of the good Samaritan, are rich with potential for new insight and even new hearings of the biblical narrative.'
11. Ibid. In his section on 'The User's Guide to Imagery', he helpfully divides various approaches to using images in preaching into: the camera model, the video-camera model and the simulator model. 146–51. See also Buttrick 1987, 63.
12. Boys 1983, 82–9. Boys argues that: 'Jesus spoke in parables because abstract, conceptual language inadequately conveyed the reorientation entailed in living in God's reign. The parables provided a means of engaging his hearers, involving them in a new way of thinking, and pressing them to a decision without provoking defensiveness.' 86.
13. See Brueggemann 1995, 313–29. 'The work of preaching is an act of imagination, an offer of an image through which perception,

experience, and finally faith can be reorganised in alternative ways.' 323. See also Brueggemann 1997a, esp. 24–37.

14. Brueggemann 1995, 313. Brueggemann continues: 'It is not that the church's theological absolutes are no longer trusted, but that the *old modes* in which those absolutes have been articulated are increasingly suspect and dysfunctional. That is because our old modes are increasingly regarded as patriarchal, hierarchical, authoritarian, and monologic.'
15. Few writers have gone so far as to suggest that good preaching is rooted in argument. Some have, however, asserted that it should be founded upon 'polar thought'. See, for example, Wilson 1995, 238–62.
16. Eggold 1980, 11.
17. See, for example, Jones 1968, 509–11. See also McClure 1995. He argues that: 'The initial result of the backlash against authoritarianism in the pulpit was the short-lived dialogue movement in the 1960s. Some preachers began to experiment with two-party dialogue sermons, postsermon feedback sessions, involvement in sermon exegesis, removal of manuscripts and pulpits, and walk-around sermon delivery.' 40. Some of these practices are still being followed.
18. Schlafer 1992, 23.
19. Ibid., 24.
20. Ibid., 22–58. See esp. 'Preaching is more listening than speaking.' 22. 'The speaking of a sermon comes from listening to all kinds of voices.' 23. This is a common theme in other homiletical texts. See, for example, Killinger 1985 'The Importance of Listening', 24–8.
21. See, for example, O'Day and Long 1993. See especially, Eugene L. Lowry's article on 'The Revolution of Sermonic Shape', 93–112. See also Craddock 1979, 51–76.
22. Craddock 1990, 8.
23. Ibid., 10.
24. Ibid., 12.
25. See Wilson 1995. Wilson makes an incisive critique on the use of inductive and deductive categories to describe the form of a sermon. He argues: ' Inductive and deductive categories may work to describe styles of preaching, but they do not work when each is attached to a particular form of sermon ... Preaching can be authoritarian in any form.' 214.
26. See Bond 1991 and Stratford 1998 for discussions of Interactive Preaching.

27. McClure 1995. See especially Chapter 2, 'Towards a Collaborative Homiletic', and Chapter 3, 'Collaborative Preaching'.
28. Rose 1997, 96. In this thought-provoking book Rose challenges the assumption that there is a 'gap between the preacher and the congregation'. 90. Instead she affirms preaching as a 'joint task' of the preacher and the congregation. 93.
29. Ibid., 30–1. See also Swain 1986, 40.
30. Barth 1991 (1963). See especially Barth's definition of preaching: 'Preaching is the Word of God which he himself speaks, claiming for the purpose the exposition of a Biblical text in free human words that are relevant to contemporaries by those who are called to do this in the church that is obedient to its commission.' 44. See also Barth 1957 and the discussion of Barth in Hilkert 1998, 20–3.
31. McClure 1995, 47.
32. For a more detailed discussion of this phenomenon see the discussion of Jacques Ellul in Chapter 9 of this book.
33. Eslinger 1995, 142.
34. Buttrick, recorded interview with Jolyon Mitchell, Vanderbelt Divinity School, USA, 29 March 1994. (Hereafter: Buttrick, Interview 1994.)
35. Buttrick 1987, see especially Ch. 10 'The Image Grid'. Buttrick argues that: 'what makes a good sermon is not one single illustration, but a gridwork of interacting images, examples and illustrations'. 153.
36. Wilson 1995, 254.
37. Ibid., 254.
38. Ibid., 254.
39. Lowry 1980. (See also Lowry 1985 and Lowry 1997.)
40. Ibid., 15.
41. See Robinson 1990. For a pioneering work on narrative preaching see: Steimle, Niedenthal and Rice 1980.
42. Wilson 1995, 208. Narrative, however, played a significant part in preaching well before the invention of television.
43. For examples of conflict and resolution in television drama see: Allen 1995, and especially Geraghty's chapter on British soaps in the 1980/1990s, 66–80.
44. Eslinger 1987, 65.
45. Lowry 1980, 6.
46. This method finds implicit support from Paul Ricoeur's fascinating discussion of 'emplotment' in 'Life in Quest of Narrative', Wood 1991, 20–33. Ricoeur argues that following a single story is a very

complex operation, and the expectation is that 'the audience readjusts as the story moves along'. 21–2.

47. Fred Zinnemann, director, *High Noon*, United Artists, 1952. Gary Cooper and Grace Kelly played the lead characters of a US marshal and a pacifist Quaker.
48. Lowry 1980, 22–3. He cites *Barnaby Jones* or *Columbo* as examples of these television series plots. See also 79 for further use of *Columbo* and the movie plot lines to illustrate his case.
49. Ibid., 23. In other words, in the same way it is assumed that 'the star will survive', so 'Jesus Christ will emerge as Savior and Lord . . . But how? In what way? for what purpose?' For Lowry, it is this 'unknown middle ground which provides the context for sermonic tension'.
50. Ibid., 50–1.
51. Ibid., 25. These five stages could be stated imperatively as: (1) Upset the equilibrium, (2) Analyse the discrepancy, (3) Disclose the clue to resolution, (4) Experience the gospel, (5) Anticipate the consequences. Underlying Lowry's argument is the belief that listeners are more likely to engage with a story for themselves, if they also move through these five stages. See Chapter 10 of this book for an example of this structure being put into practice.
52. Wilson 1995, 255. See also 183 and 132.
53. Ibid., 112. 'We become like movie directors.'
54. Chapell 1994, 180. Earlier Chapell argues: 'Relating truth through illustrative narratives, parables, allegories, and images was Jesus' method of communicating. His was not an age of visual literacy par excellence (at least in terms of modern media) yet illustrative materials pervaded his expressions. If in Christ's times illustrations were necessary, how much more, given the contemporary influences, must today's preacher weigh the need for illustrative content.' Notice how Chapell bases his argument both on imitating Christ's practice and taking the communicative context seriously. 174.
55. Rice in Wardlaw 1983, 104. Also cited by Eslinger 1987, 22.
56. Chapell 1994, 184.
57. Buechner 1977, 60.
58. Greidanus 1988, 186. Greidanus also emphasises the importance of 'using concrete, vivid language'.
59. Craddock 1985, 197.
60. Craddock 1979, 78.
61. Theissen 1995.

62. Ibid., 74.
63. Ibid., 73.
64. Ibid., 73.
65. Ibid., 185.
66. Garrison 1960, 185.
67. Markquart 1985, 184. See also Day 1998, 30–31; Davis 1958; and also Part 3 of this book.
68. Wilson-Kastner 1989, 20.
69. Wilson-Kastner highlights the 'rich ability of images to sustain many meanings'. She describes this as 'multidimensionality', ibid., 54.
70. Buttrick 1987, 56.
71. Pitt-Watson 1986, 13. Pitt-Watson argues that preaching is '*sui generis* – in a class by itself'. This is a common refrain amongst writers in homiletics.

CHAPTER 3

Radio in Crisis

> Even though radio is integral to the pattern of our lives, we rarely give it a second thought … to overlook radio is to miss the big picture.[1]

We turn now, in this chapter and the next, to radio broadcasting. As I suggested above, there are a number of interesting parallels between preaching and radio broadcasting. Both have suffered pessimistic diagnoses and prognoses: radio and preaching are said to be in crisis, to have a bleak future, to be in terminal decline. Both forms of communication have also basked in more optimistic evaluations: radio and preaching are in transition, they have a hopeful future, especially if they adapt to their new communicative environments.[2] I will propose in these next two chapters that radio broadcasting has not only survived, but also developed and even thrived through a series of crises, and that this analysis of radio is pertinent for the survival and development of preaching.

Unlike preaching, most of the crises in radio are generally considered to be things of the past. Nonetheless, the bleak predictions which commentators made about radio's future are worth considering. We will also look at some of the transitions that radio has undergone over the last fifty years that have dispelled the gloomy forecasts, and in particular at the transformations in radio technology, in listening habits, and in radio speech.

The 'Death' of Radio

'Video Killed the Radio Star'[3]

This was the title of the first music video ever played on MTV, screened on 1 August 1981. 'In a montage of exploding TV sets destroying vintage radios, The Buggles sang: "Pictures came and broke your heart ... video killed the radio star".'[4] This was not a new refrain. Over thirty years ago similar taunts were levelled at radio.[5] It had no future. The 'TV and Video Age' meant we would soon be waving goodbye to *Radio Days.*[6] They would become like a distant hazy summer vaguely remembered from childhood. Eric Rhoads, publisher of the industry magazine *Radio Ink*, believes that:

> Ever since the passing of radio's golden era, when it was the only mass entertainment medium, radio has been considered by cynics to be in decline ... Over the past 50 years, nothing has been able to overcome the perception that television's birth meant radio's death.[7]

As early as 1936 some commentators, whilst holding that radio was a 'sensational' new 'form of expression', still believed that it was 'highly probable' that television would destroy 'the new wireless form of expression even more radically than the sound film ever destroyed the silent film'.[8] It was almost as if what historian Asa Briggs described as 'the great citadel of sound',[9] the BBC's Broadcasting House, had been stormed and overrun by television.

With some 56 per cent of the United Kingdom's population, more than 20 million people, watching the Coronation Service in 1953 on television,[10] it is not surprising that the 1950s is often seen as the beginning of the crisis for radio. As early as 1950 the then chairman of the Radio Industry Council, J. W. Ridgeway, declared: 'It is inevitable that television will become the primary service and sound the secondary one.'[11] This analysis finds support in Colin Seymour-Ure's text, entitled *The British Press and Broadcasting since 1945*, in which he argues that: 'TV stole its time from radio. Radio's peak hour audience (6.00pm to 11.00pm) dived from 35 per cent of the population in early 1947 to about 4 per cent in the early 1960s.'[12] In the words of Kenneth Wolfe: 'With the arrival of a visual competitor in television ... the beguiling power of radio was over and vast tracts of the population moved rapidly out of earshot.'[13]

Consider the BBC expenditure statistics for radio and

television at this time. In 1955–6 nearly 11 million pounds was spent on radio, compared to only 7 million on television. In 1958–9 just over 11 million pounds was spent on radio, while nearly 14 million pounds was spent on television.[14] In short, television expenditure had nearly *doubled* in just over a year, whilst radio had increased by little more than half a million pounds. The signs for radio were ominous. The rapid evolution of video recording technology,[15] and the subsequent increased flexibility in broadcasting pictures looked set to 'break radio's heart'. Likewise in America, according to Jay Black and Jennings Bryant: 'The radio industry was scared'; the reason for this being that: 'Throughout most of the 1950s, the prevailing attitude in the industry was that radio was dying.'[16] In the United Kingdom,

> faced with competition from first one and then two television networks, radio went into a long decline that some thought would prove terminal. Between 1949 and 1958 the BBC's average evening radio audiences dropped from nearly 9 million to less than 3.5 million . . .[17]

Interestingly, three quarters of those 3.5 million in 1958 were without television sets. Over these nine years, many listeners in the United Kingdom might have become dissatisfied with what BBC radio offered, but not necessarily with what radio per se could offer. They were attracted to other stations such as Radio Luxembourg. Television was clearly one alternative for listeners, but it was not the only distraction.

The Renaissance of Radio

With the benefit of hindsight we can see clearly that television, and subsequently video recorders, did not destroy the wireless. As Gillian Reynolds states: 'Thirty years after commentators pronounced it dead, radio is alive and growing.'[18] Radio, to many commentators' surprise, has survived on both sides of the Atlantic. Marilyn Matelksi argues, in an article entitled 'Resilient Radio', that:

> Over and over again . . . reports of radio's death have proven

> premature ... Far from shrivelling from the media scene, there is no medium more ubiquitous than radio, no source of information, entertainment, music, sports, weather and business news more pervasive in people's lives.[19]

This bold claim for the ubiquity of radio finds some statistical support. Talk radio, for example, is currently enjoying a renaissance in many areas of the world. An optimistic article by Mary Ann Watson called 'Seems Radio is Here to Stay' highlights that: 'There are radios through all American homes – more than five on average – not just in the living room, but the kitchen, bedroom, basement, bathrooms, plus the Walkman and the one in the car.'[20] Richard Ducey, mixing his metaphors, suggests radio is the 'oldest electronic survivor' which is 'part of the American culture and continually reveals an unsinkable ability, if not to prosper, at least to maintain and grow'.[21] This position is supported by Edward Pease and Everetter Dennis who argue that 'a close look at radio demonstrates its vitality, its economic, political and social importance, as well as its staying power in the communication field'.[22]

These comments may have been written from within an American context, but they have parallels in the United Kingdom, where in the 1980s there were more radio sets than people.[23] Radio critic Gillian Reynolds states:

> Radio is part of the daily life of almost everyone who lives in the UK. People wake up to it, or switch it on first thing. We carry our radios around the house or have different sets in each room, ready to switch on. Even people with in-car CD systems listen to more radio than records. There are 40,804,000 listeners each week who take in 847,735,000 hours of output.[24]

Such isolated statistics should be read of course with some caution. Ken Garner suggests in his article, 'Reading RAJAR: Making Sense of Radio Ratings',[25] that 'year-on-year comparisons are to be favoured'.[26] If, for example, one compares the figures for the total 'weekly reach' for the United Kingdom in the third quarter in 1993 with the same period in 1995, a drop of nearly 500,000 listeners is apparent.[27] Even limited comparisons such as these should not be used as 'fool-proof' indicators of general listening trends in the United Kingdom. They should act as a warning against complacency about radio's future.

We should recognise, however, first that these general fluctuations do not indicate a haemorrhaging of listeners and, secondly, that in both the United Kingdom and the USA there is a confidence in radio's proven ability to survive and even to thrive within our rapidly evolving communicative context. Bertholt Brecht's poem on radio addressed to 'You little box', contains the plea: 'Promise me not to go silent all of a sudden.' On the basis of the statistics and sources cited in this section, it will certainly not go 'silent all of a sudden': radio is a survivor. Brecht's melancholy poem contains some clues as to why radio has survived the apparent crisis in listening provoked by the advent of electronic images. The 'little box' is 'near my bed'. It is what Brecht hears 'last thing at night and first thing in the morning'.[28]

Brecht's insights in poetic form echo the perceptions of radio critic Jacki Apple: 'Radio is seductive. It strokes the senses, wraps itself around you, whispers in the dark, wakes you up in the morning.'[29] It is an intimate medium. One of radio's great strengths is that while its 'soundscape'[30] does not demand 100 per cent attention, its pictures may still enter the listener's consciousness.

The Enduring Qualities of Radio Broadcasting

It is clear that there are various enduring qualities in radio broadcasting which have contributed to its survival. Some of these can be identified by considering two broadcasters whose work stands out from the early days of radio. The first, Richard Dimbleby, made his name as a young reporter with one of the first live radio broadcasts in 1936. He made his live report from a telephone-box near Crystal Palace as the latter was engulfed in flames.[31] Veracity and drama were added to his report both by the excited tone of his voice and, even more evocatively, by the sounds of 'shouts, firebells and the crackle of flames' in the background.[32]

This example illustrates some of the varied and non-verbal elements that can make up a successful radio report. It does not, however, challenge the importance of the verbal in radio. Without words these background sounds would have had little meaning. The crackles could easily have been mistaken for static, the bells lost music from another station and the muffled shouts a product of interference. Dimbleby's voice brought order out of potential chaos; the actuality in the background added colour and atmosphere to the verbal report.

So we should distinguish between the tools which are essential for clear communication by radio, and the additional resources which make it even more effective. For making sense of background sounds, it was essential that Dimbleby's verbal description cut through the clamour. The dramatic impact of his words, however, was enhanced by the sounds in the background, the tone of his voice and, of course the complete novelty of this form of live radio reporting.

A second figure stands out alongside Richard Dimbleby as an early master of radio broadcasting. Ed Murrow, the American war correspondent, spent much of the Second World War in London. He has been called a 'reporter-preacher'.[33] One of his greatest skills was the ability to paint what he called 'the little picture':

> One night last week I stood in front of a smashed grocery store and heard a dripping inside. It was the only sound in all London. Two cans of peaches had been drilled through by flying glass and the juice was dripping down onto the floor.[34]

It is interesting to notice his attention to minute detail. Here Murrow homes in on one scene and more specifically, on one sound. It is hard not to hear the 'drip, drip, ...' of the peach juice and to imagine that this was indeed the 'only sound in all London'. At other times Murrow would perch on rooftops during the night-time London Blitz. The result is some of the most evocative broadcasting of the war. For example, he describes how anti-aircraft barrages:

> seemed to splash blobs of daylight down the streets ... The first two looked like some giant had thrown a huge basket of flaming

> oranges high in the air. The third was just a balloon of fire ... A shower of incendiaries came down in the far distance ... It looked like flashes from an electric train on a wet night, only the engineer was drunk and driving his train in circles through the streets.[35]

He watches, he describes with the observation of a fine artist, and he communicates. It is not surprising that he was described as 'the poet of the blitz'.[36] The sounds of planes and anti-aircraft fire combine with the repressed emotion in his voice to fashion a gripping commentary.[37]

As with Richard Dimbleby the verbal expression is the backbone of the report; the actuality adds colour, dimension and vitality. In the words of A. M. Sperber, one of Murrow's biographers: 'It was *The War of the Worlds* come to life, the fantasy of 1938 become the reality of 1940, the rooftop observer, reporting on the life and death of cities, no longer an actor in a studio.'[38] Often the power of pictorial language lies in its ability to tell a story. The dripping can of peaches tells the story of bombs, destruction and the shattering of normality in parts of London life.

Two further elements add to the power of Ed Murrow's verbal report: first, the story itself was 'new' news. Secondly, Murrow himself had become part of the story. Here was no distant, objective newsreader: he was an eyewitness. He had become the eyes of the listener as he described scenes such as 'a rainbow bending over the battered East End as the all clear sounded' or a 'flower shop intact among the ruins, a funeral wreath in the window'.[39] Murrow believed that 'these things must be seen', and through his evocative use of pictorial language 'the audience saw them in vivid pictures that needed no TV cameras'.[40]

Both Dimbleby and Murrow flew in Lancaster bombers in separate missions over Berlin in 1943. They used their verbal reports to create vivid pictures and so became like TV cameras for their audiences. Dimbleby, for instance, spoke of a 'tracery of sparkling silver searchlights lighting across the face of Berlin',[41] whilst Murrow moves from specific description to imaginative simile:

> Jock [the pilot] was wearing woollen gloves with the fingers cut off. I could see his fingernails turned white as he gripped the wheel ...

> The small incendiaries went down like a fistful of white rice thrown on a piece of black velvet, ... like great sunflowers gone mad.[42]

Representational pictorial language, describing specific details of what he sees, is juxtaposed with a more poetic pictorial language, which connects what he is seeing with other pictures of reality.

The broadcasting practice of these two journalists demonstrates how they successfully utilised one of radio's enduring strengths: its reliance upon the combination of words and sounds to engage the listener's imagination. Murrow and Dimbleby painted pictures for their listeners' 'inner eye'. Their vivid and shocking accounts of their visits to Buchenwald[43] and Belsen[44] immediately after liberation are two more of their many unforgettable reports. They understood that listeners have to rely on what they hear in order to 'see' what the broadcaster is witnessing or experiencing; hence the importance of speakers using verbal pictures.

The Importance of Pictorial Language

The importance of pictorial language has by no means diminished for oral communicators today. In fact, given the multiplicity and variety of electronically produced pictures in the television age it seems likely that many images embedded in listeners' memories may be released by sounds or by word pictures on the radio. It is not surprising that certain broadcasters have worked on the assumption that there is an accumulation of images, derived from electronic sources, in listeners' minds. Ronald Reagan when President of the USA, for example, often 'evoked televised images on radio' and built his 'arguments from a visual scene that he and the nation' had 'recently experienced'.[45]

As well as recalling or reproducing images taken from an electronic source, listeners also have the ability to create or reshape mental images from their own personal experience. Adam Powell, director of Technology Studies at the Freedom Forum Media Centre, argues:

> Radio is powerful ... Television and movies may expose us to new experiences in specific detail, but radio and literature are unique in engaging the imagination, permitting us to create our own image in the mind's eye ... radio, along with the printed word forces us to collaborate with the medium as an active participant.[46]

This view of the power of radio, with its ability to engage the imagination of the listener by 'permitting' the creation of 'our own image in the mind's eye', is an important reminder to those who see the electronic visual media as entirely dominant. Perhaps one of the most significant words in this extract is 'participant'. Having the space to draw their own images liberates listeners to participate or interact with what they are hearing. This understanding of the creative and derivative powers of the imagination further shows how important it is for broadcasters and preachers to engage their listener's 'inner eye' or 'visual imagination'.[47]

The creative potential of the listener's imagination is emphasised by Adam Powell's claim for radio: 'As a result, the pictures are better on radio: What you can imagine is almost always scarier, funnier, more real and more vivid than the explicit images of video and film ...'[48] He challenges the assumption that the explicit images of video and film will necessarily be more vivid than the implicit ones of radio. Powell's generalised assertion for radio is open to contention. Nevertheless, his claim for the potential power of the imagination should not be ignored, nor should the aural quality of radio. Radio is not solely a word-based medium. Radio producers and broadcasters have a range of resources to draw upon: music, sound effects, silence and audio montages can combine to form a medium more 'visual' for the imagination than television. Even though this book primarily focuses on 'speech radio' it is important to bear in mind the wide variety of genres in radio broadcasting currently filling the air-waves.[49]

The use of pictorial language raises a number of important questions relevant not only to radio broadcasters, but also to preachers. First, how do the radio broadcaster and the preacher create the 'little picture' and the 'visual story'? Today, it is almost a 'homiletical given' to argue that 'preaching needs to become more visual'.[50] If this is taken as a prerequisite in our 'televisual age', then it makes sense to investigate how radio broadcasters practise this skill. Secondly, in portraying these verbal snapshots, how important is the choice of language? Thirdly, which communication factors can add to or detract from effective communication through these verbal pictures? These questions will be considered in the following chapter and through the case studies in part 2 of this book.

Conclusion

Radio has weathered a number of crises: the popularisation of television, in particular, was perceived as a challenge to radio's survival. The pessimistic predictions of the 1950s and early 1960s have not been fulfilled and radio has survived. On the basis of radio's recrudescence I have argued that particular intrinsic characteristics of radio, used effectively by broadcasters, have contributed towards its survival. This interpretation of radio as a survivor has fascinating connections with the first two chapters' discussions of preaching in crisis and preaching in transformation. Given that some critics have proclaimed the complete demise of preaching, the ability of radio to survive and succeed in adapting to a new broadcasting environment may have something to teach preachers. Nevertheless, survival is by no means guaranteed for either form of communication. Adaptation and transformation are vital if radio and preaching are to survive.

Notes

1. Watson 1995, 204.
2. Hoekstra and Verbeek 1994, 213. They also describe the 'new communicative environment' as the 'audiovisual culture'.
3. I am indebted to Island Records, New York, USA, for sending me a copy of the music video: *Video Killed the Radio Star* by The Buggles (duration: 3 minutes 25 seconds), and to Mark Goodman for highlighting the significance of this song.
4. Schultze *et al.* 1991, 179. It is argued 'that this was the channel that

would challenge and conquer radio's long-time dominance of the teen audience not only throughout North America but also through much of the world'. 178. See also Denisoff 1988, 54.

5. Reynolds 1994, 57.
6. Woody Allen, director, *Radio Days,* Orion Pictures, 1987.
7. Rhoads 1995, 15. It is debatable, however, whether radio has ever been the 'only mass entertainment medium', as films for mass audiences pre-date radio.
8. Arnheim 1936, 16.
9. Briggs 1995e, 30.
10. Briggs 1995d. See 'Television's Coronation', 420–35.
11. Ibid., 387.
12. Seymour-Ure 1991, 147.
13. Wolfe 1984, 537.
14. Ibid., V, 30.
15. Abramson 1995, 32–4. Abramson provides a helpful outline of the evolution of video recording machines. 'The first videotaped network broadcast was made by CBS TV with *Doug Edwards and the News* from Television City in Hollywood on 30 November 1956.' 33.
16. See Black and Bryant 1995, 266. This citation refers explicitly to the American industry, but could also be applied to the British radio industry at this time.
17. Crisell 1994, 27. Crisell believes that 'though television was clearly the major cause' of this huge decline in audience, 'there were problems with radio's tripartite programme network'.
18. Reynolds 1994, 57–61, esp. 57.
19. Matelski 1995a, 5.
20. Watson 1995, 204.
21. Ducey 1995, 164.
22. Pease and Dennis 1995, xv.
23. Seymore-Ure 1991, 147.
24. Reynolds 1994, 57.
25. Garner 1995, 6–9.
26. Ibid., 6.
27. Ibid., 8. See 'Table 1: Radio Listening Now ('95) and Then ('93)'. Weekly reach for the third quarter in 1995 was 40,514,000 compared to 41,001,000 for the third quarter in 1993.
28. Cited in Heath 1969, 62.
29. Apple 1993, 307. Apple continues: 'It is not always what you say, it is the way you say it. Radio art is about the voice as instrument, the voice as place, the voice as emotion, the voice as spirit, the voice as

body, the body of the voice, the place of a voice, the feel of a voice.'

30. Schafer 1993. Schafer writes of our 'rich and contemporary soundscape', arguing for more rigorous study of this context. 295.
31. Scannell and Cardiff 1991, 123. The fire at Crystal Palace was Richard Dimbleby's 'first big story ... listeners heard his excited voice, from a telephone booth on the spot. It was the first up-to-the minute, on-the-spot radio report of a major news story and it scooped the Newspapers'.
32. Crisell 1994, 20. Crisell interprets Dimbleby's coverage of the Crystal Palace fire in 1936 as one of the key events in the early history of British radio. It 'occurred after the evening papers had shut down and before the morning papers had appeared, and was the BBC's first scoop'. This 'demonstrated that as a news medium radio is not only quicker than newspapers but more "concrete" in the sense that it can convey the sound that it reports'.
33. W. Stott explains the title of 'reporter-preacher' in 'Documenting Media', from Crowley and Heyer, 1995 (1991), 247, 249. He argues that Murrow completely 'identified with the British cause' and so 'to avoid the term "propagandist", Murrow has been called a "reporter-preacher".' See also Shayon 1969, 51.
34. Stott, 1986 (1973).
35. Sperber 1986, 179.
36. Ibid., 179. Sperber argues that Murrow's 'reflective, impressionistic pieces ... captured the public imagination and established his image as the poet of the blitz'.
37. Ibid., 174. Sperber describes how Murrow's 'quiet narrative' of the evening of the Blitz on the programme *London After Dark* was 'underscored by the steady crashes of anti-aircraft fire'.
38. Sperber 1986, 174.
39. Ibid., 179.
40. Ibid., 179. Other examples cited include: 'A night bomber's exhaust trail was "a pale ribbon stretched across the sky", and the glasses of an anti-aircraft spotter resembled the eyes of an overgrown owl.'
41. Dimbleby 1975. His son and biographer Jonathan Dimbleby cites parts of his father's report on his flight with pilot Guy Gibson in a Lancaster bomber over Berlin.
42. Sperber 1986, 179. Note that Murrow does not highlight the deadly impact of this innocuous white rice.
43. Murrow 1945, from Caversham: BBC Archives. See also Murrow 1993, 152–4.

44. Ludovic Kennedy. *Richard Dimbleby: Voice of the Nation*, London: BBC Videos, 1990.
45. Jamieson 1988, 126–7.
46. Powell III 1995, 75.
47. See 'An Analytic of Imagination and Images', Chapter 7 of McIntyre 1987. McIntyre lists twelve functions or capacities of the imagination. Two categories, which perhaps parallel my argument here, are McIntyre's 'synoptic and integrative' and 'creative and constructive' functions of the imagination.
48. Powell III 1995, 75.
49. In the UK, Virgin 1215, Atlantic 252, Classic FM, Radio 1, 2, and 3 as well as the majority of Independent Radio stations rely heavily on music. BBC Radio 4 lives up to the name of its new rival: Talk Radio. The UK's 39 BBC local radio stations have recently been 'ordered to provide quality speech programming on ever-waning budgets'. Reynolds 1994, 60.
50. See also Wilson-Kastner 1989, 11–31, Weber 1993, 143–6, Theissen 1995, 74, and Troeger 1996, 48–57.

CHAPTER 4

Radio in Transformation

The prediction of radio's death was premature. In the face of potential crises, such as the competition provoked by television and the subsequent loss of listeners, radio has survived. It has, however, not just survived; it has experienced a renaissance, but only by being prepared to adapt to its changing cultural and technological situation. So in what ways has radio developed?

From Communal to Isolated Listening

> A profound transformation was taking place within the family, for with the transistor the radio became not only mobile but also individual. Whereas in the 1940s the family had gathered together around the radio, in the 1960s each family member pursued his or her own activities whilst listening to a separate radio.[1]

First, there have been a number of important shifts in listening habits. Radio is now *rarely* listened to in groups. In the days of crystal radio some families would cluster round a large porcelain bowl, with the headphones placed in the centre. The intended result was amplified sound. Listening to the radio was a family or communal event, the radio broadcast normally being the central focus of attention for the duration of the programme. The advent of transistors made radio a 'truly ubiquitous medium'.[2] Radio is now a far more flexible and portable medium, and can become merely a secondary or background activity for individual members of the family.

For some, however, radio still has the power to move from being a background noise to a primary focus of attention.[3] Marshall McLuhan's musings on radio as a 'tribal drum' in the early 1960s may now sound a little dated, but it is fascinating, and a little surprising, to see how he uses the common practice of having the radio on in the background as evidence of its capability to touch listeners deeply: 'The power of radio to involve people in depth is manifested in its use during homework by youngsters and by many other people who carry transistor sets in order to provide a private world for themselves amidst crowds.'[4] The potential of radio to 'involve people in depth', combined with the technological advances, have transformed listening to radio into a primarily 'privatised' activity. Increased flexibility, ease of access and radio's portability have clearly contributed to the continuing commitment to radio listening.

If we focus on one particular recent adaptation: the Walkman radio, an intriguing picture of a 'communication bubble' emerges.[5] The term itself points to an isolated and potentially mobile experience of radio. Jonathan Sacks' powerful metaphor of the 'Walkman of the mind',[6] whilst used in a different context, also resonates with this experience of a highly individualised hearing of radio. Patrice Flichy believes that the Walkman 'allows teenagers to remove themselves from adult supervision whilst still living with their parents'.[7] As Frank Gillard of the BBC remarked of the transistor: 'Radio goes with you. So it becomes a personal service.'[8]

Radio has shifted from being an experience enjoyed in community, epitomised by the picture of a family clustering around the wireless, to a far more isolated experience enjoyed by listeners who can be mobile and active whilst listening. Broadcasters can assume even less than before that listeners are hanging on their every word or are 'sitting comfortably' eagerly listening to all their broadcasts. For those seeking to capture the attention of their listeners with words on the radio, this is a significant transition.

Preachers too face a similarly difficult task as they seek to hold the attention of their listeners with words. It might also be argued that whilst preaching remains a communal event, the drift towards an individualistic spirituality may mean that individuals in the congregations listen in isolation. This finds extreme expression in the growing popularity of sermon tapes produced by some larger churches.[9] For someone who is 'house-bound', and who can no longer attend services, these no doubt can help them feel part of the congregational community. In this context, the taped sermon usually remains a highly individualised way of listening.

From Single to Many Radio Choices

Another significant transformation in radio has been the fragmentation and increased choice for listeners.[10] Carpini comments on the radio landscape in the USA:

> Radio's mix of networks and independents give it a unique ability to reach both large audiences and yet still cater to diverse cultural and political interests. On the one hand network broadcasts like *The Larry King Show* can be heard by millions of listeners over more than 1,000 affiliates. On the other hand, low-power stations allow for extremely localised community programming.[11]

A similar diversity is increasingly to be found in Europe. Audience choice continues to grow rapidly.[12] This diversity has been accentuated by rapid technological developments. These include: digital compression, regional satellite radio, internet radio, direct broadcast satellite (DBS), digital audio broadcasting (DAB) and radio broadcasting data service (RBDS).[13] In the last ten years there has been a considerable increase in the number of radio stations in both the USA and the United Kingdom, though average weekly listening has not seen a corresponding increase.[14] 'The challenge for radio broadcasters,' according to Andrew Barrett, 'will be to harness the technologies of the digital world in order to provide a variety of programmes.'[15]

Technologies such as the radio data system (RDS)[16] will allow the listener to choose a specific output, and so: 'a likely consequence of this technology is that it will *weaken* station loyalty by allowing the listener to shop around even more than push-button tuning would'.[17] This highly competitive and technologically developing media environment, combined with greater choice and ease of radio channel switching, is already making it harder to hold on to audiences.

From Proclamation to Conversation

A third significant transformation in radio is related to the style of discourse employed by broadcasters. This could be described as the shift away from proclamation to conversation. In *Media Discourse,* Norman Fairclough argues that not only journalists, but also: 'politicians or senior managers or archbishops or various categories of expert address the public in a conversationalised communicative style.'[18] This conversational approach to broadcast discourse may, according to Fairclough, suggest a: 'shared membership of the same lifeworld, and in so doing implicitly negate the differences of position, perspective and interest'.[19] This resonates with Paddy Scannell's view that: 'people did not expect to be talked down to, lectured or "got at". They expected to be spoken to in [or with] a familiar, friendly and informal manner as if they were equals on the same footing as the speaker.'[20] Scannell's understanding of how listeners expect to be communicated with is now also applicable to congregations.[21] Perhaps the evolving style of *Broadcast Talk* and *Media Discourse* has ensured that most listeners will not accept being 'talked down to, lectured or "got at"' by preachers.

On radio in the 1930s, while it was possible to 'notice a dozen times a day that speakers do not talk in a conversational tone into the microphone' but bellowed 'through the microphone to an audience of millions',[22] many, however, were delighted by those broadcasters who made you feel 'like the guest of an old friend who is looking through some dusty old correspondence by the fireside'.[23] These broadcasters were already aware of the importance of using a conversational style of discourse on the radio. Such discoveries 'accelerated the trend away from impassioned oratory and toward public conversation between speaker and audience.'[24] Scannell notes:

> Quite quickly, older public models of speaking (the lecture, the sermon, the political speech) were replaced by more direct,

> intimate, personal styles of speech. In short, broadcasting learnt that its expressive idiom must, in form and content, approximate to the norms of ordinary, everyday, mundane conversation, or talk. In talk-as-conversation participants treat each other as particular persons, not as a collective.[25]

Broadcasters had begun to learn that: 'while they control the discourse', they do 'not control the communicative context'.[26] The implications from this were that broadcasters needed to 'understand the conditions of reception' and so adapt appropriately to the fact that they were often being heard within the 'sphere of domesticity'.[27] Hence, Roosevelt's 'fireside chats' signalled a 'new model of communication: one person in the private space of his living room chatting with millions of other individuals in theirs'.[28] As broadcasters understood the medium better, and recognised the listening context of the audience, they increasingly relied upon what Fairclough described as a 'conversationalised communicative style'.

Marshall McLuhan considered this 'new model of communication' in his essay on radio:

> Radio affects most people intimately, person-to-person, offering a world of unspoken communication between writer-speaker and the listener. That is the immediate aspect of radio. A private experience. The subliminal depths of radio are charged with the resonating echoes of tribal horns and antique drums. This is inherent in the very nature of this medium, with its power to turn the psyche and society into a single echo chamber.[29]

Whilst McLuhan stresses the intimate, person-to-person and private nature of radio, his metaphors of 'tribal horns and antique drums' also point back to communication instruments of a former age, an oral culture. They evoke images of another kind of fireside chat, this time storytelling and informal conversations around the tribal camp-fire. McLuhan sees a parallel between radio and these traditional forms of communication. Both have the power to unify speakers and listeners, or to use Fairclough's terminology, to instil a sense of a 'shared life-world'.[30] One important strand within McLuhan's discussion of radio appears, therefore, to be a recognition of the strengths of the electronic 'fireside chat',[31] as a conversational model of communication.

Behind this understanding lies the belief that as a form of communication radio resonates subliminally with a pre-Gutenberg oral age. Conversational communication heard on the radio is not a new model at all. In fact McLuhan believes that with radio's electronic orality we return full circle to an 'oral culture'.[32] What is novel, however, is that radio allows speakers to cross barriers of space without moving and moreover to communicate simultaneously with thousands of private domestic spheres.[33]

In 'Poetry and the Microphone' George Orwell reflected on this and on other aspects of radio broadcasting:

> In broadcasting your audience is conjectural, but it is an audience of *one.* Millions may be listening, but each is listening alone, or as a member of a small group, and each has (or ought to have) the feeling that you are speaking to him [sic] individually.[34]

For Orwell, the imperative is to ensure that each person feels she or he is being spoken to as an individual. One way to do this is clearly by employing a conversational communicative style.

This discussion of the shift 'from proclamatory to conversational' modes of discourse on the radio has an important parallel with the suggestion made in the second chapter, that many writers in homiletics have also affirmed a move away from declamatory forms of presentation to forms which can generate intimacy or trust through a more conversational style of speaking. Most listeners to sermons have been saturated in and are accustomed to the conversational discourse of the mass media. To return to a proclamatory style of preaching is to invite a communication breakdown. A style of preaching which follows the example of radio, on the other hand, and employs a conversational form of discourse, may have a greater chance of instilling a sense of a 'shared life-world' between listener and speaker and so connecting with the congregation.

This is not to overlook the key differences between radio and preaching. These include first, the obvious point, that the radio broadcaster is a 'disembodied voice'.[35] In other words she or he is not normally there in person for the listeners, but is mediated through the radio. Or to invert the equation, the audience is rarely present when the broadcaster speaks. The opposite is usually the case with preaching, which is traditionally a face-to-face and embodied form of communication. Orwell, drawing on his own experience of broadcasting and public speaking, believes that:

> it is reasonable to assume that your [radio] audience is sympathetic, or at least interested, for anyone who is bored can promptly switch you off by turning a knob. But though presumably sympathetic, *they have no power over you.* It is just here that a broadcast differs from a speech or a lecture. On the platform, as anyone used to public speaking knows, it is almost impossible not to take your tone from the audience. It is always obvious within a few minutes what they will respond to and what they will not . . .[36]

Speakers who are prepared to improvise and respond spontaneously to the non-verbal signals of their listeners are more likely to hold people's attention. Thus preaching which is not embodied has particular inherent weaknesses. Colin Morris argues that:

> All forms of religious communication other than face to face encounters are in some way or other defective. There isn't that mystical chemical reaction which occurs when a preacher or speaker must look his or her listeners in the eye. The studio has the isolation of a goldfish bowl, cut off from humankind other than the producer or engineer who gaze on impassively through the glass. There is a vulnerability about preaching which broadcasting does not share.[37]

Secondly, with the exception of taped sermons mentioned earlier, listening to preaching is normally a less private activity than listening to the radio. Contrast a half-full church listening to a sermon, with a lone driver listening to the radio in the car. The public speaker or preacher can receive immediate non-verbal feedback. Thirdly, radio is often heard as a secondary activity, compared to the sermon which is usually listened to by a seated congregation, who are generally not involved in other activities whilst listening!

Preachers cannot uncritically imitate radio broadcasters. A conversational style may well work on radio, but using such a form of discourse needs care or else 'intimate' words can be lost in a large church amongst many other worshippers. I am not arguing that preachers should mimic radio broadcasters and turn to a more privatised, more diverse and more conversational form of communication in order to guarantee the sermon's survival. What I am suggesting is that within these transformations there are lessons for preachers. The move in radio towards a more conversational form of discourse reflects a heightened sensitivity to the hearer's situation. This is an important corrective for those who speak without imagining themselves into their listeners' world.

This point leads to the fourth and final transformation. Some radio theorists and practitioners have outlined a case for a more interactive style of radio, thereby going a step further than simply developing a conversational style of discourse. This parallels the discussion in Chapter 2 of interactive or dialogical preaching.

From Distribution to Communication

Unlike the first three transformations identified above, it could be argued that the movement from 'distribution to communication' in radio is still in its infancy. It was playwright Bertholt Brecht who argued:

> Radio is one-sided when it should be two. It is purely an apparatus for distribution, for mere sharing out. So here is a positive suggestion: Change this apparatus over from distribution to communication. The radio would be the finest possible communication apparatus in public life ... That is to say, it would be if it knew how to receive as well as transmit, how to let the listener speak as well as hear, how to bring him [sic] into a relationship instead of isolating him.[38]

Brecht's radical suggestion for radio might equally be applied to preaching, which can often be 'one-sided when it should be two'. Some writers in homiletics have drawn upon Paulo Freire's terminology[39] and as mentioned earlier described the 'one-sided' model of communication as the 'banking concept of homiletics',[40] where the 'preacher preaches and the listeners are preached at'. A radically revised approach, therefore, to broadcasting and preaching might be to 'let the listener speak as well as hear'.[41] This is happening in radio, through emails or phone-ins,[42] and to a lesser extent in preaching, through supplementary discussion groups.[43]

Brecht's idea of a more two-way style of communication is an admirable vision, but perhaps by their very nature, radio and preaching limit the development of a truly interactive or two-way form of connection. Beyond the formal and restricted channels of the post-box, fax machine and telephone, many broadcasters are simply not used to dealing with an ongoing, conversational form of critical feedback. Similarly, whilst preachers inevitably have more face-to-face contact with their listeners, they can easily remain safely ensconced in a 'distribution' model of communication, which protects them from the risk of real engagement with their listeners. Traditional communicators operating in these two fields may pay lip-service to a two-way communication model,[44] but in practice they often act as if they are operating within a simple one-way sender-to-receiver paradigm.[45] The reality may be more complex, but perceptions have a habit of shaping practice.

The advent of CD-ROMS, the Internet with its open Web page sites and the current rapid convergence of communication technologies, which are already making interactive communication more commonplace,[46] will lead to audiences becoming more used to being active receivers of information. They will inevitably be increasingly dissatisfied if relegated to the role of passive receivers.[47] Given this changing communicative context, Brecht's radical advocacy of a more interactive form of communication appears to be increasingly relevant today for oral communicators seeking to hold their listeners' attention.

Before considering further how this move from 'mere distribution' to 'engaging communication' can take place, it is important to point to another distinction between preaching and broadcasting: the context. The broadcaster usually works within the privacy of a small,[48] sound-proofed studio, often accompanied by a handful of colleagues or invited guests in the cubicle and in the studio itself.[49] She or he speaks over the airwaves normally to a mass audience, the vast majority of whom are not known to the broadcaster. Scannell has neatly summarised this double context: 'A broadcast programme has two spaces: that from which it speaks and that within which it is heard.'[50] Preachers, on the other hand, usually communicate in a single large public space, and frequently to a comparatively small group of listeners. They often know, and are known by, a large number of those listening, especially if it is their 'own' church.

By contrast in many radio stations the small enclosed world of the broadcast suite is protected from the outside world by padded doors and, depending on the size of the station, a reception desk and maybe even security guards. Occasionally the private sphere of the studio, and the media institution, venture 'the other side of the window' through outside broadcasts (OBs), through inviting 'citizens' to watch and participate, and more frequently by reporters or producers making forays into the world beyond the walls of the broadcasting centre. But as Peter Dahlgren points out: 'those media institutions which are of most significance for the majority of citizens are ... to a great extent beyond the reach of citizen practices and interventions'.[51]

As a description of a radio station this may be a caricature, but it does not go as far as the description of the Russian radio critic, Velimir Khlebnikov, who pictures it as an iron castle-like structure bearing a skull and cross bones, and marked 'DANGER': 'For the slightest halt in the working of Radio would produce a spiritual swoon of the entire country, a temporary loss of its consciousness.'[52] This may appear a trifle overdramatic, but, whilst the United Kingdom may have fallen short of falling into a 'spiritual swoon', changes on BBC Radio 4 have had a history of provoking listeners to acts of protest. Broadcasting House was in 1995 the target of a proposed march of dissatisfied listeners.[53] While the building itself does not resemble an iron castle, it was initially viewed as an old ironclad battleship, sailing up Regent Street.[54] It remains a somewhat closed environment, surrounded by the sea of people, in central London. One of the first performers to climb aboard admitted: 'My lasting impression of Broadcasting House was that it was a world of its own.'[55] In spite of many alterations, exhibitions, limited open days and programmes about the work inside, it endures as a 'world of its own', which demands a certain amount of insider knowledge to make sense of this citadel of sound.[56] It is ironic that such a relatively closed sphere seeks to distribute entertainment, information and education to so many outside in the open public sphere. We should also remember that most radio broadcasts are heard in the private sphere of the home or car.[57] The way broadcasters attempt to build a bridge between the private sphere of the studio and the private spheres of the listeners may contain some important lessons for preachers who are attempting to build bridges with their listeners.

Unfortunately, some preachers are closed to such lessons and still operate with a 'distribution' model of preaching. They simply distribute their words to their congregation. 'A lofty pulpit without stairs' is the phrase used in Herman Melville's *Moby Dick* to describe the pulpit in Father Mapple's chapel. 'It had a perpendicular ladder at the side. The preacher pulled the ladder in after him when he ascended, leaving him impregnable in his little Quebec.'[58] The pulpit is shaped like the prow of a ship, a 'self-contained strong-hold', withdrawn and isolated from the world.[59] This could easily be a metaphor for the kind of preaching which remains distant and isolated from listeners. The results of such distancing are sermons that are delivered supposedly 'in public', but in fact to private gatherings behind closed church doors. Such sermons too regularly retreat into one-way proclamation rather than espousing two-way conversation. This 'distant' style of preaching can easily slide into non-communication.

Conclusion

This chapter has demonstrated some of the ways in which radio has adapted to the television age.[60] Alongside the move away from static, communal listening patterns towards more individualised and mobile listening habits, is an increased choice of output, rapid technological developments and a shift towards a more conversational style of broadcast talk. These are only a few of the continuing transformations that have taken place in radio broadcasting since the arrival of television. While they are not necessarily conscious adaptations made by radio broadcasters to survive in the age of television, they have certainly assisted radio's survival, and perhaps given new meaning to the title of CBS's 1939 radio show: 'Seems Radio is Here to Stay'.[61]

We have also noted the importance of recognising that radio and preaching each have their own distinctive characteristics. This is one reason why preachers seeking to learn from radio broadcasters should not attempt to draw uncritically from the transformations in radio. The key word here is 'adaptation'. One reason for radio's survival has been its ability to adapt to a changing communicative environment. To affirm that it 'seems preaching is here to stay', then, preachers must not forget this principle of adaptation.

Radio's adaptation, for example, towards a more conversational form of discourse has the potential to bring about what Scannell describes as 'a de-severance',[62] which he explains means 'something like to abolish distance or farness, i.e. to bring close, to bring within range'.[63] We have seen that radio broadcasters have developed a more conversational style of communication. This helped to 'abolish distance' and bring the listener 'closer' to the speaker. Futhermore, as listeners have become immersed in this style of conversational speech, they have grown accustomed to a more intimate form of public speaking. So they will resist being 'spoken at' or 'spoken down to' by preachers.

Notes

1. Flichy 1995, 159–60.
2. Gillard 1964, 29.
3. Consider for example a BBC Radio 4 radio play, Lee Hall's *Spoonface Steinberg*, produced by Kate Rowland, broadcast 27 January 1997. 'The BBC got an unprecedented 200 calls enthusing and requesting a repeat.' One truck driver said: 'This was the most poignant piece of radio I have heard for years. I am a truck driver and I was in tears.' Another driver admitted that it 'touched him so deeply he had to stay in his car until it ended'. See Anne Karpf, 'Spoonface stirs it up'. *The Guardian*, 19 February 1997, 13: 'Most remarkably, Spoonface Steinberg is a monologue, delivered

entirely by 10-year-old Becky Simpson, who plays a seven-year-old terminally autistic child.'

4. McLuhan 1987 (1964), 298.
5. Flichy 1995, 165. This isolating tendency can be interpreted in different ways. Mark Noll, for example, argued in *Christianity Today* that the Walkman poses a serious challenge to Christianity because it represented 'one more competitor to the voice of God'. 1987, 22–3. Such 'distracting', 'atomizing' and 'alienating' views about the Walkman are challenged in du Gay, Hall, Janes, Mackay and Negus 1997. They point to Sony's own market research into the Walkman, which divides usage into 'two particular types: "escape" and "enhancement"'. 92. On these grounds they suggest that: 'There is no grand "universal" turning away from the world into privatised, atomistic distraction ... while one's listening may be private, the codes that inform listening are inherently social.' 94.
6. Sacks 1991. 'We no longer talk of virtues but of values, and values are tapes we play on the walkman of the mind: any tune we choose so long as it does not disturb others.' 41.
7. Flichy 1995, 165.
8. Crisell 1994, 29.
9. See, for example, All Souls Langham Place, London, which has a vast and popular tape library of past sermons.
10. Maggie Brown argued in the mid 1990s that: 'After decades of cosy stagnation, Great British radio is lurching towards a multi-station future of cut-throat commercialism with audiences and talent spread thin.' Maggie Brown, 'Warning: your wireless is exploding', in *The Independent*, 19 January 1995.
11. Carpini 1995, 30.
12. See Feldman 1997. Feldman describes aspects of the 'digital revolution', which is 'being forged by an accelerating move from a world familiar with analogue media to a world that will be increasingly dominated by digital media'. 1. Most relevant for the present discussion is his description of a software package called RealAudio, which gives access to '24-hour Internet Radio, which is based on the hourly output of news from ABC'. 148. See also Higham, presenter of *The Technophobe's Guide To The Future*, BBC 2, 7 May 1996, on the future of digital television.
13. Rhoads 1995, 17–19.
14. See Crisell 1994, 37–9, and Hargrave 1994, especially 33–40.
15. Barrett 1995, 157. See 'Media watch' in *The Times*, 26 March, 1999 for details of a new study by Continental Research. It claims that 'radio appears to be complementary to surfing the Web, with 25

per cent of people claiming to listen to more radio since they started using the Net.'

16. RDS here is understood to mean the same technology as RBDS, as used by Eric Rhoads. RDS, radio data system, as explained by Crisell 'exploits the large bandwidth of FM broadcasts to transmit data as an inaudible signal along with the output'. In more practical terms it is an 'automatic tuning system' which both provides the best signal of the listener's chosen station and also the facility to 'push a button for news, current affairs, rock, classical music, drama or whatever'. See Crisell 1994, 41.
17. Crisell 1994, 41.
18. Fairclough 1995, 148.
19. Ibid., 148.
20. Scannell 1991, 3. 'Manner' has replaced 'matter' in the original extract. I am assuming that this was a typographical error.
21. Miller 1995. 'Rhetoric was once the stuff of great sermons. Now the entire tone of worship should be conversation.' 73.
22. Arnheim 1936, 72.
23. Ibid., 77.
24. Jamieson 1988, 53.
25. Scannell 1996, 12–13. Chapter 5 of this book will include a more detailed analysis of the work of two religious broadcasters from the 1940s who employed 'more direct, intimate' and conversational forms of radio broadcasting.
26. Scannell 1991, 3. See also Scannell 1996. Scannell asserts that: 'A growing sensitivity to the implications of the domestic spaces of reception created a conscious readjustment of the forms of talk that radio produced, with a clear aim of being more suitable for "fireside" listening.' 19.
27. Ibid., 3.
28. Jamieson 1988, 55.
29. McLuhan 1987 (1964), 299.
30. Fairclough 1995, 148.
31. McLuhan 1987 (1964), 299.
32. This important theme in McLuhan's thought was developed more extensively by Walter Ong. See for example, Ong 1982, 5–77.
33. Scannell argues that: 'It is not just that radio and television *compress* time and space. They create new possibilities of being: of being in two places at once, or at two times at once.' Scannell 1996, 91.
34. Orwell 1970 (1958), 374–82. Also in Strauss 1993, 167.
35. Shingler and Wieringa 1998, 43. See also Dyson 1994, 172–8.
36. Strauss (ed.) 1993, 167.

37. Colin Morris, Letter to Jolyon Mitchell, 25 August 1998.
38. Brecht 1993 (1932), 15.
39. Freire 1971, 67. Freire argues against 'banking' education, which is merely concerned with 'transferrals of information', and argues for a more dialogical approach which blurs the teacher–student divide.
40. See discussion of Craddock in Chapter 2 of this book; and see also Bond 1991, 58–60.
41. Listeners already do this within the black preaching context. See Mitchell 1990a, 92–3. Mitchell describes, affirms and interprets this practice.
42. Scannell perceptively points out: 'Audience members who elect to take part in phone-ins enter the discursive space of the programme but not its physical place. They remain in their own place while dialling into a public discourse.' Scannell 1996, 141.
43. See, for example, the 'collaborative' methodology espoused in McClure 1995, 59–72.
44. For a clear outline of such an approach see McQuail and Windahl 1993, 19.
45. Ibid., 17.
46. Feldman 1997. 'For many the shift to digital means a move from passive to interactive media. But it is already clear ... that interactivity is only a thread in the fabric of change and development.' 18.
47. 'In about the first decade of the new century we will have a transition from the information society to the experience society. It will be about "being there" ... Instead of buying a television set, a camcorder, a computer and a telephone, you will buy one terminal that will integrate all of those capabilities together.' Professor Peter Cochrane cited by Harrison 1995, 7.
48. This description of the studio as a 'private space' is a qualification to Scannell's belief that 'the radio or television studio is a public place into which people come to take part in a variety of political, cultural, educative or entertaining programmes'. Scannell 1996, 140.
49. 'Cubicle' refers to the room linked to the studio where the producer and the studio managers normally sit during broadcasts.
50. Scannell 1996, 139.
51. Dahlgren 1995, 155.
52. Khlebnikov 1993, 32.
53. 'To have provoked the middle classes into threatening to march on Broadcasting House to protect a much-loved service from its

own top managers sounds like an implausible achievement, but that is exactly what happened when the BBC threatened to remove Radio 4 from long wave.' Maggie Brown, 'Warning: your wireless is exploding', in *The Independent*, 19 January 1995.

54. Reid 1987, 20. Reid attributes this to Newson, one of the engineers who helped install the equipment in the original control room.
55. Ibid., 46, attributed to pianist Jean Melville who had joined the BBC in 1927.
56. For insider knowledge, see Schlesinger's fascinating study on the workings of Broadcasting House's (BH) newsroom in the late 1970s. Schlesinger 1987 (1978). This text covers not only BBC radio news at BH, but also BBC television news at White City, and was based on ninety full days' observation.
57. Loktev 1993, 204.
58. Melville 1956, 55–6.
59. The Moby Dick analogy is also made use of by Sleeth 1986, 94.
60. For a far fuller account of how this took place in America, see Fornatale and Mills 1980.
61. Norman Corwin wrote and produced, 'Seems Radio is Here to Stay' for CBS, 1939. See also Watson 1995, 195–6.
62. Scannell 1996, 167. This is how Scannell translates Martin Heidegger's *entfernung*, Heidegger, 1962, 138 n. 2.
63. Scannell 1996, 167.

PART II

Case Studies from British and American Religious Radio

CHAPTER 5

Radio Padre and Radio Academic

We turn now to a detailed examination of the work of some outstanding British religious radio broadcasters. Obviously such a study has to be highly selective and limited to a few practitioners. We then consider some examples taken from the very different radio environment of the USA. The question of how to communicate orally and effectively in an environment where audio-visual stimuli compete for the listeners' attention remains at the heart of the discussion.

First we examine two religious radio broadcasters from the 1940s, Ronald Selby Wright and C. S. Lewis. We do this for several reasons. Both were broadcasting during the Second World War, a time of upheaval and insecurity. Audiences had urgent needs at a traumatic time. Religious broadcasters had to adapt themselves to this changing situation, and both Lewis and Wright did so with considerable skill. As well as being important in its own right, their work provides an insight into religious radio prior to the popularisation of television. Compare their broadcasts with examples from *Thought for the Day* discussed in the following chapter and it is possible to see some of the ways that religious broadcasting has transformed over the past fifty years.

Ronald Selby Wright and Clive Staples Lewis were extremely popular, broadcasting at the same time as Richard Dimbleby and Edward Murrow. Like Dimbleby and Murrow they provide a useful exemplification of the power of speaking visually. R. S. Wright was commonly known as the 'Radio Padre' and C. S.

Lewis could be described as a 'Radio Academic'. They make a fascinating contrast. The former was a down-to-earth Church of Scotland padre, who became the BBC's Radio Padre in April 1942. The latter was an Oxford don whose radio talks would later be published, with a few amendments, as the best-selling *Mere Christianity*.[1] Both broadcasters became household names, and built up considerable followings. Such was their popularity that both had their radio talks published. Their broadcasting styles, and in particular their use of conversational and pictorial language, are illuminating.

Radio Padre – Ronald Selby Wright

> The Radio Padre is recognised all over the country as easily the finest thing religious broadcasting has ever done for us ... here is a man who really knows the people he is talking to; he knows their lives and really understands their difficulties.[2]

Ronald Selby Wright, ordained in the Church of Scotland, was seconded from an Edinburgh Army Unit[3] to the BBC at the partial instigation of the Head of Religious Broadcasting, Reverend Dr James W. Welch.[4] Wright's weekly fifteen-minute radio broadcasts began on 1 April 1942, though he had previously given four talks in November 1941. Whilst C. S. Lewis, according to *Time* magazine, had an average audience of 600,000,[5] Wright would eventually attract around 7 million listeners every Wednesday.[6] 'His talks continued into 1944 and became increasingly popular in broadcast and printed form.'[7] These talks became 'as much a wartime institution as Tommy Handley's *It's That Man Again*'.[8]

A number of factors contributed to Wright's popularity and effectiveness as a broadcaster. First, Wright travelled extensively. As he was concerned not to become out of touch with his soldier audience, he visited soldiers stationed at 'lonely posts dotted all over the country'.[9] He claims:

> I slept in more beds than Mary Queen of Scots ever slept in. I was

> travelling by trains, buses and everything else. I never stopped travelling. The result was that I got to the most remote places, up in the Highlands and down Devonshire and Somerset. They all welcomed me because they all listened.[10]

He was keen to meet as many soldiers as he could. He 'met troops living in lonely valleys and moors, in Highland glens, on islands or round our coasts'.[11] He heard many of the questions and problems of ordinary soldiers, who had had limited contact with Christianity and the church. Hearing the concerns of his listeners at first hand informed his work as a broadcaster. The combination of extensive travel and regular broadcasting was an 'exceedingly exhausting assignment'.[12] Nevertheless, leaving the studio to enter the world of his listeners inevitably nourished his broadcasts.

Over forty years later the radio broadcasting consultant Robert McLeish would forcibly advise: 'It is a positive duty for the broadcaster to escape from the confines of his [sic] building into the world which is both the source and target for all his enterprise.'[13] Wright needed no such advice, as he took this 'duty' extremely seriously and regularly escaped the confines of his broadcasting bases in Bedford and London.[14]

A second reason for his attracting such a large audience was his broadcasting manner. 'He was friendly and pleasant to listen to;' according to radio producer Ronald Falconer, 'the listener felt he was speaking directly and personally to him.'[15] This evaluation is echoed in the BBC radio documentary on his life:

> Ronald Selby Wright was a consummate professional when he got into a radio studio. In an era when many of the best-known voices on the radio treated the microphone like a public meeting, he grasped intuitively that it could be used to say intimate things in a very personal way.[16]

Wright's own understanding of why his radio talks were so popular provides further support for Falconer's evaluation. Wright admits:

> I think really because I'm not a deep theologian. I like people and talk to people and I just talked to them, I didn't preach to them. I

> just chatted to them. In fact the very first time I did the Radio Padre, Dr Welch, [who] was head of Religious Broadcasting, put a coat at one side of my table and said 'Now there is somebody over there. You are talking to that person' and as a result I didn't shout, I just chatted to somebody, who was there ... I just talked to the people as though they were beside me.[17]

It is clear that Wright understood one of the fundamental characteristics of radio: the perceived proximity of the speaker for the listener. This insight ensured that he tried to speak in a natural and conversational fashion. He believed that 'what one was doing was just talking to somebody sitting round the fire beside me. They were more like fireside talks.'[18] In Wright's eyes this intimate discourse, where one is just chatting to one's listeners, is the 'splendid secret of the whole business'.[19]

A letter cited in his unpublished personal diary provides some evidence of the natural, conversational form of his first radio talk on 1 April 1942. One John McVie described how members of the Edinburgh Mess of Wright's former regiment were seated at dinner at 9.25pm about to listen to the new Commanding Officer, when, in an adjoining room: 'came that marvellous voice of yours and it was so real and natural that you might have been speaking to us from that little central table instead of from a studio down South'.[20] Wright believes that he wasn't modelling on anybody in particular, but simply being himself and 'talking naturally'.[21]

This sense of speaking naturally, personally and directly to his listeners can be seen in many of his introductions. For example, when setting out his talk on fidelity he begins by creating a feeling of intimacy: 'I think we know each other well enough and understand each other well enough now for me to speak out pretty strongly about it.'[22] He is attempting to create a sense of 'mediated' friendship between his listeners and himself. The reality is that he knows few of his 7 million listeners and few know him as anything more than a disembodied voice. In short, they 'know' him, not in the 'flesh', but as a broadcaster 'well enough' not to be surprised if he is frank or straightforward in his talks. This fictional or illusory intimacy is at the heart of much successful mass communication, and may further explain Wright's popularity.

Engaging Images

In one talk, aptly entitled 'The Message Must Get Through',[23] he tells a story about when he was 'tramping over our own Border hills with some Scottish soldiers'. He recounts how:

> We'd been on the hills for some days, marching, sleeping in the heather with nothing but the sky above us; . . . [we] came to a lonely valley lost in the midst of these green hills near Lauderdale, where we stopped and rested. I went up to a lonely cottage on the side of the hill to get some water. The old woman came to the door to give me what I wanted, and then seeing the fellows below in the valley, she looked up at me and said. 'This is the second time only that the King's men have ever been in this valley.'[24]

The specific details add power to this narrative. For example, 'sleeping in the heather with nothing but the sky above us' is an easy image for the listener to recreate, especially for the thousands of soldiers who were regularly sleeping outside. Or notice the repetition of 'lonely' in consecutive sentences. The placing of 'lonely valley lost in the midst of these green hills' and 'lonely cottage on the side of the hill' adds to an emerging picture of isolation. It is important to recognise, however, that visual detail is but one of the tools skilfully used by Wright. Short sentences, active verbs and intriguing dialogue all contribute to the force of the story.

This can be seen later in the same talk, with an image that makes for a strong contrast with his earlier picture of the Border hills:

> I walked again last week in London through row after row, street after street of ruined, battered houses. I passed the great Church of St. Paul's standing majestically amid a mile of ruins.[25]

Active verbs such as 'walked' or 'passed', rhythmic repetitions such as 'row after row', and developing parallelism such as 'street after street', all combine to create a picture of an embattled London, where St Paul's remains 'standing' defiantly surrounded by destruction. This is on a far grander scale than Ed Murrow's London Blitz report, discussed in Chapter 3, which focused on a dripping peach can. It lacks Murrow's observation of minute detail, but compensates with the powerful image of St Paul's 'standing majestically'. Wright's description of Blitz-torn London is another example of how pictorial language can create a memorable scene, which would have had the potential to touch the listeners' imaginations, especially for those who knew London or who were living through the Blitz.

Wright's skill in engaging his listeners' attention was partly founded upon his ability to step into their shoes, and articulate their experience. For example, in 'Cairo Calling', a talk which evolved from his short tour of the Middle East forces in 1943 and 1944 he evokes the atmosphere of home with a few simple word-pictures:

> It's folk at home, and home itself, that makes up life; and beds with sheets, and tea round our fireside, and slippers, and 'to hear our names or voices we love'...[26]

He engages not only the visual imagination, but also aural memories by evoking the 'voices we love'.

In the same talk he once again returns to the Scottish hills to create a romantic vision of home:

> I remember one frosty evening shortly before I left to come out and see you, tramping over Scottish Border hills with Wallace Campbell, these hills that are green to the top and, to me, the friendliest of all hills, and when we came to a certain spot we saw a shining streak of silver glittering diamond-like in the now darkening hills – St. Mary's Loch in the distance. [27]

Specific representational imagery: 'tea round our fireside', give way to more impressionistic imagery: 'silver glittering diamond-like'. In both cases particular details are used to heighten the sense of presence. The travelling to a certain spot, followed by the 'we saw', adds immediacy to this dusk viewing of St Mary's Loch. He continues: 'Of course, had we gone that night we would have found that the silver of the loch had turned to blue.'[28] Notice how he has used specific colours: green, silver and blue. The result is, literally, a more colourful set of scenes. The glittering silver is meant to represent the romantic memory of home, the blue the colder reality.

The point Wright is making is a simple one: 'many of you out here have got an almost exaggerated view of the land you'll return to one day'.[29] In other words, it may be like 'silver glittering diamond-like' in the memory, but on return, home may be a more mundane colour. Wright in these examples demonstrates the ability to create a series of scenes with a few simple verbal brush strokes. The result is a simple, but powerful message.

Wright's Keener Sight

Thomas Troeger emphasises the importance of alerting 'the eye to keener sight'.[30] As it has been argued above, Wright demonstrates such 'keen sight' in many of his other broadcasts. In a talk on 'Prayer', his 'visit to a lonely Gunners' site' provided another noteworthy image:

> I saw two promontories jutting out into the sea-loch. One was bleak as ever bleak could be – jagged, stony ground with but one sad bent tree. The other, not 200 yards across the water from it was a glorious medley of colours from flowers and coloured shrubs and trees white with blossom or green with freshness of the first leaves.[31]

It is as if Wright has becomes the listeners' camera: snapping two contrasting shots that become crisper in definition by being placed next to each other. The image of 'one sad bent tree' becomes even more desolate when placed alongside the image of 'trees white with blossom or green with freshness of the first leaves'. He not only demonstrates 'keen sight' for detail and colour, but also makes subtle changes to what David Buttrick describes as the 'focal field'. Buttrick defines this phrase in these terms: '*Focal Field* can best be understood by imagining a camera lens which widened, can take in a large screen, or, narrowed down, will pick out particular objects.'[32] In this example Wright has shifted or narrowed the attention of the listener, from the 'bleak promontory' to the 'bent tree', thereby narrowing the 'focal field'.

If we turn to some of Buttrick's other categories, it is possible to analyse further elements of Wright's pictorial discourse.

Buttrick writes of 'lens depth' which he defines as 'the degree of self-engagement involved in point-of-view'.[33] In this example, Wright keeps a distance from involvement in the scene, and maintains the point of view of an observer or static camera.

Apart from 'focal field' and 'lens depth', Buttrick speaks of 'focal depth' in discourse, which 'refers to the degree of penetration into what we are observing'.[34] In the case of the two contrasting landscapes, they initially have a flat 'focal depth'. In other words, there is little 'penetration into what we are observing'. This, however, changes as Wright makes a move to explore the disparity between the two promontories. In his eyes the transformation from 'bleak stony ground' to a 'glorious medley of colours', is the result of 'vision' and 'hard-work'.[35] He is attempting to give his picture 'focal depth', and so penetrate the surface. In a transition, which is not entirely successful, he argues that prayer, which inspires vision and hard work, can transform the rocky ground of people's lives.

In the discussion so far, we have seen that Wright's conversational style and his use of engaging and 'homely' pictorial language are but a few of the many broadcasting tools he used in his talks.[36] His success was perhaps due to this variation of style, as well his 'keen eye' and his ability to recreate scenes for his listeners. In most of his talks, however, his point of view, and the point of view the listener is encouraged to take, remain static.[37]

In Buttrick's terms Wright was skilled with 'focal length' and 'focal depth' in his pictures, but less at ease with 'lens depth', or allowing himself to become deeply involved in and through his word-pictures. Even after the tragically premature death of his friend Sergeant James Dalgleish, only a few hours after being on air with Wright,[38] he resorts in the following week's talk to the second hand 'poetic imagery' of 'green pastures' and 'still waters' of Psalm 23.[39] Such 'distance'[40] may reflect raw emotions rather than a lack of feeling for the death of his friend;[41] that he was moved is clear from the fact he delivers a talk not on the subject announced in the *Radio Times,* but one entitled: 'On the Death of a Friend'. His description of the last time he saw James Dalgleish, whilst possibly too romanticised, is nevertheless easy for the listener to visualise:

> When he left me that night, as he shook hands, he smiled that grand smile of his. 'Goodnight, Sir,' he said. 'See you in the morning.' And then we parted, and looking round again was a setting sun of a glorious summer evening in his face. He waved ... Some words I'd spoken a week or two back seem now almost strangely prophetic: 'He's gone. I do not understand. I only know that as he turned to go and waved his hand, in his young eyes a sudden glory shone, and I was dazzled by a sunset glow, and he was gone'.[42]

In a number of other talks Wright adds pathos and insight to stories of loss and separation by the addition to the scene of visual details.[43]

It is worth noting a further reason for Wright's popularity amongst certain listeners, notably British prisoners of war. He was used in 1943 by MI9 to pass on coded messages.[44] He relates that:

> when I started the talks 'Good evening forces' in fact I was coding the message and when I came to the word 'but' it meant the code was over ... so I did that for a considerable time. It nearly drove me mad.[45]

It is hard to imagine the use today of a preacher coding a sermon for her or his congregation to decode later at home.

Wright's 'direct and simple if somewhat patronising talks' were not, however, without their critics. W. E. Williams, one of the writers for 'Critic on the Hearth' in *The Listener,* was initially, in late 1941, highly critical.[46] By mid-1942, however, he would be more positive and was 'impressed' by 'the tactics' of one of Wright's talks. In Williams' opinion this was 'a matter which too many wireless speakers fail to study'. On one occasion, he also applauded the way in which the 'Radio Padre wisely delayed his exhortation until he had provided a homely analysis of the state of being "browned-off"'.[47] Given Williams' earlier critique of the Radio Padre,[48] this is a surprisingly positive review. A more significant point, besides this single example of a critic tempered by Wright's 'tactics', was that according to Wright himself he received between 100 and 1000 letters a *day* in response to his broadcasts. On this basis alone, assuming the general accuracy of these figures, it is fair to deduce that the Radio Padre made a considerable impact.[49]

Radio Academic – C. S. Lewis

> Lewis had no interest whatsoever in the radio as such, a harsh contraption the sound of which he cringed at every time he heard it bellowing from his gardener's bungalow.[50]

It is ironic that C. S. Lewis, an Oxford academic and Christian apologist, who initially 'hardly listened to radio',[51] should have become a popular war-time broadcaster.[52] In 1944 Anne Fremantle claimed in *Commonweal*: 'Miss Dorothy Sayers, Father Ronald Knox, Miss Barbara Ward and above all, Mr C. S. Lewis, are definitely religious radio stars.'[53] This particular 'religious radio star' likened his broadcasting to a 'procrustean bed'.[54] Despite his apparent dislike for radio work, his broadcasts provide an interesting parallel to the radio style employed by Wright, who, surprisingly, is not mentioned here by Fremantle.

Like Wright, Lewis was invited by the then Head of Religious Broadcasting, James Welch,[55] to broadcast: 'The microphone is a limiting, and often irritating, instrument, but the quality of thinking and deep conviction which I find in your book [*The Problem of Pain*] ought surely to be shared with a great many other people.'[56] Neither Welch nor Eric Fenn his producer defined Lewis's broadcasts, but he was influenced and even constrained by their advice.[57] It is impossible to divorce the broadcasting of either Lewis or Wright from Welch and the Reithian institution that provided them with their platform, or in this case with their microphone.[58]

James Welch wanted 'something like *The Christian Faith as I See it* – by a layman'.[59] The result was a series of four broadcasts which 'began in the late summer of 1941',[60] and was billed in the *Radio Times* as *Right and Wrong: A Clue to the Meaning of the Universe*. Lewis was 'overwhelmed by letters even before finishing his four talks'.[61] His second series, this time of five talks, was entitled *What Christians Believe* and was broadcast in early 1942.[62]

The fact that he was invited to do more broadcasts suggests a certain degree of perceived success. These were entitled *Christian Behaviour* and ran for eight consecutive Sundays in 1942. His earlier sets of talks were all delivered live, but his final seven-part war-time series, *Beyond Personality*, was prerecorded and broadcast weekly in 1944.[63] All of his talks would later be published, without much adaptation, as *Broadcast Talks* (1942), *Christian Behaviour* (1943) and *Beyond Personality* (1944).[64]

Appropriate Pictures?

> Lewis has received so much acclaim for remarkably apt and visual analogies in illustrating complex issues, it's worth noting that he took trouble over these.[65]

William Hooper's assertion finds support from a careful reading of Lewis's original scripts. For example, one point, which Hooper also notes, is to be found in the script for *Right or Wrong: A Clue to the Meaning of the Universe: Materialism or Religion?* This was broadcast on 20 August 1941. Lewis had originally written:

> If there was a controlling power outside the universe, it could not show itself to us as one of the facts inside the universe – no more than an author of a play could walk in as one of the characters in the play.[66]

Intriguingly, above the typed script Lewis has altered the analogy, adding in his own writing: 'no more than the operator in a cinema could himself appear on the screen'. The analogy is altered yet again in the published book, to read: '. . . no more than the architect of a house could actually be a wall or staircase or fireplace in that house'.[67] Unlike the first two images, where it is possible to imagine the author or cinema operator appearing in the drama, it is harder to conceive of the architect in the building itself (unless, peradventure, he were to fall into the cement mixer). The point to stress here is the care with which Lewis refines his analogies.

This can be seen elsewhere in other original broadcasting scripts. For example, in a talk broadcast on 15 February 1942, he again adapts his original image. In this talk on *What Christians Believe* he explores what it means to have the 'Christ-life' dwelling inside. In the original typed script he suggests that 'it's not merely the spreading of an idea; it's more like evolution – a biological or super-biological fact'. In pen, he has crossed this out and replaced it with a more specific analogy: 'it's more like transforming, like a caterpillar becoming a chrysalis'.[68] Later in the same talk, where he argues that 'God never meant man to be a purely spiritual creature', he has put a line through the general phrase 'the bodily process of eating and drinking' and above, written in pen the more specific and active phrase: 'he [God] uses physical things like bread and wine' to make his point that: 'He [God] likes matter. He invented it.'[69]

These adaptations in Lewis's own handwriting on his original scripts provide direct evidence that he did 'take trouble' over selecting the appropriate visual analogy. In these amendments, we catch a glimpse of Lewis the English scholar, author of the groundbreaking *Allegory of Love*,[70] wrestling to create visual analogies which will both connect and communicate appropriately with his listeners. It is useful to bear this craftsmanship in mind as we concentrate on a number of specific examples from Lewis's broadcasts.

Consider the images that build this metaphor:

> Why is God landing in this enemy-occupied world in disguise and starting a sort of secret society to undermine the devil?[71]

It is almost as if Lewis has turned God into an undercover agent, stealthily penetrating a war-zone. Such a surprising transference of roles is at the heart of many of Lewis's analogies. In this example, the question is brought alive by the graphic picture of 'God landing' and a phrase redolent with meaning in the early 1940s: 'enemy-occupied'. Given the German occupation of much of Europe at this time, his inquiry gains force through topicality, the provocative image of God in disguise, and the echoing of an earlier phrase where he had stated: 'God has landed on this enemy-occupied world in human form.'[72] The Lewis critic, Joe R. Christopher, describes this as an 'interesting image that runs throughout *What Christians Believe*'. Christopher believes that the use of 'landed' in this talk suggests an 'invasion from the sea', which 'was not unusual for saboteurs in Europe during that time in the war'.[73] Lewis has made an intriguing, and some would say inappropriate, pictorial connection between his understanding of the Incarnation and an image easily recognisable to the listeners of that day.

Another example of Lewis's attempt to make his theology

more accessible through analogy can be found in his later set of talks, *Christian Behaviour*, where he makes the imaginative link between humanity and a fleet of ships:

> Think of us as a fleet of ships sailing in formation. The voyage will be a success only, in the first place, if the ships don't collide and get in another's way; and, secondly, if each ship is seaworthy and has her engines in good order.[74]

Lewis develops this 'extended analogy'[75] further as he articulates the view of those who believe that it: '... doesn't matter what his ship is like inside provided that he doesn't run into the next ship'.[76] He will later critique such an individualistic view, arguing that morality is relevant not only to the creation of harmony inside personalities, but also between individuals, and within the whole of humanity. His method in this extract is based on an attempt to invite his audience to make an imaginative leap. The 'imaginative shock'[77] is created here by the encouragement to think that we as humans are like a 'formation of ships'. In other words, the power of this image is created, not simply by resonating with wartime worries about the safety of naval convoys,[78] but also by the extraordinary connection between ourselves and a fleet of ships. In this case, the basic pictorial language, of the 'ships sailing in formation' is the building block of Lewis's analogy.

A further example of Lewis's ability to create 'shocking' connections between images is to be found in his discussion of 'sexual morality':

> You can get a large audience together for a strip-tease act – that is, to watch a girl undress on the stage: now suppose you come to a country where you could fill a theatre by simply bringing a covered plate on to the stage and then slowly lifting the cover so as to let every one see, just before the lights went out, that it contained a mutton chop or a bit of bacon, wouldn't you think that in that country something had gone wrong with the appetite for food?[79]

This argument by analogy partially depends upon the use of pictorial language, and the graphic revealing of the mutton chop. Joe Christopher rather generously describes this as a 'delightful analogy' of a 'country in which food is gradually revealed striptease fashion'.[80] Such an assessment fails to recognise the surprising and ultimately shocking nature of this picture. Lewis's aim is to show how the 'sex instinct' has in some way gone wrong or become corrupted. Once again it is the specific details, such as the unmasking just 'before the lights go out', which add to the atmosphere of this memorable and somewhat strange imagined event.

Approximate Pictures

Another extract provides a useful insight into Lewis's own understanding of creating pictures in the mind. In his talk where he has been discussing 'What Christians Believe', he moves into the world of science and a consideration of how scientists explain the atom. Lewis argues that they:

> give you a description out of which you can make a mental picture. But then they warn you that this picture is not what the scientists actually believe. What the scientists believe is a mathematical formula. The pictures are there only to help understand the formula. They are not really true in the way that the formula is; they don't give you the real thing but only something more or less like it.[81]

This provides insight not only into Lewis's understanding of scientific method, but also perhaps his view of the role of pictorial language. It is a pointer to reality, rather than the reality itself. It does not 'give you the real thing but only something more or less like it'. Borrowing his own analogies, it might be argued that Lewis used pictorial language in his broadcasts to entice the listeners to step 'through the wardrobe' and move 'farther up and farther in',[82] encouraging them towards a new view on the world and their own lives. His verbal pictures are intended to provide an approximate view rather than an exact representation.

Another extract, this time from his talk on ' Right and Wrong as a Clue to the Meaning of the Universe', in August 1941, underlines his quick-fire use of pictorial language. In this talk Lewis argues that humanity is on the 'wrong road', has been 'making some big mistake', and needs to change direction. To reinforce this point he uses three common images: first, the picture of 'putting the clock back' is followed by a rhetorical question: 'Would you think I was joking if I said that you *can* put a clock back, and that if the clock is wrong it is often a very sensible thing to do?' Secondly, a new picture is introduced to support this point: 'If you're on the wrong road, progress means doing an about-turn and walking back to the right road.'[83] Thirdly, the previous images are reinforced by an example from arithmetic: 'When I have started a sum the wrong way, the sooner I admit this and go back and start again, the faster I shall get on.'[84]

This series of pictures is a good example of how in many of his radio talks Lewis often paints a picture in the air, and immediately reinforces it by painting another. It is as if he creates one picture, only to lay it aside or discard it and sketch a new one. The result of such an approach is to create a temporary or impromptu feel to many of his images and analogies. This observation provides a qualification to those, like A. N. Wilson, who critique the effects of Lewis's style. Wilson may be correct to challenge Lewis's theology in the picture of humans becoming 'slugs or crabs' as a parallel to the incarnation,[85] but his critique fails to recognise the nature of many of Lewis's verbal pictures. These may be refined images, but they are basically offered as quick spontaneous sketches rather than carefully executed masterpieces. 'Lewis, in these radio addresses,' according to Joe Christopher, 'explains matters simply and uses an analogy for every difficult idea.'[86] The reason for this approach is not simply to explain difficult ideas, but also surely because Lewis is attempting to hold his listeners' attention by using provocative and startling analogies. These often rely on pictorial language for their form.

Oral Pictures

It is not entirely surprising therefore that Lewis's three books, *Broadcast Talks, Christian Behaviour* and *Beyond Personality,* which were closely based on his radio talks, retain much of their oral character. Lewis admitted: 'In the printed versions I made a few additions to what I had said at the microphone, but otherwise left the text much as it had been.'[87] Later he wisely suggested that 'a "talk" on the radio should, I think, be as like real talk as possible, and should not sound like an essay being read aloud.'[88]

Lewis attempted to put this into practice throughout his radio talks. One of the most explicit examples of 'real talk' is when he offered an apology at the start of a broadcast in August 1941:

> I must begin by apologising for my voice. Since we last met I've managed to catch an absolute corker of a cold. Should you hear this talk suddenly interrupted by a loud crash you needn't jump to any rash conclusion. It'll probably only be me sneezing or coughing. Well, the point I got to last week was ...[89]

Unsurprisingly, this apology is not included in the published text. By suggesting that he and his listeners have met before, and through gentle irony about his cold, he establishes a sense of intimacy or connection between himself and his listeners.

Like Wright, Lewis normally employed a conversational tone of voice. One critic observes:

> He neither whispers nor shouts. Never does he display the vocal antics of the high-powered salesman, the fiery orator, or the impassioned evangelist, but he uses force and emphasis on a conversational level to intensify meanings and to sharpen contrasts.[90]

It is impossible in a written text to recreate Lewis's baritone, resonant, and conversational tones,[91] but it is important to read the pictorial language in these three short books as the product of oral discourse, rather than as prose which is intended to be read as a carefully considered literary piece. Moreover, it is vital to recognise, with Carolyn Keefe, that:

> unless Lewis' voice captures the pathos, the humour, the irony, unless from the analogies, instances, and illustrations it evokes sensory images within the mind of the listener, even his most excellent script will remain nothing but a sheaf of splendid writing.[92]

The skill with which Lewis 'evokes sensory images within the mind of the listener' partially resides in the use of his voice, but also in the way in which he edited and clarified his expression for his radio talks. He himself admits: 'If you are allowed to talk for only ten minutes pretty well everything has to be sacrificed to brevity.'[93]

Behind this familiar style and rich voice is a rhetorical objective. Lewis confesses: 'I'm not preaching ... I'm only trying to call attention to a fact; ... we have failed to practise ourselves the kind of behaviour we expect from other people.'[94] Just as Wright sought to stimulate his listeners' imaginations by using verbal pictures, so Lewis attempted to construct a familiar world for his audience and then extend it: 'This world is a great sculptor's shop. We are statues and there is a rumour going round the shop that some of us some day are going to come to life.'[95] Lewis's use of pictorial language is often tightly integrated into the fabric and logic of his talks. He appears to create verbal pictures not simply to connect with his listeners, but also to lead them on, 'into something beyond' and to 'catch a glimpse' of another 'country'.[96] This evocative and neo-Platonic language is typical of Lewis, and sets his apart from Wright's more straightforward style.

In a later radio talk, published in *Beyond Personality*, Lewis explores the idea that acting in a certain manner can be transformative of character. He asks: 'May I once again start by putting two pictures, or two stories rather, into your mind?' First, he draws from the fairy tale of *Beauty and the Beast*, and then, secondly, he tells a story which:

> is about someone who had to wear a mask; a mask which made him look much nicer than he really was. He had to wear it for years. And when he took it off he found his own face had grown to fit it. He was now really beautiful. What had begun as a disguise had become a reality.[97]

Lewis initially describes this as a picture and then corrects himself to describe it as a story. Perhaps a 'pictorial story' would be a more accurate description. Behind this visual tale is a profound understanding of how practice or action can be formative. Using language in this pictorial fashion may also have a transformative effect on the listener.

The frequency with which Lewis uses and refines his pictorial language to form his metaphors, sharpen his analogies, and also develop his arguments suggest that this was more than a rhetorical device, it was at the heart of how he himself envisaged and imagined the 'Christian revelation'. It seems that it was also the foundation stone for his narrative method. He admits:

> One thing I am sure of. All my seven Narnian books, and my three science fiction books, all began with a picture of a faun carrying an umbrella and parcels in a snowy wood. The picture had been in my mind since I was about sixteen. Then one day, when I was about forty, I said to myself: Let's try to make a story about it.[98]

Lewis's ability to develop a whole story from a simple mental picture may further explain the ease with which he made surprising pictorial connections, topical pictorial allusions, and swift pictorial transitions in his broadcast talks.

Some biographers are extremely positive about this aspect of Lewis's radio work.[99] Such positive evaluation should be read critically as there is at times a tendency in some of the vast literature surrounding Lewis's life and work to slip into hagiography or even 'Lewis idolatry'.[100] According to his Presbyterian producer, Reverend Eric Fenn,[101] the BBC research highlighted how Lewis's broadcasts divided people. He wrote to Lewis: 'They obviously either regard you as "the cat's whiskers" or as "beneath contempt".'[102] Interestingly, out of thirty-three contemporary reviews of these radio talks, the majority were positive reviews.[103]

Conclusion

Lewis and Wright both drew upon common experience as source for their broadcasting. The end result, however, was often contrasting. It is illuminating to place Wright's representational descriptions of lonely promontories, deserted valleys and blitzed London streets beside Lewis's more metaphoric word-pictures of fleets of ships, strip-tease acts and God in disguise. It could be compared with putting a Constable beside a Turner, with Constable concentrating on graphic detail to create the impressive landscape, Turner going beyond the scene itself, focusing instead upon the light swirling amongst the clouds.[104] Wright often used the details of scenery to create an atmosphere and root his story in reality, while Lewis frequently created surprising connections to lead his listeners beyond the mundane to a new vision. Obviously as broadcasters they relied not on paint but on words to create mental pictures in their listeners' imaginations.

This chapter has not attempted to provide a comprehensive analysis of their popularity, nor detail the continuing critical discussion about Lewis's work.[105] Instead, a few reasons for their popularity have been suggested. The focus, in both cases, has been on a small selection of a larger corpus of work. Lewis was a prolific writer of popular theology, children's books and scholarly works. Wright was a frequent preacher, speaker, writer and editor.[106] For Lewis, broadcasting was a small part of his work, for Wright it was a significant, but by no means the only element. In the midst of the confusion of the Second World War, Lewis was a confident academic apologist for Christianity attempting to decode theology for his radio audiences, whilst Wright was primarily a pastor who used simple and unambiguous verbal pictures to reawaken or reinforce his listeners' faith.[107]

Before attempting to identify specific lessons for preachers from the radio broadcasting practices of Wright and Lewis, we should highlight the considerable gap between communicating effectively in a studio in the 1940s and doing so in a pulpit in the 1990s. During the Second World War, radio broadcasting had a distinct advantage over many other forms of communication. For Anne Frank and her family radio gave rhythm to their long days in hiding; it became a great 'morale booster'.[108] Wright admits that part of the reason for his popularity, and this almost certainly applies to Lewis as well, was that:

> people had nothing else to do. There was a blackout and people didn't go out, they didn't go to the pictures, they didn't go to the theatre and for long periods they just had to sit at home and so they listened to the radio.[109]

Wright and Lewis had a potentially 'captive audience'. Nevertheless, given the substantial amount of mail that they both received it was clear that they successfully engaged many of their listeners. One of the key arguments of this chapter is that two reasons for their success were, first, their use of conversational discourse or 'real talk' as Lewis describes it, and secondly, their use of pictorial language which had the potential to engage their listeners' imaginations.

It is unlikely that, if Wright or Lewis attempted to repeat their broadcasts today, they would hold many present day listeners' attention. On one level both of their approaches are dated, and even for their times their broadcasts are far from flawless. Any straightforward imitation of the techniques or style of either Wright or Lewis would almost certainly fail to work with the very different audiences of today. A much more sophisticated hermeneutic approach to their work is required. Nevertheless, there are three primary principles to draw out from their practice that will translate into our different cultural and communicative context. They can be summarised in three simple words: knowledge, conversation and engagement.

First, knowledge: one of the marks of Wright's work was that he made a considerable effort to know his listeners. It was obviously impossible to meet them all, but travelling round the country ensured that he developed a strong sense of the difficulties and fears that many of his listeners were facing. Lewis was not such a prolific traveller, but many of his analogies draw on his imaginative travels into other people's worlds. Preachers who withdraw from the world into the safety of their study or ecclesiastical community, and fail to understand their listeners' world, are in danger of not being heard. Preachers need to engage critically with their communicative environment. It is another way of knowing our listeners.

Secondly, conversation: Wright and Lewis developed a conversational style of speaking on the radio, which allowed the listeners to feel they were being spoken to directly. Speakers today can learn from these early examples of broadcasters who tried not to write literary pieces, but attempted to create 'real talk'. Behind Lewis's conversational, 'casual and spontaneous flow of words lurks a calculated and meticulously constructed text'.[110] Rarely, however, did either Lewis or Wright wear their heart on their sleeves, and make themselves vulnerable to their listeners. The obvious exception can be seen in Wright's talk on the death of Jimmy Dalgleish, but even in this case, the grief is to be inferred rather than made explicit. More often Wright and Lewis maintained a sense of distance from their audience, at times sounding over-confident, authoritative or even magisterial in their broadcast talk. This marks a sharp contrast with the work of many contemporary broadcasters as we will see in the next chapter.

Thirdly, engagement: Wright and Lewis recognised the intrinsic and potential effectiveness of radio in involving the listeners more actively in the communication process. In different ways they both attempted to connect with their listeners through a variety of easily accessible images, pictures and stories. The pictures they engaged with and used reflect a little of their own characters. Wright, the army chaplain, in his own words, may not have been a 'deep theologian', but one of his great skills was to observe scenes and replicate them verbally, thereby creating a picture which could resonate with his audience's experiences. Lewis, the academic, demonstrates a greater precision with his pictorial language, sometimes refining his analogy a number of times before using it. Topical, shocking or approximate pictures were used not only to engage his listeners, but also to lead them further into an alternative view of reality. Preachers seeking to be heard today can learn much from Wright's and Lewis's attempts to engage with their listeners through painting pictures with words.

In the next chapter we will consider two more British broadcasters operating in our contemporary communicative environment. They will provide some evidence that stands in contrast with this chapter and they will therefore offer further useful insights for preachers who hope to connect with their listeners today.

Notes

1. C. S. Lewis 1977 (1952).
2. Professor A. C. F. Beales in *The Universe,* cited by Wright 1980, 49–50.
3. Wright was assigned to 7/9th Royal Scots, attached to the 8th Battalion. See also Briggs 1995c, 564 n. 124.
4. Rev. Dr James Welch was Head of Religious Broadcasting for the

BBC from 1939 to 1947. It is fair to argue that not only Wright, but also Lewis, owe their broadcasting opportunities to James Welch. C. S. Lewis's and R. S. Wright's broadcasts should not be considered separately from the BBC's religious broadcasting policy of the time. Welch significantly shaped this. He wrote passionately in *The Listener:* 'Religious broadcasting is, remember, an extension of the Church, its primary task is to supplement and strengthen the Church's work and try to do what the Churches cannot do. We are all partners.' Welch 1942, 53. From this statement it may be inferred that Welch regarded broadcasters such as Wright and Lewis as partners in the Church's work.

5. Henry R. Luce, editor, 'Don–Devil', *Time,* 8 September 1947, 27–9. See also the front cover for a memorable image of Lewis in the foreground and a devil-like figure in the background. The caption is: 'Oxford's C. S. Lewis. His heresy: Christianity'.
6. Wolfe 1984, 278. *Let's Ask the Padre* broadcasts 'were sufficiently well received by the Corporation and the Chaplain General to encourage his secondment for six months beginning in February 1942'. Wright claimed that: 'The numbers went up to about ten million according to Melville Dinwiddie [head of Scottish Religious Broadcasting] and the average was about seven million.' R. S. Wright interview by a member of the Imperial War Museum Staff, date not known. (Hereafter: Wright, Imperial War Museum Interview)
7. Ibid., 280. See also Wright 1942, and Wright 1943.
8. Foot and Langley 1979, 115. By his own reckoning Wright did about seventy fifteen-minute talks. He also participated in morning prayers, *Lift Up Your Hearts,* and even took part in the variety show, *Ack Ack Beer Beer.* Wright, Imperial War Museum Interview 1.
9. Wright 1980, 47.
10. Wright, Coulter Interview 1993, 1. See Coulter 1997, esp. Chapter 6: 'Alternative War-Time Ministries'.
11. Wright 1941–3. In this unpublished report he describes what Dr Welch, Head of Religious Broadcasting, wanted him to do: 'He wanted me, with the Army's permission, to get around as many of those, at that time very many, lonely posts dotted all over the country and meet as many of the men as I could and every week talk to them over the air, taking the place in some sort of a way of their own Padres.' (See Unpublished Reports section in bibliography.)
12. Wolfe 1984, 278.

13. McLeish 1988, 160. This advice could be adapted for preachers. 'It is the positive duty for preachers to escape from the confines of their church into the world...'
14. Wright admits that: 'almost every railway carriage contains at least one sermon'. Wright 1942, 34.
15. Falconer 1977, 79. Falconer argues that one of the wartime developments in radio was the 'direct and personal communication of the radio talk'.
16. McKay, *The Radio Padre*, BBC Radio 4, 1993. The commentary continues with a significant observation: 'his [Wright's] distinctive style which sometimes rendered him virtually inaudible as a preacher was ideally suited for the wireless'. This remark correctly highlights how different styles of speech may suit radio broadcasting or preaching. Preachers seeking to learn from radio broadcasting should bear in mind that radio is an intimate medium of communication, where projecting to 'fill the hall' is not necessary or appropriate.
17. Wright, Imperial War Museum Interview, 4.
18. Ibid., 4.
19. Wright, Coulter Interview 1993, 10.
20. Wright, *Personal Journal/Diary*, 1942.
21. Wright, Imperial War Museum Interview, 5. 'I think I was just myself. I wasn't modelling on anybody, simply talking actually as I am talking to you just now. I just would be talking to somebody sitting on another chair over there and that's all that happened really and I still do it with schools. I still preach at schools quite a bit and I can talk to them the same way. I find that's what people seem to like. They just want you to be natural, talk naturally.' Notice how Wright claims to use a similar speaking style for broadcasting and preaching.
22. Wright 1942, 38–9.
23. This talk was based on a sermon preached by Wright at St Giles' Cathedral at the first parade and dedication of the colours of the Civil Defence Messenger Service, and was 'later broadcast to the Empire'. See Wright 1943a.
24. Wright 1943a, 82. He continues, by making a theological connection: 'as I went down to join them again, and I remembered. I remembered how not two thousand years ago a small company of young men, most of them in their early twenties, had started the movement that has changed the face of the world.' This needs to be heard aloud to be understood. Notice how he repeats 'remembered' and thereby interrupts his own discourse.

25. Ibid., 83.
26. Wright 1944, 90.
27. Ibid., 90–1.
28. Ibid., 91.
29. Ibid., 92.
30. Troeger 1990, 33–52.
31. Wright 1943a, 98.
32. Buttrick 1987, 59.
33. Ibid., 59.
34. Ibid., 61.
35. Wright 1943a, 98.
36. Another device he used frequently was the interview. See, for example, 'The Padre Asks the Archbishop', in Wolfe 1984, Appendix 3, 543–6.
37. For useful discussions on 'Point-of-View' in homiletics see Buttrick 1987, 55–69; and for its relationship to ideology see Simpson 1993.
38. Wright 1943a, 35–41. Wright notes, at the end of the interview/talk entitled 'Sgt. Jimmie has more Questions' that 'three hours later and not 500 yards from where this talk was given Sgt. Dalgleish was killed by enemy action'. He was putting out incendiaries.
39. Wright 1942, 98.
40. Buttrick 1987, 59. '*Distance* is a peculiar category that is spatial, temporal and perhaps even emotional.'
41. His diary entries effectively conclude after 'Jimmie [James Dalgleish] was killed'. Wright, *Personal Journal/Diary*, 1942, 212.
42. Transcribed from McKay, producer, *The Radio Padre*, BBC Radio 4, 1993.
43. See, for example, Wright, 1970. He graphically describes a scene prior to the Dunkirk evacuation where a young dispatch rider joined Wright and several others who 'prayed under the trees that summer evening'. He movingly relates how one of the last requests of this dispatch rider was that they should pray, not for themselves, but for their relatives worrying at home.
44. See Foot and Langley 1979, 115. 'The whole talk was thereupon taken down in shorthand – accidents allowing – in several prisoner of war camps, and the text was puzzled out afterwards.'
45. Wright, Coulter Interview, 7. It is clear from this interview that Wright was uneasy about this practice, partly because there was something 'two faced' about using a religious talk for passing on coded messages and also because he believed it was 'ruining' his

talks at the beginning as he 'had to alter' parts 'in order to fit in the code'.

46. Williams 1941, 800 and see Wolfe 1984, 279.
47. Williams 1942, 695. Williams' comments concluded with advice to include 'fewer anecdotes', take '10 minutes instead of 20' and 'temper' his voice with a 'less reverberating note'. For Wright's talk see Wright 1942, 44.
48. Williams 1941, 800 and see Wolfe 1984, 279.
49. Wright 1980, 109.
50. Green and Hooper 1974, 201.
51. Griffin 1988 (1986), 184.
52. Joseph Dowell, for example, in a letter to Walter Hooper would describe C. S. Lewis's broadcasts on *What Christians Believe* as 'magnificent, unforgettable', see Green and Hooper 1974, 209.
53. See Keefe 1974 (1971), 148. For more on D. L. Sayers' contribution to radio see Coomes 1992, 146–62, and Reynolds 1993, 298–307 and 317–28.
54. Lewis 1988 (1966), 198.
55. See Wolfe's chapter on 'New Approaches: James Welch', in Wolfe 1984, 145–204. He provides a useful insight into Welch's 'bipolar ministry', in which he attempted to serve as a 'priest of the Church of England and as a servant of the Corporation'. 145. Welch, according to Wolfe, 'wanted the single Christian message, however difficult to define, plainly broadcast without the suggestion of a species of "BBC religion" which was but a spurious mixture of the simplest Protestant ethic.' 154. Nevertheless, Welch's selection of broadcasters was *predominantly* white, male and middle class, and almost always what he viewed as orthodox Christian. This inevitably shaped the form and content of religious broadcasting to be heard on the BBC during the Second World War.
56. J. W. Welch letter to C. S. Lewis, 7 February 1941 cited in Green and Hooper 1974, 201.
57. See, for example, Eric Fenn's letter to Professor C. S. Lewis, 29 December 1943. Fenn encloses Lewis's seven talks on 'What Christians believe about the nature of God' and advises Lewis about timings: 'we usually reckon 1,750 words for a 15 minute talk'. He asks Lewis to expand them. Fenn also suggests a significant change to Lewis's third talk, using the candle metaphor to start his broadcast as a bridge for the 'listener who has not heard the previous talks without damaging your arguments'. It appears that Lewis took Fenn's advice regarding timings, but

not regarding the controlling metaphor. Lewis was clearly 'pro-duceable', if not malleable.

58. See McIntyre 1993. This biography provides useful insights into how Reith's understanding of Christianity influenced religious broadcasting in the BBC.
59. Wolfe 1984, 200; and see letter from Welch to Lewis, 7 February 1941.
60. Wilson 1990, 180. Lewis travelled by train from Oxford to London every Wednesday night to broadcast between 7.45 and 8.00. See also Green and Hooper 1974, 202.
61. Green and Hooper 1974, 203.
62. 4.45–5.00pm, on 11, 18 January and 1, 8, 15 February 1942.
63. Green and Hooper 1974, 210–11.
64. Lewis 1942, 1943 and 1944.
65. Hooper in Lewis 1984, xv.
66. Lewis, *Right or Wrong: A Clue to the Meaning of the Universe: Materialism or Religion?* BBC Archives 4.
67. Lewis, *Right or Wrong,* 21.
68. Lewis, *What Christians Believe.* 4.45–5.00pm, Sunday 15 February 1942, BBC Archives, 4.
69. Ibid., 4.
70. Lewis 1936.
71. Lewis 1942, 61.
72. Ibid., 51. This image recurs throughout this talk, appearing at the end of the second chapter, in the fourth and at the end of the fifth.
73. Christopher 1981, 71.
74. Lewis 1943.
75. Christopher 1981, 69.
76. Lewis 1943, 9.
77. Riegert 1990, passim.
78. Christopher 1981, 69.
79. Lewis 1943, 27.
80. Christopher 1981, 70.
81. Lewis 1942, 53.
82. Lewis 1980a (1950), 12–13. 'Farther up and farther in' is a recurring statement in Lewis 1980b (1956), 153–73.
83. Lewis 1942, 29, see also Lewis 1977, 35.
84. Ibid., 29. See also Lewis 1977, 35.
85. Wilson 1990, 181.
86. Christopher 1981, 72.
87. Lewis 1977 (1952), 5.

88. Ibid., 5.
89. Hooper in Lewis 1984, xiv–xv.
90. Keefe 1974 (1971), 173–4.
91. Ibid., 173–4.
92. Ibid., 176–7.
93. Lewis 1943, 7.
94. Lewis 1942, 12. In a letter to Sister Penelope on 15 May 1941, Lewis explains how his radio talks 'are *preparatio evangelica* rather than evangelism, an attempt to convince people that there is a moral law, that we disobey it'. Lewis 1988 (1996), 193.
95. Lewis 1944, 14.
96. Lewis 1943, 64.
97. Lewis 1944, 35.
98. Lewis 1966. 'It all began with a picture'. 42.
99. See, for example, Green and Hooper 1974, 209. 'The clarity of Lewis's thought, his ability to encapsulate a great many facts into a few words is perhaps nowhere better illustrated than in these broadcasts.'
100. Dorsett 1990, 213. 'Since his death almost 60 books have been written and edited on Lewis' life and work, hundreds of magazine and journal articles have appeared, and almost one hundred and fifty master's and doctoral dissertations have been prepared on this author.' See also Wilson 1990. In his Preface Wilson speaks of 'Lewis idolatry' and concludes that: 'We do Lewis no honour to make him into a plaster saint.' xvi, xviii.
101. Wolfe 1984, 145, 147 and passim.
102. Fenn, letter to Lewis, 23 March 1944, cited in Griffin 1988 (1986), 221. 'For each of these BBC talks, Lewis was paid ten guineas and offered vouchers for the train. The vouchers he took; the fees he asked the BBC to send to a number of worthy and needy people.' 202.
103. Keefe, 1974 (1971), 152. Keefe analysed 3 Protestant, 10 Secular, 20 Roman Catholic reviews.
104. See *The History of British Art,* written and presented by Andrew Graham-Dixon, BBC 2, 19 May 1996. On Constable: 'By painting so large he dared to suggest the most ordinary subjects might also be the most profound ones.' On Turner: 'He was more concerned with the light than the subjects.'
105. Contrast, for example, A. N. Wilson's evaluation in 1990, 180–1, with George Sayer's in 1997, 277–8. Sayer describes a memorable scene: 'I remember being at a pub filled with soldiers on one Wednesday evening. At a quarter to eight, the bartender turned

the radio up for Lewis. "You listen to this bloke," he shouted. "He's really worth listening to." And those soldiers did listen attentively for the entire fifteen minutes.' 278. See also Carpenter 1997 (1978). 'Lewis was not exactly at his best at the microphone; or rather, his use of the medium emphasised the more dogmatic side of his character. Radio brought out neither his stentorian power nor his flashes of wit, and his broadcasting manner was formal and rather restrained. But he spoke clearly and unhesitatingly, and the talks were considered a great success, not least because of the large number of letters which resulted from them.' 183.

106. Wright edited the *Scottish Forces Bulletin* during the war. 'The Church of Scotland had a supplement for the Scottish forces and they asked me to take it up. I made it into a kind of booklet. It came out originally every month and was like a little magazine. I put in anything I liked. I did that for a long time, for several years.' Wright, Coulter Interview 1993, 11.
107. This may further explain Wright's unease about being used to communicate coded messages.
108. Anne Frank wrote in her diary Monday 27 March, 1944: 'The radio therefore goes on early in the morning and is listened to all hours of the day, until nine, ten and often 11 o'clock in the evening.' See Frank 1989 (1986), 572–3.
109. Wright, Imperial War Museum Interview, 4.
110. Shingler and Wieringa 1998, 37. This reference is to radio in general.

CHAPTER 6

Thought for the Day

Religious radio has travelled a long way since the heady days of Lewis and Wright before the challenge of television and the explosion of the mass media. The past fifty years have seen a number of significant shifts within BBC religious radio. First, the move away from the Reithian ideal of proclaiming a 'thoroughgoing, optimistic and manly'[1] Christianity towards a more secular Birtian 'mission to explain'.[2] Secondly, the development from mainstream Christian broadcasting to multi-faith religious broadcasting; the idea that public service religious radio was an extension of the churches, and had an evangelistic function, was firmly rejected by the BBC in the 1970s. Thirdly, the erosion of the protected 'God Slots' on both national and local stations;[3] and fourthly, the reduction in airtime specifically assigned for religious broadcasting.

The implications of some of these developments have received little attention from scholars.[4] The changes, however, are significant for contributors to *Thought for the Day*, which is found on BBC Radio 4's *Today* programme at approximately 7.48am on Monday to Saturday. There can be no question of proselytising.[5] Broadcasters on *Thought for the Day* are by no means exclusively Christian and no speaker is allowed to challenge other faith traditions.[6] Following a recent internal review, however, agnostics and atheists are still not given access to broadcast on *Thought for the Day*.[7] This is a short slot, which like other 'God Slots' faces competition. *Thought for the Day*, commonly referred to by the *Today* staff as *Thought*, has been repeatedly cut down in length, now lasting only two minutes and forty-five seconds. David Coomes, the BBC's series producer responsible for *Thought*, believes that 'it has become much sharper and tighter and has benefited from being shorter.'[8] It is clear that the style and content of *Thought* have altered since the 1970s:

> The slot has changed a lot . . . it used to be much more pious. So also has the *Today* sequence, it was much more varied, you had *Keep fit with Eileen Fowler* . . . and much more magazine-type items on. And it's now very hard news. So what *Thought* stands for has shifted quite heavily.[9]

This has inevitably had editorial consequences for *Thought*. Coomes, a newspaper journalist before joining the BBC, is clear about what he is looking for in a contributor:

> someone who can think theologically, someone who will represent a particular religious perspective, because you know we try and fulfil balances of denomination and religion and male and female, and so on . . . And you want someone who can actually engage with a *Today* audience at ten to eight in the morning and not sound completely out on a limb, who doesn't sound pious, who doesn't sound like a vicar delivering a sermon.[10]

Thought regularly provokes debate over its contributors, its content and its future.[11] Its situation, embedded in a fast-paced current affairs programme, ensures that its contributors are speaking alongside highly skilled broadcasters. *Thought* is normally preceded by a summary of today's 'papers', a package illustrated by short clips and actuality, and is often then followed by an interview, brief trails for some of the day's programmes and the weather forecast. The 8am news that follows simply cannot be 'crashed', so time is strictly limited. This is a highly competitive and time-conscious broadcasting environment. Contributors to what Paul Donovan describes as 'The Breakfast Pulpit'[12] cannot assume an attentive audience.

Nevertheless, its listeners are not to be underestimated. As Coomes emphasises:

> Contributors have to accept that this is a Radio 4 audience which means it's not particularly young, and it's quite conservative, but they are able to think very deeply, and they are able to reflect, and they are able to appreciate clever thoughts and ironic thoughts and humorous thoughts . . .[13]

The picture emerges of an intelligent, critical audience, likely to be listening to radio only as a secondary activity.

Polly Toynbee argues that it is out of place in *Today*: 'We get a warm soup of unctuous "Thoughts" that jar oddly with the brisk tones of the *Today* programme.'[14] Other commentators are more positive. Paul Donovan, for example, argues that *Thought* 'is an invaluable daily reminder of transcendence', though he balances this affirmation with the comment that: 'although the slot has an influence out of all proportion to its length . . . it alienates as well as attracts'.[15]

As a 'God Slot',[16] *Thought* may be a soft target for commentators' criticisms, but even the majority of listeners who do not reach for the 'off dial' are likely to be preparing to leave the house, eating breakfast, in the bathroom, snoozing in bed or en route to work. Some find it an unwelcome interruption:

> I want a radio with a *Thought-for-the-Day* inhibitor, a radio that will turn down the volume automatically at the first mention of their god-slot, but which will monitor the silent broadcast and turn the volume up again as soon as the voice says, 'That was *Thought for the Day*.' I want a radio with a bishop-filter, a cardinal-canceller, a vicar's voice-vanisher, a radio programmed to replace these two minutes of tosh with some item from the repertoire of short piano pieces.[17]

Journalist James Fenton wrote this 'affirmation' of BBC Radio 4's *Thought for the Day* in *The Independent.* His comment suggests that at least part of the audience is not exactly sitting on the edge of their beds, anxious to hear the next *Thought.* In spite of such entertainingly negative evaluations, I will suggest that preachers do have lessons to learn from this strand of religious broadcasting. To test out this assertion we will analyse in detail the approaches taken by two experienced and respected broadcasters who are regular contributors to *Thought for the Day*: Angela Tilby and Lionel Blue.

Radio Iconographer – Angela Tilby

> Radio taught me about preaching first because I did some broadcasting in my twenties. The discipline of having to think about every word, cut out the superfluous, *to use images, pictures and stories,* that

> was a huge, huge benefit when I first started as a lay reader to preach sermons; because I never ever took for granted that anybody wanted to listen to me at all ... in fact rather the reverse.[18]

Angela Tilby is an experienced radio broadcaster and television producer who joined the BBC in 1973.[19] She feels she has had a 'long relationship' with *Thought for the Day*, because one of her first tasks as a producer in the mid-1970s was to produce it. Now as a regular contributor to *Thought*, her role has changed:

> I work as a colleague along with colleagues who actually produce me ... it's a good experience to be produced because you realise what dreadful things you put other people through ... If they're tough and revolting it reminds me I quite often am too, [laughing] so it's a kind of penitential experience for me.[20]

She has produced numerous episodes of *Everyman* and *Horizon* for the BBC – topics have ranged from Anorexia to the Survival of the Soul – and a four-part documentary with Mark Tully on *Lives of Jesus*.[21] Interestingly, she does not see any obvious links between her work as a TV producer and her radio broadcasting. She even believes that the two media 'rather fight each other', since television 'is so much about the immediate emotional impact', as opposed to radio which depends more on words and painting 'pictures in people's minds'.[22] Self-effacing about her skills as a television producer and director, Tilby considers herself to be 'much more of a word person, a writer, and a hearer of words' who does not have 'very much visual sense'.[23] Assuming that self-assessment is accurate, it raises a question about what Tilby draws upon for her word-pictures. The threefold answer she gives illuminates much of her work as a radio broadcaster.

First, she is a self-confessed introvert who is dependent on her memory:

> Like living in a rich and fertile forest out of which you take the bits that will shine or work or make sense out there ... [my] inner life is made up of all sorts of things ... TV programmes, old films, places been to, [all of which is] somehow recorded.[24]

This memorable picture explains the rich diversity of her imagination and the ease with which she moves in and out of pictorial language.

Secondly, her theological understanding finds its roots in pictures rather than abstract concepts. She admits that she is not: 'a good philosopher, which means I don't understand theology through a series of flow charts, of highly logical constructs which are somehow not clothed with pictures. I don't think you can do anything without pictures.'[25] Tilby finds support for her approach from a theologian 'from North Africa'[26] born in the fourth century, who was himself a highly skilled word-artist:[27]

> Augustine ... made it quite clear [that he] couldn't envisage God without mental imagery.[28] He just had no capacity to think of God in abstract, and I think that's true for me as well. I do conjure up images ... even though I know all images are inadequate.[29]

This inability 'to think of God in the abstract' may partially explain why she found biblical Hebrew so alluring. She finds that: 'Hebrew is very rich and it works on imagery, and parallels of imagery, in a very profound and interesting way.'[30] In one *Thought,* following a 'vicious bomb' in Jerusalem, she challenges the image of God 'who can never hurt anyone, never be angry with anyone and never condemn anyone' with a graphic extract from a psalm rich in parallelism:

> 'Pour out thy indignation upon them ... add to them punishment ... let them be blotted out among the book of the living.' ... What is real about the *Psalms* is that they come from an imperfect world, where the basic crookedness of the human heart is recognised. God doesn't just look on regretfully, but gets into battle himself. He fights, he judges, he delivers.[31]

Tilby has clearly been angered by this atrocity in Jerusalem. She finds some of the resources for her response in the uncompromising pictures and language of the Psalms. She is not afraid to make an explicit challenge to the theological position which argues that 'God himself can do nothing except sympathise with our distress'.[32]

A third, and slightly surprising, facility which Angela Tilby draws upon is her ability to link colours with words: 'I am one of those people who does see some words, particularly names, in colour.'[33] She believes that this intriguing and slightly strange skill of connecting colour with words provides a further useful resource: '[It] sometimes means you have an imaginative capacity with language which people on the whole find interesting to listen to . . .'[34] We will examine Tilby's 'imaginative capacity with language' later. The way she actually draws upon each of these resources in *Thought* will provide an avenue by which to approach her radio broadcasting.

Before turning to a detailed analysis of extracts of Tilby's broadcasts it is worth considering her own views about radio broadcasting and, in particular, pictorial language on the radio.

> I don't think I'd start with saying paint pictures with words. I'd say: 'What will you want to say?' And then what you wrote I'd cut down to the core. When doing something like *Thought for the Day,* every word counts, you cannot afford to have superfluous adjectives, you cannot afford to have superfluous subordinate clauses and all the rest of it.

Tilby demonstrates a ruthless attitude towards verbosity:

> First of all, you shred it really, and then you build on, draw on, colour [and then ask] how can I make it more attractive, more engaging. There's a kind of asceticism about writing this kind of radio. It's got to be thin.[35]

Angela Tilby's response to a hypothetical broadcaster asking for advice reveals an editorial rigour and a caution towards attaching too much importance to painting pictures with words. She believes this is only a secondary skill for broadcasters aiming to do successful *Thoughts.*

She does argue, however, for a 'respect for the medium' of radio, and a respect for 'what ears are for'. She believes that 'when people are not using their eyes, you call upon the eyes of the mind' and you can 'approach the eye through the ear'.[36] A single sentence best summarises her understanding of one of the strengths of radio: 'Through the ear you see, and that is the extraordinary gift of radio.'[37] Earlier she spoke of another 'gift' of radio, closely linked to this observation. In her eyes, radio is really a 'kind of incomplete medium' which does 'call out from the listener a kind of imaginative response and . . . radio broadcasting is really about that'.[38] How does Angela Tilby draw upon these closely linked 'gifts' or inherent strengths of radio in practice? 'It is much easier to write a *Thought* when you call on a piece of experience which you can see in your mind.'[39]

We will consider the ways in which Angela Tilby develops and uses pictorial language to engage the 'eyes of the mind' through an analysis of five *Thoughts* broadcast between March and July 1996. In an interview she explained the process of building her *Thought* for 16 July 1996:

> I was seeing in my mind's eye a picture of what I heard on the radio, which was a group of children with the headmistress singing a hymn. What was interesting was that when I got the paper this morning there was a picture that was almost more like I had imagined than I had imagined! It was right back to the 1950s with these little kids, hands clasped together, their eyes shut. It was enchanting.[40]

Into this *Thought*, exploring the theme of prayer, Tilby integrates what she sees in her 'mind's eye' with the picture in the newspaper. This broadcast is constructed around four graphic scenes of school assemblies. Her opening scene deftly takes us back to her own school experience in the 1950s where they had prayers 'twice in the school day':

> There was no doubt in my five year old mind that prayer was talking to God, someone bigger than the very large headmistress in her black dress, high heels and seamed stockings. She was so fierce and frightening that I was impressed that she talked to God with deference. It gave me hope.[41]

Tilby here makes use of the specific details of a 'black dress, high heels and seamed stockings' to highlight the character of her headteacher. This is balanced in the following scene in which she leads her listeners to her next school 'where prayers were called Assembly, and happened once a day, in a bright, sunny hall'. The listeners are introduced to her next 'rather gentle head teacher in a bluebell coloured suit'.[42] She uses the colours of clothes to distinguish the respective personalities of the head teachers.[43] This illustrates how her 'imaginative capacity' for linking words and colour, noted earlier, contributes to her text.

The third scene portrayed is from her 'grown-up school' in the 1960s. Tilby skilfully reflects how 'prayers had become embarrassing'. She does this through her descriptions of 'solemn agnostic rows of sixth formers stood with eyes unblinkingly open, sullenly examining their illegal nail varnish'.[44] These three scenes help listeners to 'see', to return to the words of Paul Scott Wilson, 'by creating' images 'as though making a movie'.[45] In this example, Tilby creates what we could describe as a 'slowed-down' verbal 'movie'. She achieves this by recreating simple scenes with little movement but with specific, almost photographic, detail. Listeners are encouraged to recreate in their imaginations this scene of teenagers standing in rows. The carefully selected adjectives 'unblinkingly' and 'sullenly' create a mood and further demonstrate how Tilby attempts to put into practice what was noted earlier that she believes about radio: 'Through the ear you see, and that is the extraordinary gift of radio.'[46]

Her fourth and final scene lacks any explicit pictorial elements. She merely states:

> When the pupils returned to St Luke's Primary School in Wolverhampton yesterday, the headmistress led them in a hymn of praise to God, not denying their recent trauma, but reassuring them of a strength and comfort beyond what fallible adults can ever hope to provide.[47]

Perhaps Tilby assumes that her listeners will already have the images of the school lodged in their minds. This is not an unreasonable assumption given that the horrific knife attack on children and teachers had been a lead story in TV news bulletins and newspapers of the preceding week. In this *Thought* Tilby demonstrates discipline over the use of pictorial language. She chooses specific details in order to evoke images in the listeners' minds. In her own words, she is attempting in different ways to 'call out from the listener a kind of imaginative response'.[48]

This is also the case in her *Thought* for 27 May 1996, which focused on her adventures on Mount Sinai. An imaginary dialogue with the camel that carried her half-way up the mountain is followed by a graphic description:

> From the camel's back I could see the harsh face of Sinai, the sun overhead. The rock face was implacable, a granite wall ... You lose

> sight of the peak when you get near, and then, quite suddenly, you're there. You stumble into light and sky, and, where the elders of Israel 'beheld God and ate and drank' there's a Church and a kiosk and you can have a cup of tea.[49]

Her entire *Thought* is built around this picture. She shifts the subject from 'I' to 'you' and therefore subtly changes the 'point of view'[50] of the listener. David Buttrick argues that 'varied points of view in a sermon will be intrinsically interesting'.[51] This is equally true of radio: Tilby's shift in the point of view cannot fail to add interest, as it has the effect of inviting the listener to join her on Mount Sinai itself. In other words, whereas an objective third person description might distance the listener, Tilby's switching between the first and the second person encourages listeners to 'stumble' into the 'light and sky' of the top of Sinai for themselves.

Her description of the descent include moves from the first person pronoun, 'I', through the plural, 'we', and back to the singular 'I':

> I dreamed of a bath and a cold beer ... When we finally got down, the light had almost gone. Only the summit was lit and I could see that the harsh shape was lined and scarred. I was marked by the mountain, I was tired and sore.[52]

So we sense both her personal, individual experience, and a group experience. Tilby is also sensitive to the light and the shapes that Sinai creates. Rather than turn it into a distant but beautiful Ansell Adams style photographic representation, she parallels the marks or scars of the mountain with her own marks of weariness. The result is that once again she encourages her listeners to participate in the picture for themselves. Tilby as the foot-weary explorer allows herself to become the person we can identify with. It is almost as if she has allowed herself to become a bridge into the picture itself.

She performs a similar role in a third *Thought,* broadcast on 13 May 1996. This focused on the 'garden experience' of Augustine and paralleled her own memories of reading in the garden:

> I'm thinking of 'summer gardens' because this time of year reminds me of the weeks I spent in the garden years ago trying to revise for

> exams. Bird song, cherry and magnolia bring back a frisson of fear. Yet they also bring a sense of grace. Gardens in May were the places I learned to learn ... I remember sitting on my own with a book, following the letters along a line with my finger, mouthing the sounds, and then suddenly the sounds in my head gripped the letters on the page and I understood.[53]

With a few swift verbal brush strokes, references to 'bird song, cherry and magnolia', Tilby's garden is visually established. As in the earlier examples, she uses pictorial language as a tool for drawing the listener into a new world. The distant story of Augustine and the garden in Milan where he heard a voice cry '*Tolle, Lege*' (Take, Read), becomes more accessible to the listener through Tilby's vivid pictures which evoke her own experience.

In a fourth *Thought* during this period of March to July 1996 Tilby reflects on the difficult experience of divorce and of dividing up the possessions. This one does not have the pictorial language of the three other examples already cited. Perhaps only two sentences reveal Tilby's skill at evoking pictures with words. Her very first sentence sets up a contrast: 'What is united by a priest with prayers and confetti is unravelled by a judge in a welter of paperwork.'[54] In these provocative oppositional phrases a 'welter of paperwork' contrasts with 'prayers and confetti'. She does not develop these references explicitly, but gives only the briefest of visual hints, to illustrate the painful reality of how 'we do put asunder, over and over again'.[55]

The final words of the *Thought* are another example of pictorial language pared down to its minimum: 'Like a death, the end of a marriage requires a funeral, and then for the ghosts and the bones to rest in peace.'[56] This is a powerful and moving *Thought* which implicitly draws upon Tilby's own personal experience. Some ten months before, she had made herself extremely vulnerable with another *Thought*, where she mentioned that her 'marriage to a clergyman had ended in divorce'.[57] In both *Thoughts* her insights gain authority not only through the use of pictorial language, but also by her willingness to be vulnerable on air. I would argue that, as Tilby's memory appears to be highly visual, these two factors are closely intertwined.

In contrast to this example, pictorial vulnerability is almost entirely absent from a fifth *Thought* broadcast on 1 July 1996. The 'topical tag' or news basis for this *Thought* was the previous day's debate in the House of Lords over the asylum bill. Tilby's broadcast centred on the 'difference between law and justice'.[58] In only 434 words she attempts to explore the collision of two 'moral concerns': first, anger towards those who come to 'milk the benefit system', and secondly, worry for those who 'flee here seeking safety'.[59] She raises the difficult question of how we can discern the difference between these two types of people. The complexity of the issue, and the far from visual terms that Tilby employs, make it a hard *Thought* either to identify with or to construct pictures of in the mind. The result is a less than gripping broadcast.

Only in the last sentence does she build an evocative metaphor: 'In the high court of eternity, justice judges law.'[60] This concluding sentence is a provocative attempt to inject tangible life into abstract concepts. It may be language used with finesse, but as a metaphor it relies on connecting the abstract noun 'eternity' with the potentially visual image of 'high court'. The personification of 'justice' judging law is an active phrase, but it still lacks explicit pictorial language. This broadcast serves as a balance to the four other *Thoughts* considered, where she makes more consistent use of pictorial language. It illustrates that whilst Tilby favours this device, it is by no means the only approach that she employs. Her pictorial language works in alliance with other discursive devices.

Another device Tilby employs is the 'enticing' structure of her *Thoughts*: often she does not immediately reveal the point of what she is going to say. This is an attempt to draw her audience into listening, and could be described, in Fred Craddock's terms, as an *inductive* approach to speaking. David Coomes's description and evaluation of Angela Tilby's *Thoughts* provides support for this assertion.[61]

> [Y]ou hear the start of her talk and you think: 'I will listen to this because it's going to have *a twist in the tail,* it's going to have something novel to say, it's not going to be run-of-the-mill at all', and she develops it, unpacks it, and in the last paragraph gets there.[62]

Coomes likens this sense of narrative uncertainty to: 'a two-and-a-half minute detective story, where you're waiting for a surprise or waiting for some development that's not actually predictable'.[63]

Without actually using Craddock's terms, he compares what could be described as an *inductive* approach with the *deductive* method employed by other contributors who:

> say what they are planning to say in the first couple of paragraphs, then unpack, and it's fairly predictable, even if it can be quite well done. But those that actually set the subject at the top, rooted in human experience or story, and then develop, and then come to a firm conclusion which is not absolutely predictable from the first paragraph, that's what I look for.[64]

Tilby's *Thought* on divorce, for example, begins by rooting itself in human experience: 'Ending a marriage is one of the hardest things in the world to do well.' From the first few sentences it is not predictable how she will conclude. In her penultimate sentence she suggests that 'real forgiveness comes when you regain distance'. Her last line carries weight and poignancy connecting 'death' with 'the end of a marriage' which she believes also 'requires a funeral' so that the 'ghosts and bones' can be laid to rest. This is an example of Tilby's ability to create a surprising twist in the conclusion of a story.

Tilby's broadcasts, however, are not universally successful. Sometimes she allows conceptual detail to obscure her message. In the discussion of the asylum bill, in contrast to the other *Thoughts* considered, Tilby eschews vivid language and relies almost entirely on abstract concepts and generic nouns. The result is a *Thought* that lacks accessible language or a surprising narrative. This should be a useful warning to preachers: the danger of employing over-abstract discourse is that it offers few points of connection with listeners.

I have proposed that Tilby's skill at creating pictures with words is usually augmented by other devices, such as creating inductive or surprising narrative structures. My main point, however, is that Tilby creates what she describes elsewhere as a 'visual theology' through her word-pictures.[65]

Radio Rabbi – Lionel Blue

Rabbi Lionel Blue is a reformed rabbi, with a History degree from Oxford University and a degree in Semitics from London University. He has worked as the European director of the World Union for Progressive Judaism in Brussels, he has been an editor of liturgy for over thirty years for the reformed synagogues and a lecturer at the Leo Baeck College in London since 1967.[66] He is best known, however, for his work as a radio broadcaster on both BBC Radio 4 and Radio 2. He became a 'household name' in the 1980s, just as C. S. Lewis and R. S. Wright were in the 1940s, through his idiosyncratic broadcasts.[67]

> Lionel Blue, let's face it, is a one-off really because he just tells stories. Often quite disjointed stories I have to say, but he's just a great character and he gets away with things that no other contributor, frankly, can get away with.[68]

In 1994 Blue was awarded an OBE partly for his services to broadcasting. To date, apart from Charles Handy, he is the only contributor to *Thought for the Day* who has had a taped collection cassette made of his Radio 4 *Thoughts.*[69]

In some informal advice to young broadcasters, based on his own broadcasting experience which began in 1967, he emphasises the importance 'of being yourself', and of letting 'weaknesses' and 'doubts' come through.[70] Many of his broadcasts follow these suggestions, and are based upon an endearing 'frankness'.[71] Whether speaking about his time in hospital,[72] his operation,[73] his homosexuality,[74] or his insomnia,[75] he is not afraid to speak with candour about what he has felt or is feeling. Such vulnerability marks him out from the *Today* presenters and reporters, as well as from many of the other contributors to *Thought.* His open approach has created a broadcasting persona that is an exemplification of what Norman Fairclough describes as the 'foregrounding of personality'.[76] In other words, Lionel Blue has become more than simply another 'religious-sounding' voice on *Today*; through his style, he has established a strong individual identity for himself. Blue's own understanding of why this 'frankness' is useful for religious broadcasters is illuminating:

> If you say what's really in your mind, not what ought to be in your mind, this is the secret of radio religion! Terry Wogan, Derek Jameson are themselves.[77] You don't have to be the brightest, the most mystical but it does have to be you. One of the problems in radio religion is that people are not themselves ... religious people stand a little above themselves. They don't speak from their real centre. This is OK from the pulpit, where they're expected to speak for their tradition, but radio is totally different. Even though you might be speaking to millions, it is very, very personal. The good preachers on radio have ceased to give sermons.[78]

By speaking with 'frankness' from his own 'centre', Blue has created for himself an identity not of a preacher, but rather a popular conversationalist. Such a mode of discourse is very much in keeping with the 'populist, common-sense style'[79] of the *Today* presenters. Blue also recognises, nevertheless, that when he does *Thought* he is 'in the middle of a very fast news programme' where 'what you say has to be very tight'.[80] Part of Blue's skill is his ability to combine a sense of conversation with a 'tight' script.

He repeatedly distances himself from seeing his broadcasting in traditional preaching terms: he perceives it as a 'much more intimate' form of preaching, 'without the robes and choirs'.[81] As an experienced broadcaster and preacher, however, he does make a surprisingly over simple distinction between broadcasting and preaching styles:

> In radio you are forced to be one thing which you are not in an ordinary pulpit. In the ordinary pulpit, you can be grand, mystical, that sort of thing; but in the radio you have to be relevant, and you have to fit in with the actual circumstances. You can't put on the plummy voice or preachy voice or a special one to show you are saying special thoughts ... It is the same world as the bed, the traffic jam and everything else.[82]

As a broadcaster Lionel Blue certainly avoids the 'plummy voice or preachy voice'. His resonant and warm East End London accent is distinctive, but also reassuringly 'normal'. This adds to the apparent normality of the pictures he creates. He has a simple objective:

> We are really trying to break down that wall between the ghetto and the boulevard. In practice, it all seems rather light, low, but in fact

> what we are trying to do, all religious broadcasters, we are trying to *translate* a religious ghetto into modern life – without any presuppositions, without assuming things, we are trying to tell people about religion who don't have Scriptures, pray or anything like that at all. And I think we are succeeding, because people who are not religious, who do not pray, listen . . .[83]

Rabbi Lionel Blue has a unique approach towards breaking down the wall between 'the ghetto and the boulevard', and trying to 'translate' the religious language of the ghetto into the discourse of 'modern life'.[84]

This combines with a simple but imaginative process, where he thinks not of the huge audience but of 'someone in my kitchen' who he is 'talking things over' with, 'over a cup of tea'.[85] As a preacher he never uses notes because he wants to see his listeners' faces and believes he is involved in a 'dialogue', a 'conversation'. Obviously he cannot precisely replicate this flexible process in the radio studio, but Blue does believe himself to be involved in a 'conversation' with his listeners:

> I'm not quite sure why it happens, and it sounds a bit precious, but it's as if I am seeing people through the mike and I realise this isn't working. 'No, I'll put it to you this way.' You are constrained by the fact you have to have a script, of course time is important.[86]

This highly visual experience, of 'seeing people through the mike', and of imagining a few of his listeners across the table, appears to help him 'fit in with' what he describes as their 'actual circumstances', as well as make last-second minor alterations to his script.

The picture that emerges of Lionel Blue is of a skilled broadcaster, who believes that openness, a conversational style and seeing his audience all help him to communicate. Blue is a religious broadcaster who accepts that he is involved in a 'dialogue' and that the 'time of telling people what their problem should be and what their answers are, that time is gone'.[87] His self-declared aim is to 'help people write the Scriptures of their own lives' and to explore the 'metaphysics of happiness', rather than do PR for his 'own religion'.[88]

He also appears to delight in his radio audience, his 'nicest congregation', as he still identifies with 'non-religious people' because he was a Marxist in his youth 'and an ideological anarchist', and he believes that part of him is 'still like that'.[89] This identification is also assisted by his strong visual imagination, which allows him to imagine specific individuals in his audience. As with Angela Tilby, his gift for seeing also provides resources for his broadcasts. It is to this that we now turn.

> I nearly became an artist once. I had this sort of small exhibition, then decided I wouldn't go on with it because it was either full time or nothing, but pictures do come into my mind, for instance pictures of the East End of London. Whenever I painted it was pictures of the East End of London, people I remember and memories ... I want to paint now. In painting the synagogue meetings of forty years ago ... I'm beginning to understand ... what these things are saying to me. And it's as if my mind takes snapshots of things.[90]

Lionel Blue admits to being a 'failed painter', but he believes that his sensitivity to what he sees, to take 'snapshots of things', has considerably 'influenced him as a broadcaster'.[91] He is acutely observant of details whether he is 'watching the people in the underground station' or wondering 'why that man is wearing odd socks in the concourse of Euston'.[92] There seems to be a clear link between Blue's interest in painting and the 'snapshots' in his memory.

His understanding of the role of such pictures is intriguing:

> I think these pictures are trying to tell me something. It's as if life is a series of pictures which stay in my mind and each of them has a message, like the stations of the cross or something, except that mine are jolly.[93]

In each picture that he remembers he therefore sees the potential for a message. These snapshots or pictures derive not only from what he saw, but also from what he read. He was a 'very lonely child' who read a lot. This has also stocked his 'mind with images and all sorts of things'.[94] He does not develop these identifications of some of the sources of his broadcasting into a theory of verbal pictures, but instead grounds his theory in terms of practical advice to new broadcasters:

> You've got to take up a story or incident that keeps on coming into

your mind, that's very important to you ... it might be important to the listener. If it's not important to you it will always be contrived.[95]

This advice echoes his early thoughts on the importance of speaking from the 'centre' of the personality and 'of being yourself' as a broadcaster.

Two potential sources for Blue's broadcasts have therefore been identified: first, snapshots from his memory, and secondly, personal experiences. Throughout his broadcasts he draws primarily not from the Scriptures, but from his own experience. He explains this approach with a rather generalised observation about both preachers and listeners:

[A]ll preachers sort of live in a religious ghetto. They assume that everybody knows a certain religious terminology or believes certain things. Most of the people don't believe and they don't have Scriptures. They don't know what Scripture is ... [Scriptures] are marvellous, but too long ago and too far away to matter, what happened to you yesterday is far more important than what happened to Moses 4,000 years ago or Jesus 2,000 years ago.[96]

One other source for Blue he describes as his 'Divine Friend'. This has been a 'construct in my mind' since 'my Quaker days' at Oxford.[97] In his own words he claims to see the friend sometimes: 'Sometimes we put our hands around each other, it looks like a Guardian Angel, sometimes like a Jesus figure, sometimes like Anne Frank or somebody like that.'[98]

Blue's 'Divine Friend' is not a surrogate scriptwriter, producer or editor for his broadcasts. In Blue's eyes, his friend is someone he wants to please, who has given good advice, and has not led him into 'cloud cuckoo' land.[99] It is hard to locate precisely the role that this elusive 'friend' plays in Blue's broadcasting, nevertheless it is clearly understood to be another more indirect source for his verbal pictures.

In one early *Thought* he is candid about how he draws upon his own personal experience. Blue admits:

A major source of ideas for sermons and spirituality came to me in airport lounges, bars, cafés (not always the genteel ones) and bus queues. To my astonishment the still, small voice of God spoke to me through the clamour of a juke-box.[100]

In the following paragraph he speaks of a Marlene Dietrich song: 'Where Have All the Flowers Gone?' In short sentences, he summarises the song: 'Young Girls pick them. They give them to their men. The men had gone to war, and got killed. Out of their graves little flowers grew. Where had they gone, those flowers? Well, young girls had picked them …' This *Thought* concludes with a powerful picture built around what he saw in a café in Germany. The unstated suggestion is that this poignantly repetitive song is playing on the jukebox in the background of the café:

> I looked up and saw a young boy and girl at the next table. A vase of flowers separated them. The full tragedy of Europe came home to me, and I knew the work I must do. So many people had to be reconciled to break that terrible repetition. God had spoken.[101]

The three scenes are skilfully woven together. The flowers act as a connecting sign, which signify how war separates, and how the tragedy repeats itself. This provides a good example of how his 'painter's eye' draws on a memory of his personal experience. The normality of the café scene is undermined by what has gone before it: the song highlighting the tragic waste of war and the need for reconciliation. The meaning of a simple vase of flowers separating a girl and boy is therefore invested with new meaning by the preceding song. An easily recognisable scene is therefore extended to explain how Blue learned that 'the still small voice of God' speaks from unexpected sources.

In this *Thought*, the idea of God is introduced through an everyday discourse, which draws heavily upon pictorial language. The central point of the *Thought* is that God is not necessarily found in the midst of religious institutions and religious discourse. Blue is implicitly inviting his listeners, through pictorial language, to extend their horizons and to be open to the possibility of God speaking to them in and through their everyday lives.

This is a central element of Blue's message. In one *Thought*, entitled 'A Tall Story from the Talmud', he makes this point explicit:

> When you pray, hold up your ordinary life to God, and you will find something extraordinary on it – His fingerprints. Among the confusion of voices in your mind is His still small voice.[102]

Blue is not afraid of naming God in his broadcasts, but does so less frequently than Tilby. Occasionally it is embedded in a traditional blessing or prayer, but more often it is within a picture of everyday life.

One of Blue's most memorable and characteristically humorous word pictures is his description of what he did when he fell into a grave:

> Climbing out of a grave is not easy, or dignified. I am not athletic, and I was tangled up in my black robes of black bombazine and my velvet hat. They passed down the ropes, but it was as difficult as a ski lift, and I kept on falling and bouncing back on that awful coffin lid. I peered up at the mourners and they down at me, and at last I knew what it was like to be at the receiving end of a funeral.[103]

Blue describes this unforgettable event graphically. He uses it as a device to highlight the dangers of taking our dignity and ourselves too seriously. Blue's use of humour is almost one of the defining characteristics of his *Thoughts*. In this he stands in a great tradition of Yiddish religious humour. Sometimes his stories are free-standing. Mostly they are woven into the pattern of his talks, showing both his humanity and his appreciation of the incongruities of the human situation. In this 'falling into the grave' *Thought* there is an endearing self-mockery and then a natural turning to God in prayer in a café over a cup of coffee after the funeral. It is interesting to notice how the discourse of prayer is placed visually into the ordinary context of a café. The result is to transform prayer into an activity that need not be restricted to the confines of an explicitly religious building or occasion.

These *Thoughts* illustrate how Blue uses pictorial language as a device for attempting to translate the discourse of the 'religious ghetto' into the discourse of modern life. He uses it to bring colour to his humorous stories, which aim to break down the wall between 'the ghetto and the boulevard'. As with Angela Tilby, pictorial language is but one of a number of verbal devices which Blue employs. As Shingler and Wieringa emphasise, Blue employs 'informal and colloquial' language; he speaks in 'relaxed and familiar tones', assumes an air of 'mutual understanding and sympathy', displays a 'keen understanding of "ordinary life"' and usually addresses his listeners as an 'audience of one' in an intimate and dialogic fashion.[104]

Some of these devices provoke strong reactions. Journalist Andrew Grimes, for example, is clearly dissatisfied with Blue's attempt to be colloquial:

> Rabbi Lionel Blue's occasional stints on *Thought for the Day,* the little God-slot which holds up Radio 4's *Today* programme every morning, are not always worth more than five seconds' attention. He has many irritating mannerisms – prefacing every sermonette, for instance, with a pseudo-colloquial 'Well, now' – and he makes embarrassingly awful jokes.[105]

For other listeners these are seen as endearing idiosyncrasies. The criticisms, if a little harsh, serve as a useful warning to broadcasters and preachers about the dangers of verbal idiosyncrasies,[106] or what could be described as 'studied spontaneity'.[107]

By contrast David Coomes appears perhaps unrealistically positive:

> Rabbi Lionel Blue is the character, he's the one-off who'll go on for ever. He can't fail to please. People feel comfortable with him. He almost performs what Hugo Gryn did on the *Moral Maze*: you want to hear the voice of comfort and humanity and so on.[108]

Coomes might be claiming too much for Blue, but he does illustrate how Blue's success is based on far more than simply using pictorial language. James Jones argues that: 'the reason why Rabbi Lionel Blue is so successful is because he is so descriptive, and sometimes you wonder where he is going in the *Thought*, but his success is that he tells a good story.'[109] His stories, his humour, his openness and his vulnerability in the content of his broadcasts all contribute to his performance. Even the searingly critical Andrew Grimes was 'quite impressed'[110] by Blue's thought-provoking honesty in one of his *Thoughts.* It has been argued in this section that Blue's ability to speak pictorially, from what he describes as 'the centre', strengthens the quality of many of his talks.

Conclusion

We should recognise that *Thought* can be a communicative failure, and the use of pictorial language does not guarantee success. Even established figures in religious broadcasting, such as Tilby and Blue, are by no means faultless broadcasters. They themselves admit that they can sometimes alienate some of their audience,[111] though this may partially reflect individual listeners' bias. There are lessons to be learnt from their mistakes as well as their successes, Tilby's over-abstract discourse, for instance, or Blue's studied spontaneity.

I have in fact focused primarily on their strengths. We have seen that in different ways 'painting pictures with words' is an important element in the work of these two regular contributors to BBC Radio 4's *Thought for the Day.* The technique is, however, more than simply a device for adding colour and interest to a 'lengthy' monologue. It is used to extend the listeners' fields of discourse, and to encourage new thoughts about both theological and moral issues. God is often unashamedly named, and rather than being surrounded by theological jargon, is located in the context of pictures and stories of everyday life.

These conclusions have importance for preachers attempting to communicate effectively today. As radio critic Tom Gardiner asserts: 'Religious information and the church context can easily get in the way of the religious communicator.'[112] Both broadcasters discussed in this chapter have shown how pictorial language, metaphors and stories can be used by speakers to liberate themselves from the insider-discourse of a particular faith community.

Tilby and Blue, of course, do not stand alone. James Jones, the Bishop of Liverpool, for example, also sees himself as an oral interpreter of our audio-visual culture. He believes that he acts as a verbal 'iconographer', 'impressionist' and 'photographer' depending on the subject matter and the speaking situation.[113] As a regular contributor to *Thought* James Jones often creates recognisable but surprising scenes. His description of a visit to a night-club with 'pounding music that invaded your body through the feet more than the ears' shatters stereotypical views of how bishops might spend their Friday nights.[114]

Reflecting on his broadcasting work, Jones also emphasises the importance of preachers surprising their listeners, 'of taking people in a direction where they're not quite sure of':

> I think the parables of Jesus are like this . . . If you want to know what the parables are about, you tell a story till you get to that moment when you say: 'Surprise! Surprise!' The priest ran by, he didn't help, the Levite ran by, he didn't help, but surprise, surprise, the dreaded Samaritan stopped . . . And I think too there's got to be an element of surprise in a sermon.[115]

Speaking visually can become one of the building blocks for helping speakers to surprise their listeners.

John Newbury, who has produced James Jones and also been a contributor to *Thought* himself, offers the following advice:

> When you broadcast on radio you need to paint pictures with words, you need to tell stories, you need to eschew abstract concepts . . . When you're broadcasting you only have one chance. There's no such thing as a rewind button.[116]

Angela Tilby and Lionel Blue are clearly part of the school who when they are broadcasting 'paint pictures with words' and usually 'eschew abstract concepts'. Tilby acts as a disciplined verbal iconographer shaping pictures on the basis of the images already lodged in her own colour-sensitive imagination. Blue works as a pictorial storyteller, weaving everyday images together to create compelling narratives which aim to help us interpret our own situations and recognise that we are not alone in our difficulties. This illustrates Coomes' observation that one of Blue's strengths is his ability to root what he is 'saying in human experience or a story'.[117] Both Blue's and Tilby's stories and insights into human experience are enlivened by their use of pictorial language and vivid stories. They point preachers to the importance both of rooting discourse in concrete experiences or stories and of enlivening such speech with pictorial language.

In both his theory and his practice, Blue echoes his former producer John Newbury's reminder that radio is a 'one to one medium', with listeners in 'the bathroom, in the loo, in the lounge, in the bedroom and in the kitchen' and that 'no one wants someone in their breakfast room to start preaching to them'.[118] As suggested earlier, preachers have a potential advantage over radio broadcasters, as they can normally see their listeners. Eye to eye contact with the chance to assess how their words are being received through the body language of listeners is a useful tool in the communication process. While preaching is not a 'one to one medium', the act of stepping imaginatively into or even visualising the world of individual listeners remains an important imaginative move for preachers. It will help them to create verbal images which resonate with their listeners, as well as preventing them from talking down to their congregations.

Colin Morris, a former head of religious broadcasting for the BBC and contributor to *Thought* for some thirty years, offers personal reflections on preaching and religious broadcasting pertinent to the current discussion:

> I regard the two activities as quite distinct skills and if either approach encroaches too much on the other, the result is either a *Thought for the Day* which is a sermonette or a sermon which is a commentary on topical events ... The goals are also different – that of *Thought* is to bring someone up short and make them think; that of the sermon is to get them to act, to make life-decisions. The very occasional *Thought* may do that too but usually the best we can do is to help the listener to get through that one day, by giving him or her a glimpse of a workaday world alive with God.[119]

I do not entirely agree with Morris's belief that preaching and doing *Thought* require 'quite distinct skills'. Nonetheless, his distinction between broadcasting and preaching goals serves as a useful reminder that *Thought* is a significantly distinct communicative event from a sermon.

It is also worth noting that compared to Wright and Lewis in the 1940s, those doing *Thought* face new pressures as they operate in an increasingly secular context where faith is often privatised and where some argue that 'agnostic pluralism reigns'.[120] This has serious theological implications for broadcasters. Rabbi Jonathan Sacks, for example, believes that one of the characteristics of our culture is that 'we no longer need, nor would we even think of invoking, God in order to understand nature or history'.[121] Angela Tilby argues that it is important on *Thought* 'to remember the word "God"' and to be prepared to 'open a window on the transcendence of God'. She perceives that there is sometimes now 'pressure to turn it into a nice little talk about morality' or allow it to become 'an opinion piece' which is 'not offensive to agnostics'. She believes this pressure is part of a contemporary process, where 'the name of God is being erased from public speech'.[122]

Public service religious radio, and perhaps *Thought* contributors, are under considerable implicit pressure to reflect this type of world-view, where the name of God is absent, and where listeners construct their own moral universe. Pluralism of moral beliefs and religious expression has become part of what is sometimes described as 'the post-modern condition'.[123] On this basis we could say that, along with other religious radio, *Thought* now operates within what Old Testament theologian Walter Brueggemann describes as a 'new interpretative situation'.[124] There is now a new moral context in which, as Woody Allen suggests in *Bullets Over Broadway*, the artist constructs his or her own 'moral universe',[125] without reference to God. At their best, both *Thought* and preaching can offer a counter story to such a secular world-view. How to relate with theological integrity to current issues in a non-secular way is a pressing question for preachers. Richard Harries, Bishop of Oxford and another regular *Thought* contributor, points to the challenge of 'teasing out a theological dimension of something that is in the news' and in 'a way which is neither political nor platitudinous and which is accessible to people of a wide variety of beliefs and none, rushing off to work'.[126]

Few assumptions can now be made about listeners' belief systems. On these grounds any approach to religious communication must take seriously the diversity of belief or indeed absence of faith. It cannot ignore the fact that the listener is, according to Tom Gardiner, 'often more secularised than the religious communicator'.[127] The challenge is to develop approaches that allow speakers and listeners, often from contrasting faith worlds, at least to understand their divergent fields of discourse.[128] There is a need to employ forms of discourse that enable those who are experienced in theological modes of discourse and who perceive themselves to inhabit a particular 'realm of meaning',[129] to communicate with those for whom such discourse is at best incomprehensible and at worst irrelevant, meaningless or even offensive.[130]

Preaching has another advantage over a radio *Thought*: time. Few sermons are as short as two minutes forty-five seconds. Usually preachers have time to develop a theme more fully in ten, fifteen or even twenty minutes.[131] Nevertheless, this extra time can become an excuse for overlong, ill-disciplined or poorly constructed sermons in contrast to Tilby or Blue's tight scripts. Coomes asserts of *Thought*:

> It's not just a straight sermon style, but actually manages in two and a half minutes to say one thing, it's very important that it's one thing. It's not *Thoughts for the Day*, it's *Thought for the Day*. Well argued, well constructed . . .[132]

Preachers, he argues, can learn from this practice and become more disciplined and imaginative in their speaking.[133]

We have seen that pictorial language plays a significant role in the work of a verbal iconographer and a pictorial storyteller. We have seen that it is by no means the only verbal device that they employ, but that it combines with other approaches such as editorial self-discipline, vulnerability through personal stories, conversational and humorous discourse to enable them to build bridges between themselves and their listeners. Listeners are often implicitly and explicitly invited to participate imaginatively in the discourse.[134] At their best these broadcasts become co-creative acts, which have the feel of two-way conversations. Compared with Wright and Lewis, Tilby and Blue are more tentative in their claims of faith and more apt to 'wear their hearts upon their sleeves'. Using a term loosely adapted from George Lindbeck's categories, they could be viewed as 'expressivists',[135] attempting to use pictorial language as a means to extend, transform or even counter their listeners' fields of discourse.

Preachers can learn from the variety of ways in which Tilby and Blue use pictorial language. On some occasions they use it as a bridge to go from one discursive field where God is not mentioned to another where God is named.[136] At other moments they use it to demonstrate that embedded in the normality of everyday life there are what Peter Berger described as 'signals of transcendence'.[137] Pictorial language can act as a 'verbal icon',[138] pointing beyond itself to these signals. It can also be used to uncover hidden values from the 'school of suffering'.[139] Pictorial language has the potential therefore to perform a range of functions. These include acting as a bridge, as a signpost, as a verbal icon and as a teacher for listeners. It can also function parabolically, illustratively, or simply as a 'wake-up call' for a distracted congregation. Through pictorial language, and in other imaginative ways, each broadcaster is attempting not simply to connect with his or her audience, but also to expand the listeners' fields of discourse, realms of meaning, and even horizons of faith.

Notes

1. Reith 1924, 191–2, 194.
2. This phrase 'mission to explain' originates from a series of articles written by John Birt (Head of Current Affairs, LWT, 1974–77) and Peter Jay (Economics Editor, *The Times*, 1967–77) in the 1970s on a '"bias against understanding", which they believed to characterize television news and current affairs.' See Eldridge 1993, 5.
3. Gillian Reynolds' case that 'religious broadcasting is hanging on by its finger-nails' was supported by a number of examples from Radio 4. *The Daily Service* (Radio 4) has been marginalised to Long Wave, and *Morning Worship* (Sundays, Radio 4) is sometimes reduced by fifteen minutes to make room for Test Match coverage. Note also how James Boyle, the controller of Radio 4, has cut *Ten to Ten* from the schedule, as well as bringing *Prayer for the Day* and *Sunday* forward to earlier and less popular listening times.

4. Peter Elvy in his unpublished PhD thesis touches on some of these developments. See Elvy 1995, especially Appendix 1, 'The Future of Independent Christian Broadcasting', an address by Peter Meadows, 22 February 1994, 307–8. Meadows highlights the shift in the BBC's religious broadcasting policy philosophy by comparing a paper by Rev. Francis House in 1948 and CRAC's submission to the Annan Committee in 1975.
5. 'The one thing you just cannot do is proselytise'. Coomes, Interview 1996. This ideal contrasts with the philosophy espoused by a former director and controller of BBC Scotland, in Dinwiddie 1968, 92–103. The underlying assumption of Dinwiddie's Chapter 8 is that a legitimate use of religious radio is for evangelism. He does however emphasise the importance of caution in this area: 'before the microphone could be used to bring in the lapsed and lost, some hard thinking and bold experiment was necessary to determine the target and the scope of radio evangelism'. 95.
6. Radio critic, Paul Donovan, explained how: 'New voices soon to be heard [on *Thought*] include those of Akhandadhi Das, the principal of the Hindu establishment Bhaktivedanta Manor in Hertfordshire, and Clive Lawton, employed by the Chief Rabbi on Jewish renewal' and the Islamic educationalist Nadeem Kazmi. (Donovan 'No more holy than thou', in *The Times*, Radio Waves Column, 14 July 1996.) An unnamed report in the *Daily Mail* a month earlier had asserted: 'Radio Four's Thought for the Day was under attack yesterday for handing a platform to the Hare Krishna religious sect,' in the *Daily Mail*, 12 June 1996.
7. This controversy was covered extensively in the press. See, for example, 'Radio 4 "God slot" to keep the faith', in *The Times*, 14 April 1995; 'BBC keeps faith with listeners', in the *Daily Telegraph*, 14 April 1995; 'Radio slot closed to atheists', in *The Guardian*, 14 April 1995; 'Radio God Slot ban on atheists', in the *Daily Express*, 15 April 1995. In all of these articles the BBC's Head of Religious Broadcasting, Rev. Ernest Rea, is cited: '*Thought for the Day* is there to give a distinctiveness and to throw a different light on news events, if you secularise it then you dilute that special perspective.'
8. Coomes, Interview 1996.
9. Tilby, Interview 16 July 1996.
10. Coomes, Interview 1996. He continues: 'And who has something ideally provocative to say, and I suppose takes something that can be quite ordinary and something that's being covered a lot in the

Today programme and just give it a tweak and look at something from a different perspective, you know, without being pious ...'

11. Recent debates have centred on: Anne Atkins' broadcast on homosexuality (see Polly Toynbee, 'Give us hellfire, not opiate, in the God slot', in *The Independent*, 14 October 1996, 15); or Gabrielle Cox's politically biased *Thought* (see 'Thought for the Day: Don't let Lefties lecture', in the *Daily Mail*, 28 August 1996); or the exclusion of atheists and agnostics on *Thought*; or the controversial 'resting' in 1996 of seven 'white, male, Christian and ordained priests', who used to contribute to *Thought*. David Coomes admitted: 'We have 30 contributors to *Thought* at the moment, and probably I'm going to build that up to about 40.' He explains why he rested the seven contributors: 'the basic reason, absolutely, the truthful reason was I wanted to bring in some new names, a bit of new blood, and slowly shift things around a bit'. Coomes, Interview 1996.
12. See Paul Donovan's useful chapter on 'The Breakfast Pulpit' in Donovon 1997, 149–73.
13. Coomes, Interview 1996. 'I have looked after *Thought* for the last three years or so.' Before being in charge he was one of several producers who were responsible for producing it.
14. Toynbee, 'Give us hellfire', 15. In this entertaining article she provocatively argues: 'You know something is wrong from the moment they start to speak. Sometimes they are perky and facetious, sometimes they ooze with improper social concern for the Bosnians or the homeless. Even when it is a Sikh, you do not get the authentic tones of the rebels besieged in the Golden Temple, the fanatics who shot Indira Gandhi. You get a soft-voiced gentle soul who may carry a dirk in his turban, but sounds as if he, too, has been through a C of E theological college. This is a conspiracy of the religions to present themselves as agreeable, reasonable people, despite the mayhem religion causes wherever in the world people actually believe in it.'
15. Radio critic Paul Donovan cites BBC audience research into the 7.30–8am section of the programme in April 1994: 'Thought for the Day was something that nearly a fifth of the Today audience did not want to hear.' Donovan, 'No more holy than thou'.
16. The 'God Slot' is a common way of describing *Thought*. See, for example, Diana Pulson's story on: '"God Slot" Rabbi's Revelation', in the *Liverpool Echo*, 7 October 1995.
17. James Fenton, 'Thought for the day: dispense with bishops', *The Independent*, 13 March 1995.

18. Tilby, Interview 1996 (italics mine).
19. She has recently taken early retirement from the BBC, and was ordained deacon in 1997, and priested in 1998. Since the Autumn of 1997, she has been a lecturer in Spirituality for two-thirds of the year at Westcott House, Cambridge. For the remaining third she makes programmes as a freelance producer and/or works as a broadcaster.
20. Tilby, Interview 1996.
21. Angela Tilby, series producer, *Lives of Jesus*, BBC 1, 4 Sundays in December 1996. Presented by Mark Tully. See also Tully 1996.
22. Tilby, Interview 1996.
23. Ibid.. On the basis of viewing a number of Tilby documentaries, she appears to be being more than a little self-effacing. For example, the visually imaginative juxtaposition of desert shots with Mark Tully walking up the mountain in the final episode of *Lives of Jesus* created a number of memorable scenes for this final programme in the series.
24. Ibid.
25. Ibid.
26. Tilby, *Thought for the Day*, 13 May 1996.
27. See, for example, the graphic manner in which Augustine describes his conversion in *Confessions*, 1961 (c. AD 397), 177–9.
28. 'The point that Augustine was not very at ease with purely abstract thinking is usually made, and more tellingly I think, in relation to his difficulties in thinking of God as a purely "spiritual" being without imagining some spatial dimension to God's existence. This difficulty is explored in Book 7 of the *Confessions* . . . [and see also] Books 10 ff. of the *Confessions* for the way he agonises about the reality of time, space and form and in what sense God created the world.' Letter from Angela Tilby to Jolyon Mitchell, 10 April 1997.
29. Tilby, Interview 1996.
30. Ibid. See Alvin C. Rueter who argues 'we should strive to preach like a Hebrew', in other words, visually. Rueter 1997, 67. See also Achtemeier 1980, 99–100. Achtemeier, an Old Testament scholar and homiletician, highlights the wide range of metaphors, similies and images to be found in the Bible.
31. Psalm 69:24a, 27a, 28a and Angela Tilby, *Thought for the Day*, 4 March 1996.
32. Angela Tilby, *Thought for the Day*, 4 March 1996.
33. Tilby, Interview 1996.
34. Ibid.

35. Ibid.
36. Ibid.
37. Ibid.
38. Ibid.
39. Ibid.
40. Ibid.
41. Tilby, *Thought for the Day*, 16 July 1996.
42. Ibid.
43. See for another *Thought* which notes the colour of clothes: Angela Tilby, *Thought for the Day*, 20 May 1996. Tilby begins her *Thought* about Tibet with passing attention to the colour of the Dalai Lama's robe: 'We've got used to seeing the Dalai Lama patiently travelling the world, with his red robe and unwearied smile ...'
44. Tilby, *Thought for the Day*, 16 July 1996.
45. Wilson 1995, 225.
46. Tilby, Interview 1996.
47. Tilby, *Thought for the Day*, 16 July 1996.
48. Tilby, Interview 1996. Also cited above.
49. Tilby, *Thought for the Day*, 27 May 1996.
50. See Buttrick's discussion of 'points of view' in 1987, 55–68.
51. Ibid., 68.
52. Tilby, *Thought for the Day*, 27 May 1996.
53. Tilby, *Thought for the Day*, 13 May 1996.
54. Tilby, *Thought for the Day*, 9 July 1996.
55. Ibid.
56. Ibid.
57. Tilby, *Thought for the Day*, 18 September 1995.
58. Tilby, *Thought for the Day*, 1 July 1996.
59. Ibid.
60. Ibid.
61. See Chapter 2 of this book for a discussion and evaluation of Fred Craddock's inductive and deductive categories for preaching.
62. Coomes, Interview 1996 (italics are mine). He admits: 'And I have Angela Tilby [on *Thought*] not so much for her theological standpoint, as the fact she writes very clever scripts, complex scripts, but not too complex and clever.'
63. Ibid.
64. Ibid.
65. Tilby uses this phrase in reference to a Coptic Monk Father Benjamin's explanation of the Coptic cross in 'Who owns Jesus?' Episode 1 of *The Jesus Diary*, Radio 3, 2 December 1996, produced by Norman Winter, written and presented by Angela Tilby.

66. Lionel Blue sees his editing work (*Forms of Prayer)* with Dr Johnathan Magonet as his most important. See also Blue 1985a (1979).
67. Blue 1985b.
68. Coomes, Interview 1996.
69. Newbury, producer, 1990.
70. Blue, Interview 1995.
71. Blue 1985b. In the introduction he admits after reassembling and reading a number of his *Thoughts* through, he was pleased with their 'frankness. My only regret was that I hadn't been franker'. 7. Compare these sentiments with Phillips Brooks' well-known assertion that: 'Preaching is the bringing of truth through personality.' Brooks 1989 (1877), 5.
72. Blue, *Thought for the Day,* 14 September 1987.
73. Blue, *Thought for the Day,* 6 March 1989.
74. See Diana Pulson, '"God slot" Rabbi's revelation' in the *Liverpool Echo,* 7 October 1995. Some critics have argued that Blue has abused his platform, and used *Thought* for his own personal agenda, and as a psychological mirror for helping him understand his own complex personality.
75. Blue, *Thought for the Day,* 30 January 1989.
76. Fairclough 1995, 147. 'This is often perceived and portrayed in a way which harmonizes with the core contemporary cultural value of individualism, in terms of a foregrounding of the unique and individual personalities of, especially, different presenters.'
77. Rabbi Lionel Blue has often shared the same studio as these two presenters, Terry Wogan and Derek Jameson, as he regularly does the 9.15am *Pause for Thought* on the 6.30–9.30am Radio 2 morning sequence. For an extreme example of a radio broadcaster who speaks all that is on his mind see the film about the American DJ or 'shock jock', Howard Stern, director, *Private Parts,* 1997.
78. Blue, Interview 1995.
79. Fairclough 1995, 142.
80. Blue, Interview 1995.
81. Ibid.
82. Ibid.
83. Ibid. 'to these' follows the final word 'listen' and refers to *Thought for the Day* and *Pause for Thought* (italics mine).
84. This phrase echoes Lamin Sanneh's fascinating text on translation, 1989. Lionel Blue, however, uses it differently from Sanneh. For further discussion of translation see Chapter 8 of this book.
85. Blue, Interview 1995.

86. Ibid.
87. Ibid.
88. Ibid.
89. Ibid.
90. Ibid.
91. Ibid.
92. Ibid.
93. Ibid.
94. Ibid. He continues: 'bits of Bunyan come out, Blake, Diaries, all sorts of things.'
95. Ibid.
96. Ibid.
97. Blue 1985, 1985b, 64–6.
98. Blue, Interview 1995.
99. Ibid.
100. Blue 1985b, 11.
101. Ibid., 12. Compare R. S. Wright's observation, also cited in the previous chapter, that: 'almost every railway carriage contains at least one sermon'. R. S. Wright, *Personal Journal/Diary*, 34.
102. Blue, 1985b, 40.
103. Ibid., 19. 'I was burying an old lady in winter, and the ground was icy. I stood around the ground with mourners. They passed me a spade to throw in some earth, for this is part of the Jewish ritual. In my fervour I got carried away, and slipped – the earth went in first, then went the spade, and then me.'
104. Shingler and Wieringa 1998, 116–17.
105. Andrew Grimes, 'Radio News', in the *Manchester Evening News*, 11 February 1995.
106. One fellow broadcaster, who asked to remain anonymous, argues that Blue is in danger of becoming a caricature of himself, and has become trapped into playing his own public persona. This view does not do justice to Blue's own emphasis upon the importance of 'speaking from the centre'.
107. The danger of Blue's studied spontaneity became transparent when on one occasion he turned to the second page of his *Thought* and it was not there. In spite of prompting from John Humphries he was unable to continue his *Thought*. It highlights the danger of being entirely script-bound in a live communicative setting. Nevertheless, he received many letters of support after this broadcast. He believes it illustrates the 'danger of becoming over slick' as a religious communicator. Blue, Interview 1995. This is also a pertinent point for preachers today.

108. Coomes, Interview 1996.
109. James Jones affirms Blue's descriptive broadcasting style, by criticising his own: 'The great thing about *Thought* is to be descriptive and not prescriptive, and what you're doing is putting yourself into the shoes of people and trying to describe what they are. And *Thought* fails and I'm afraid that there are too many of us who do it, prescribing, saying: "We must this and we must that," and those prescriptive things are terribly hectoring and, I think, very alienating.' Jones, Interview 15 June 1997.
110. Andrew Grimes, 'Radio News', in the *Manchester Evening News*, 11 February 1995. Grimes goes on to confess that he was 'quite impressed' with a particular *Thought* by Blue which touched on feelings of patriotism, sexual frustration and guilt, connected with the Second World War victory celebrations. Grimes admits: 'I was impressed by the rabbi's little talk because it was most unusually, attached to a genuine thought. Paradoxically, *Thought for the Day* is usually short on thought.'
111. It is important to emphasise that listeners may be alienated not simply by tedious or inappropriate broadcasts, but also because iconoclastic discourse may lead some to 'switch off ' in disagreement.
112. Tom Gardiner, on 'Songs in Space' in the *Church Times*' radio review, 29 September 1995. He continues: '*Thought for the Day* on Monday had Bishop Richard Holloway, who began by telling us about his going to confession. I think you can talk like that to "the Sunday people", but it gives the rest a feeling of remoteness.' I would suggest that even to 'Sunday people', preachers who use inappropriate theological and/or abstract language can inculcate a 'feeling of remoteness' amongst many of their listeners.
113. Jones emphasises the importance of iconic language and also hypothesises: 'I would have thought that when you're talking about God in images you are being impressionistic. When you are describing situations in which people find themselves you're being more like a photographer.' Jones, Interview 1997.
114. Jones, *Thought for the Day*, 24 February 1997. He goes on vividly to describe the 'strobe lighting' which 'seemed to hold the gyrating, air-beating dancers in an experience of religious intensity. But the ecstatic look in their eyes vanished as they left the club into the cold dark night – their faces gaunt and empty. It was as if they'd left their souls behind on the dance floor.'
115. Jones, Interview 1997.

116. Newbury, Interview 1995. Newbury is a former editor of BBC Religious Broadcasting.
117. Coomes, Interview 1996.
118. Newbury, Interview 1995.
119. Morris letter to Jolyon Mitchell, 25 August 1998, 1.
120. Newbigin 1991, 60.
121. Sacks 1991, 27.
122. Tilby, Interview 1996. See the following chapter for the contrasting experience in the USA, where the name of 'God' is still found regularly in public discourse.
123. See Lyon 1994; Harvey 1989; and Lyotard 1984.
124. Brueggemann 1993: vii. 'There can be little doubt that we are in a wholly new interpretative situation.'
125. Woody Allen, writer and director, *Bullets Over Broadway*, 1995. A frequent refrain in this film was that 'the artist creates his own moral universe'.
126. Harries letter to Jolyon Mitchell, 18 August 1998. See Harries 1984, 24–7; English 1996, 18–22.
127. Tom Gardiner, on 'Songs in Space', in the *Church Times*' radio review, 29 September 1995.
128. This challenge is found in a heightened form in the BBC World Service. See, for example, how the English religious current affairs programme *Focus on Faith*, soon to change its title to *Report on Religion*, attempts to present weekly religious news to an internationally diverse audience.
129. Phenix 1975 (1964), 165–73. 'Human beings are essentially creatures who have the power to experience *meanings*. Distinctively human existence consists in a pattern of meanings.' 167. Phenix's understanding of the object of general education could be usefully adapted to highlight one of the objectives for *Thought for the Day*: 'To lead to the fulfilment of human life through the enlargement and deepening of meaning.' 167.
130. This argument resonates with Hans-Georg Gadamer's understanding of the 'fusing of horizons' in hermeneutics. See Gadamer 1989 (1960), 302–7. 'In the process of understanding, a real fusing of horizons occurs'. 307. See also Thiselton 1980, and Van A. Harvey's useful essay on 'Hermeneutics', in Eliade 1987. Van A. Harvey suggests, echoing Wittgenstein and Heidegger, that: 'explanation and interpretation make sense only within a horizon of presuppositions, practices, and assumptions that our culture mediates to us – our tradition, so to speak'. 285.
131. See Stephen Ward, 'Preachers decide time is right to cut back on

tradition', in *The Independent*, 3 May 1994. Ward reports on a survey that found that sermons are getting briefer. Survey not cited.

132. Coomes, Interview 1996.
133. Ibid. Richard Harries, Bishop of Oxford, admits that he has learnt from doing *Thought* that 'it is possible to communicate what one wants to say in a very short slot'. Richard Harries letter to Jolyon Mitchell, 18 August 1998.
134. This important point finds support from American writer, William Hethcock, who argues that: 'Rather than looking at a picture or watching a play from the outside, the [listeners (word missing)] must become part of the scene the sermon sets. They must be helped actually to have an experience as they listen!' Hethcock 1995, 45.
135. Lindbeck 1984. Neither Tilby nor Blue fit precisely into Lindbeck's widely cited three categories of how doctrine works. For brief but helpful discussions of these i) Cognitive–Propositional, ii) Experiential–Expressivist, and iii) Cultural–Linguistic models see: Wells 1998, 54 and Ford 1997, 347–8.
136. See, for example, David Winter discussing the 'Weather Channel', on *Thought for the Day*, 3 June 1996. Winter believes that: 'if speakers name God too soon or inappropriately, then many "secular" listeners may "switch off" from following the *Thought* to its conclusion'.
137. Berger 1970. 'I would suggest that theological thought seek out what might be called *signals of transcendence* within the empirically given human situation ... By signals of transcendence I mean phenomena that are to be found within the domain of our "natural" reality but that appear to point beyond that reality.' 70.
138. See Wimsatt, Jr 1970 (1994). 'The term icon is used today by semeiotic [sic] writers to refer to a verbal sign which somehow shares the properties of, or resembles, the objects it denotes. The same term in its more usual meaning refers to a visual image and especially to one which is a religious symbol.'
139. See, for example, Blue 1985b, 62.

CHAPTER 7

American Radio Preachers

We now move across the Atlantic to consider some examples of religious broadcasting in the very different cultural context of the United States of America. The examples are drawn from my own fieldwork in the USA. It was originally encapsulated in a programme produced for a BBC Radio 4 documentary, *Garrison Keillor's Radio Preachers.* Since I made contact with over 100 religious radio stations, and carried out more in-depth visits and detailed interviews at another twenty stations, there was a wide choice of local radio preaching material from which to select. As a way of narrowing the focus to within manageable parameters, I will limit the discussion in this chapter to the radio preachers who appeared on *Garrison Keillor's Radio Preachers.* I will also draw on extracts from interviews with the preachers and recordings of their preaching not heard on the programme itself. The central criterion for inclusion in the programme was the extent to which they exemplified significant characteristics of American radio preaching.

Garrison Keillor provides a number of useful observations about the context, character and durability of this type of radio preaching:

> It was always thought that mass media would gradually erase regional and ethnic differences – that radio and television would lead inevitably to a vast homogenisation in society – but this may not be true. The Southern radio preachers ... represent an extraordinary American oral tradition, an extemporaneous style of preaching that can be traced back to the early seventeen-hundreds, and radio has helped it survive. These are preachers from the backwoods, far off the beaten path, and if you wanted to go visit their churches,

> you'd have a hard time finding them. But you can find them on the radio across most of America.[1]

Radio preaching is clearly a complex, multi-faceted phenomenon. It provides windows on to a number of American religious subcultures. Some of them you can find on the back roads, 'off the beaten path', preaching on the 'airwaves of Zion',[2] others you might discover working in large cities. Some can be found in what Mark Ward describes as the 'hall of fame',[3] others are known to only a few local listeners. Whilst their varying expressions of faith reflect the wide range of Christian beliefs found in America, the vast majority of radio preachers are working from a fundamentalist or an evangelical position,[4] sometimes within a para-church organisation, or occasionally as independents. Leonard Sweet observes:

> The way in which radio brought together orality and electricity in the charged atmosphere of evangelism is yet to be fully explored as a factor in the evangelical dominance of the airwaves, where today it is estimated that three-fourths of all religious broadcasting is either evangelical or fundamentalist.[5]

They not only use a distinctly idiosyncratic broadcasting style, but they also represent a theologically distinctive tradition. They are descendants of the revival tent tradition, operating from what could be described as an electronic revival tent.[6] J. B. Lineberry, an evangelist who built churches in Arizona and who has been broadcasting on the WHHV radio station in Hillsville, Virginia, since 1972, comments:

> I've done it because of reaching people. I feel that you can reach more people by the means of radio than any other way. And I also go on tent revivals because I feel that you can reach more people that won't go inside of a church. They come to a tent, because it's different. You can draw people in that's never heard the Gospel.[7]

Radio preachers can all too easily be portrayed as an irrelevant and discordant sound in the American mass media context. Irrelevant, because most radio preachers work within what Quentin Schultze describes as the 'religious radio ghetto'.[8] Discordant, because many only speak to the ghetto from the ghetto about the ghetto in the language of the ghetto.[9] The result of such in-group language is that most radio preachers have tiny audiences, serve a 'small religious subculture', and frequently fail 'to attract even their own kind to the medium'.[10]

This marks a sharp contrast with the preachers of the 'golden age of radio',[11] where the likes of Father Charles E. Coughlin[12] and Charles E. Fuller attracted millions of listeners.[13] For example, 'when a Philadelphia station asked its listeners if they would like to hear Coughlin or the New York Philharmonic on Sunday afternoons, the vote ran Coughlin 187,000, Philharmonic 12,000.'[14] Charles Fuller was also extremely popular, drawing an estimated audience of 20 million.[15] According to broadcasting historian Mark Ward: 'At the peak of his radio ministry in 1943, Fuller was heard on more than a thousand stations at a cost of about thirty-five thousand dollars per week.'[16]

Today religious radio works with much smaller budgets and audiences. Nevertheless, the view of religious radio in America and especially radio preaching, as discordant, dying or even dangerous, has to be placed alongside other noteworthy facts. The number of religious radio stations has been steadily increasing; some affirm that it has been 'mushrooming',[17] over the last two decades. In 1972 there were some 399 stations carrying 15 hours of religious programmes or more each week in the United States. In 1982 this number had nearly doubled to 736. By 1992 it had increased to 1156 stations,[18] increasing to 1566 in 1994.[19] These figures suggest that stations and broadcasters still have faith in religious radio. One station manager based in New Orleans admitted to me that he had changed station policy and now accepted the broadcasts of radio preachers, partly because it was more lucrative than his previous music-driven schedule.[20]

Religious radio, and radio preaching in particular, remains a significant broadcasting phenomenon, an important topic for investigation. Fred Craddock believes that:

> Radio is making a comeback in a sense of becoming a more used vehicle for preaching than television. Television is very expensive, and television has gotten a bad reputation because some of the tele-evangelists were guilty of an assortment of things. So the radio has

> the benefit of being an old traditional way of reaching the secular public. 'How do I reach beyond the walls of the church?' Use the radio![21]

Robert Duvall's sympathetic cinematic portrayal of a devout Pentecostal preacher from Texas in *The Apostle* (1997) provides a dramatised insight into the way a local preacher uses a small radio station to draw attention to the independent church he is setting up.[22] As with many of the radio preachers I met, broadcasting is but a small part of his preaching ministry.

One of the most memorable characteristics of this form of radio broadcasting is its extremism, both verbal and vocal. This is hard to capture in a written form: some of their discourse has to be heard to be believed. I will attempt, however, to show something of this by using the following notations.

Key to Transcription Conventions:[23]

1. Standard Type Face:
   Ordinary conversational volume and intonation
2. **Boldface Type:**
   Increased volume and intonation used for dramatic/projected speech
3. **BOLDFACE CAPITALS:**
   Greatly increased volume and intonation range

Underlining words or syllables: words/syllables spoken with emphasis

* thumps or pounds on rostrum/pulpit

+hah+ loud expulsion of breath that punctuates chant/sermon

bounds quickly spoken speech

[] bounds transcriber's comments

I will use these notations sparingly and only when they advance the general thrust of the argument. One reason for placing emphasis on para-linguistics and appropriate literary notation is the importance of delivery for evaluating this kind of broadcasting.[24]

At first sight many of the examples to be discussed may seem to be laden with negative implications. The kind of discourse we encounter seems alien and distant from contemporary British culture, creating obstacles rather than bridges to understanding. Nonetheless, it has a raw vitality, a liveliness that is in contrast to the calm urbanity exhibited by the broadcasters considered in Chapters 5 and 6.

In order to engage critically and sensitively with the exclusivist nature of certain aspects of their discourse, we need to make an imaginative leap into these preachers' discursive worlds. In his ethnographic study, *The Airwaves of Zion*,[25] Howard Dorgan describes Brother Arnold Noles of Neon on WNKY, a Kentucky radio station, as an 'impassioned speaker' who: 'seemed to lose himself in exhortation. Standing in one spot throughout his sermon, he placed his hands on the long studio table, leaned over the microphone, and concentrated exclusively on his radio audience, whoever they might have been.'[26]

I witnessed similar scenes in 1994 when I visited a number of radio preachers in their small, often poorly equipped studios. Many of the radio preachers currently broadcasting in rural America make a striking contrast with the high profile TV evangelists made infamous in the 1980s. Broadcasting to their small, local audiences, far from national attention, they express their beliefs and passions 'through a regional vernacular that is often foreign to mainline denominations'.[27] With a few exceptions, they tend to describe themselves in self-deprecatory tones, acknowledging the paucity of their formal education. Their audiences, in Appalachia for example, according to Dorgan are also 'generally below the national average in educational and other socio-economic measures'.[28] One radio preacher who is still preaching after thirty years on his local radio station, described himself as only 'a country boy' with 'no college education'.[29] This humble refrain echoed through the words of many of the rural radio preachers I met and interviewed.

The Singing Radio Preacher[30]

One preacher who saw himself as a 'good awle country boy' was Curtis Stoops.[31] I drove west from Richmond, Virginia, for eight hours into the Appalachian Mountains to meet him. Based in Max Meadows, Virginia, he has been radio preaching for over twelve years. He has converted his garage into a studio, where he has produced numerous shows for the local radio stations. His aerial resembled an old bent coat hanger, his tape library consists of a large cardboard box overflowing with cassettes. His studio – which, for all its rough edges, he is proud of – acts like a magnet to dozens of other local radio preachers. They come down from the mountains to preach, to sing and to broadcast.[32]

Stoops is part of what Nancy Ammerman calls an 'evangelistic people', and more specifically, a 'pragmatic evangelist'.[33] Radio broadcasting provides the best means of reaching a world which, in his view, needs to hear the words of a preacher.[34] Stoops's small broadcasting community works independently of 'mainline' denominations. He is part of a 'regional common man's phenomenon' which originates 'from heavily independent religious subgroups that owe little or no allegiance to hierarchical structures'.[35] These two factors, a desire to evangelise and a loyalty to his small independent religious subgroup, are reflected in his preaching.

On the one hand, Curtis Stoops uses accessible autobiographical pictorial language in his singing and his speaking, both of which are vehicles for his preaching. After nearly dying of a stroke he composed a song called *Too Many Treasures.* In flat and yet strangely mesmerising tones he transports his listeners into barren deserts, down ice cold rivers and through other metaphors of trauma. Memorable pictorial language is 'born out of a personal trouble',[36] in this case his stroke.

At the heart of these images lies a message of rescue and relief. His discourse is passionate, full of hope, and at times lightened by humour. Perhaps most memorably, he describes in detail a baptism, which culminated in his inadvertently falling into the river.[37] As with many other rural radio preachers, behind these simple autobiographical verbal pictures lies his desire to evangelise, 'to reach out' and to communicate the simple call to conversion. This rhetorical objective is perhaps made clear by his use of pictures of hope, rather than judgement. On the other hand, Stoops often employs biblical language and a 'stylized sermonic technique' that is 'distinctly Appalachian'.[38] In a programme from 1993, he persistently uses religious terms such as 'covenant', 'gentiles', 'plan of God' and 'Prince of Peace', with no explanation.[39] His transitions between these apparently unconnected biblical terms make it difficult to follow the flow of his preaching. 'This was a clear display of in-group language on an in-group audience. It probably reached none of those it was intended for. It never left the ghetto.'[40]

These two sides of Stoops's radio preaching, autobiographical and biblical, could be described as outsider-accessible discourse and insider-friendly discourse. The tension between these two strands within Stoops's broadcasting is accentuated by his repetitive rhetorical style. Like many other Appalachian radio preachers, he tends to repeat words, phrases and images for emphasis.

In one broadcast, for example, he attempts to describe his listeners' life in a world which is bristling with difficulty, and to highlight the peace which only the 'Prince of Peace' can bring. In his delivery he hardly pauses, even to breathe:

> # That world of trouble and sorrow,
> **that world of being upset continuously,**
> **that world of having nerve problems,**
> **that world of having financial problems,**
> **that world that seems like things are just so tough that you can't make it through, but <u>JESUS</u> come,**
> **the Prince of Peace,**
> **THAT YOU MIGHT FIND PEACE, EVEN LIVING IN THE MIDST OF THIS WORLD,**
> **WE CAN PUT THE WORLD BEHIND US WHEN WE'RE <u>IN</u> JESUS CHRIST, WE CAN LET IT GO RIGHT BY . . . #** [41]

Curtis Stoops builds up a poetic crescendo in this breathless series of statements. Pace and volume increase as he develops his theme. It is clear that he is attempting to step into the world of a listener who is in crisis, and he is also attempting to point them towards the biblical image of 'the Prince of Peace'. The troubled world is placed in sharp contrast with the peace of Jesus Christ. In Stoops's eyes, there is only one way to qualify for this peace: 'You <u>must</u> be **born again**, and that's the only way.'[42]

This represents his, and many other rural radio preachers', central appeal.

In another radio sermon he develops this point at length in a semi-dramatic, semi-shouting form, marginally quieter than the previous extract:

> Nicodemus said: 'Why, how can I be born again? Can I enter into my mother's womb a second time?' That's not what He's talking about! He's talking about inviting Jesus into your **heart!** That He'll give you a renewing of the mind, that you won't **no longer** be called the uncircumcision, **but you can be called a very CHILD of God, no more aliens from God** ...[43]

Even in this quieter extract, the force with which he hits each phrase indicates that he is passionate about proclaiming this message. His shouting style, however, combined with his use of insider language tends to blur the clarity of his message.

Alongside this blurring, there is once again a conflict between insider discourse and outsider-accessible imagery. Compare a word like 'uncircumcision' which has little resonance for outsiders, with words like 'mother's womb', a universally familiar term. Again note how biblical imagery is a central source for much of Stoops's broadcast talk.

In an extended extract from later in the same broadcast he links the 'born again' language from John 3 with an allusion to the Pauline concept of 'the renewing of the mind'.[44] He is obviously quite content to fuse images from Johannine texts with assertions from Pauline literature:[45]

> # I like that Scripture, you know when you get into trouble. I like that Scripture that talks about: 'I know my sheep, and my sheep know my voice.' **Do you know the very voice of God?** You know, I have **heard God speak**. A lot of people say well that's the Bible. It says: 'You know we need a preacher, and he needs to be sent.' It says: 'Faith comes by **hearing**!' And you know when you're reading the bible, you're not hearing it, but you're reading it. **But when you hear the preacher or you hear someone that's been CALLED, that's been anointed, by the PRECIOUS Holy Ghost, then they can unlock the key of the MYSTERIES OF GOD, THEY CAN REVEAL THEM TO YOU.** #[46]

This provides an insight into the theological foundations of Curtis Stoops's radio preaching. First, as I suggested above, at the heart of his message is a fusion of biblical quotes or paraphrases. Secondly, he has an extremely high view of the spoken or preached word of God. He even appears to place it above the reading of Scripture itself, on the basis that 'faith comes by hearing'.[47] For Stoops, the aural nature of radio preaching is clearly part of its attraction to him. In an endearing example of confused metaphoric language he proclaims that an anointed speaker can 'unlock the key of the mysteries of God'.

At first it appears that Stoops's 'primary audience'[48] is made up of those 'without hope', who need to hear a preacher.[49] Towards the end of a sermon broadcast in December 1993, however, he obviously perceives a second group of listeners who are already sympathetic to his cause. This is clear from his frequent use of prayer in his broadcasts. In fact the divisions between preaching, prayer and singing are not always clearly defined in Stoops's broadcasts.[50] Accompanied by music, which sounds akin to the tinkling of a saloon piano, he moves from preaching to prayer with little announcement.

> Got a little baby and a mother we've been praying for all week. And we want you to reach out to that little child. We want to see it dead healthy. And we want to see that family together and happy. And we can see it in the name of Jesus ... O **God** how we need you today – can't do without you. [We] **need the power of the Holy Ghost, that you sit upon this world, that dwells inside of me, that dwells inside of these ministers as they come into the pulpit. O God pour that fire, let those bones get on fire on the inside, that they'll preach a sermon in the pulpit that men could not resist, that they'll come to you.**[51]

Stoops uses the word 'see' three times: he encourages his listeners to visualise a restored infant. In active and graphic terms he describes the Holy Ghost who 'sits' and who 'dwells' in the ministers as they 'come into the pulpit'. In words which echo the prophet Jeremiah, he implores that the 'bones get on fire on the inside'.[52] This is Stoops at his most pictorial, but with the synthesised piano music and the increasing force of his delivery, it is easy to be distracted.

Pictorial language does play a role in his radio talk and singing, but a limited one. Stoops uses both autobiographical and biblical pictorial language, but he does not rely on it for effective communication. At the heart of his radio preaching is the force of his delivery combined with his 'spontaneity',[53] his partial memory of scriptural verses and his obvious 'personal involvement' in what he speaks, shouts and sings about. Whilst his spoken discourse includes little explicit representational pictorial language, through a mixture of vocal force, biblical allusions and a passion for his message, he conveys the impression of a preacher earnestly attempting to persuade his audience to respond.

The Athletic Radio Preacher

Toby Powers is another radio preacher who seeks to evoke a response from his listeners. At only twenty-one years old, he was already the minister of a small Congregational Methodist church in Union Hill, Georgia. He broadcasts regularly from the gospel station WGMI in Bremen, also in Georgia. This is a small station, which claims a potential audience of 10,000 people and a station cat called Segue. It is situated so close to the railway tracks that the rumble of a train going by can often be heard on radio. The small size and the unsuitable location of the station do not deter Toby Powers in his extraordinary style of preaching.

> # Peter looked at the Lord in the verse number five, of Mark Chapter **nine, he looked at him, he said 'Master', his first words were these: he said 'MASTER, IT'S GOOD FOR US TO BE HERE'** [laughs] **'WOOOH!' he said, 'IT'S SO GOOD FOR US TO BE HERE.' WHENEVER THE GLORY OF GOD COMES ON THE SCENE, erY'UR FIRST REACTION WILL BE * 'I'M NOT WORTHY OF THIS'. BUT PETER SAID: 'MASTER, IT'S GOOD FOR US TO BE HERE.' erBLESS YOUR HEART, WHEN YOU REALLY SEE GOD'S GLORY, erYOU'LL REALISE IT'S A GOOD PLACE TO BE # when you're seeing the glory of God. Amen.** [Laughs][54]

A written text cannot begin to do justice to the unforgettable passion and intonation of Toby Powers. For a listener not used to this style of discourse, for someone outside Powers's discursive community, it would be impossible to ignore the style of his broadcast talk. He switches rapidly between the biblical story and his imagined listeners' experience of seeing the glory of God. Different listeners will respond differently. For me, Powers's picture of the glory of God is overwhelmed by the excitement and pace of his delivery.

On the radio, he displays an energy that borders on the comic to those outside his discursive community, and yet his usual speaking voice is calm, straightforward and normally modulated. He admitted, surprisingly:

> I would say that I have mellowed some, and that I, I have slowed down some of my athleticism and some of my er acrobaticism in the pulpit. I don't jump around and, and maybe run as fast and as hard and as much, and jump as many pews, and banisters, and pulpit as what I used to.[55]

Powers may not 'swing from the banisters or rafters' as much as he used to, but he makes up for this with a verbal athleticism, which leaves many listeners breathless.[56] The contrast between Powers in the radio pulpit and Powers in conversation is striking. It is as if two different people are speaking.

He admits he owes a debt to an American evangelist from earlier this century:

> My hero has always been Billy Sunday and I have studied a lot of his works and things. Some people said that when he was seventy years old he was swinging from the rafters and preaching hard, and he was criticised often for preaching too dramatic, and too dynamic and too much on money even.[57]

As an evangelist Billy Sunday 'charmed the crowds with his baseball stories, saloon impersonations, and vaudeville antics'.[58] Powers's radio preaching is not a precise copy of Sunday's style, but he clearly moves into performance mode as he steps behind the microphone.

It is fascinating to see how the highly experienced broadcaster Garrison Keillor handled these recordings of Powers. Almost by counter-suggestion, Keillor invites his audience, who are about to hear another part of a Powers sermon, to consider how this preaching would sound in a more traditional context. Keillor speaks gently: 'It's hard to imagine sitting in an Anglican church in London, York or New York and see the vicar lean out from his high gothic pulpit and say':

> # You know folks lots of times we go through some hard things in this world, and we face some troubles and trials, we face some heartaches, we face some tr-tribulations in this world. But let * me remind * you of something, let me remind you *, let me remind you: * **There's good times waiting on the other side. There's <u>good</u> stuff waiting on the other side where Jesus is. And there's so much glory over there.** You know sometimes we getting good meetings here, and the Bible even said: 'We were allowed to sit with Christ in heavenly places on this earth.' But folks let me remind you of something – **WOOOH**, that this ain't ev'n anything to compare with what is waiting on the other side. **Hallelujah**. Sometimes it gets so good I heard people say: 'Well it don't get any better than this.' It does too bless your heart. It's going to get so good till our bodies **we've got here won't even be able to handle it. God will have to give us a <u>brand</u> new one to be able to handle the glory that's a-coming and waiting for us on the other side**. # Amen. Glory to God. Hallelujah.[59]

The juxtapositioning of Keillor's and Powers's styles highlights their radically different approaches to radio broadcasting and, more specifically, the contrasting ways they use their voices and create pictures with words. Keillor is gentle in his delivery, and he invites his listeners to make an imaginative leap. By describing an Anglican preacher leaning out over the 'high gothic pulpit' he encourages his audience to imagine a specific picture.

Powers has, in radio production terms, a faster and much more 'up-front' or 'in-your-face' broadcasting style than Keillor.[60] He uses more general terms such as 'good times', 'good stuff', or the 'other side' to illustrate his preaching. These phrases do not paint such vivid pictures as Keillor's. Powers tries to create a scene through drama and re-enacted speech. He shifts, to borrow a phrase from Erving Goffman, 'from monologue to the enactment of dialogue'.[61] Behind these sermons is his conviction that one day some of his listeners will see the glory of God. His tone of voice and variation of pitch, combined with shouts of delight and ecstasy, make it difficult for an outsider, not used to this style of communication, to engage with the worlds he portrays. His extreme vocal outbursts make his radio preaching intriguing, but ultimately outsider-unfriendly.

The Blowing Radio Preachers

Many of the American Bible Belt's rural radio preachers are at their most graphic when describing how Jesus Christ will return and bring an end to this 'restless' and 'evil world'. Brother Clarence Brown, for example, a Pentecostal minister based in Raven, Virginia, leaves his listeners in no doubt as to what will come to pass:

> He is going to come with <u>vengeance</u> and with <u>wrath</u>,
> He is going to pour it out on a <u>world</u> that has forsaken <u>him</u>,
> **He is going to pour it out on a world that has denied him.**[62]

Brown's pictorial language is drawn from biblical apocalyptic literature. In a passionate attempt to 'warn the people to flee the wrath to come', he describes 'signs in the sun, moon, and earth ... the sea and waves roaring ... the sea turning to blood ...' He implies that the atomic bombs of the Second World War are 'like the flickering of a candle' or 'the lighting of a match' compared to the destructive potential of this day of wrath.[63]

This view, of the imminence of the second coming and a world bound for destruction, is often combined with a negative evaluation of the general American public. Another similar radio preacher is Winnifred Garner, the owner of station WGMI in Bremen, Georgia.

> There's lots of people act like babies <u>today</u>, +hah+
> Act like they haven't grown an <u>inch</u> since God saved them, +hah+
> **Shame on you,** +hah+
> If you're still a <u>baby</u>, +hah+
> Bottled baby – I'm sorry for you, +hah+
> Somebody has to burp you every
> once in a while to make you, +hah+ er belch +hah+
> Something is wrong with you,
> Why don't you just come home? +hah+
> So many people knows more about movie stars,
> they know about the sport characters, +hah+!

than they do about the word of God, +hah+!
Oh I tell you friends, its come just about time for me to leave you again, but this is brother Winnifred Garner saying thankyou for letting me come in your place of listening.
You tune in er – er – er – the tomorrow,
same time, same station. May the good Lord be with you.
And I want to say to you, since I have said different times before:
We're planning on being back on the air tomorrow, but who knows?
Jesus may come back in the air before I come back on the air.
[More and more distant, as he moves away from microphone][64]

Breaking his exhortation into 'short, punchy, 'hah'-accentuated lines',[65] Garner draws on a simple picture: a baby drinking milk, images found in Paul's first letter to the Corinthians[66] and the fifth chapter of Hebrews.[67] He updates the picture to include 'bottled baby' and burping on the back. This imagery is used almost to insult his audience, goading them into facing their spiritual immaturity. In Garner's eyes, part of growing up spiritually means facing the power of Hollywood, which he sees as a 'false idol' that distracts people from the word of God.

Other radio preachers, both rural and city based, go further in their cultural critique. They see an America bound for the same destiny as the ancient Roman Empire, in terminal decline, as a tide of immorality sweeps across the United States.[68] Vernon Williams, a former alcoholic, now a preacher at Welcome Hill Baptist Church, Carrollton, near Bremen, believes that a key factor for connecting with listeners who are in need, is personal experience:

> You can't talk to a drug addict unless you've really been where they've been, and you can't talk to er, er an alcoholic unless you have been there. And by that, and through the experiences I've had, I can come to their level . . . and let them see, and try to make them understand someone does care for them and understand them.[69]

In this interview Williams came across as a thoughtful, restrained speaker. As a preacher Williams is as passionate as Toby Powers:

Friend this restless world today, +hah+
These hungry hearts, +hah+

This suffering, +hah+
In agony and in feet of the devil, +hah+
Friend these folks today, +hah+
Is starving to death, +hah+
For the word of God, +hah+
And friend we need to preach the Word, +hah+
The Paul said: Be instant in season +hah+
Out of season +hah+
Reprove, rebuke, +hah+
With all unsuffering doctrine, +hah+
My friend, we need to preach, we need to preach JESUS . . .'[70]

Once again the radio preacher's phrases are punctuated by an explosive 'hah', almost like tapping a 'foot to keep time'.[71] According to Thomas Long, the radio preachers see the 'blowing' or suck and blow style as a sign that they are under the power of the Holy Spirit.[72] In other words a 'hah' at the end of each line is proof for some preachers that they are literally blowing out the word of God as they speak.

These apocalyptic radio preachers' style of discourse implies that they are speaking only to those 'insiders' who view passion, shouting and rapid intake of breath as a sign of the anointing of the Holy Spirit. Their approach suggests that they have forgotten their own self-stated desire to reach 'outsiders' listening in radio-land. They ignore the heterogeneous character of their 'invisible' audience,[73] many of whom would inevitably find their manner of speaking entirely alien. At moments these radio preachers have failed to follow Goffman's injunction that radio 'announcers must conjure up in their mind's eye the notion of listeners, and act as if these phantoms were physically present to be addressed through gaze, body orientation, voice calibrated for distance', as 'broadcasting involves self-constructed talk projected under the demands, gaze, and responsiveness of listeners who aren't there'.[74] The aim of these radio preachers, the 'country boys', with their limited pictorial language, is to reach out to and connect with *all* their listeners; but in reality their oral idiosyncrasies act as a barrier to this process.

It is a mode that contrasts strongly with the more conversational broadcasts of the Radio Padre or Rabbi Lionel Blue.[75] I would propose that the 'country boys' content and style of preaching on radio is primarily insider-friendly, and, in spite of their stated aims, is unlikely to attract sustained, regular listening from those outside their particular discursive communities.[76]

The Radio Faith Healer

Now meet two city-based preachers. Both are skilled and experienced communicators. Both have a college education and draw from the black preaching tradition. Both make limited use of pictorial language, and tend to adapt images from the biblical texts. Both sometimes have their services recorded to be broadcast at a later date.

Dr Gregg Thomas is a minister at the 'Christian Faith Temple Family Worship Centre', based in a shopping mall on the outskirts of New Orleans. He has two doctorates and is a certified Clinical Christian Counsellor. He also has experience in business, where he 'did a lot of speaking motivating people'.[77] In his eyes, this wide-ranging experience has shaped his radio preaching:

> You're going through your greatest battle right now, and its hot, and your land has been scorched, and you wanna dive in the pool, but you need to stop, and you need to allow God to pour himself into you, so he can walk with you, he can let you know which way to go.[78]

In this extract he contrasts a hot, scorched land with diving into a pool. He does not, however, develop either image. They are bracketed by reference to being in a battle and God pouring 'himself into you'. The extract is a good example of how Gregg Thomas, to borrow a term from Henry Mitchell, is 'linguistically flexible',[79] in that he attempts to involve his audience as he moves rapidly from image to image.

This linguistic flexibility can also be seen in the way in which Thomas tackles the whole area of healing. He recognises that 'people are hurting' and 'those that are hurting just go round hurting others'. He also believes that God is the 'counsellor' who can heal and 'resolve' people's pain.[80] He expresses this faith in vivid terms:

> Some of you may have loved ones, this morning, that may have AIDS, that may have cancer, that may have incurable, with the doctors, that praise God, according to them are incurable diseases, **but I want you to know whether they're lost or whether they've been found, God still loves them, Oh! Glory to God**, and because He loves them, he will **what**? He will heal them. I am here to tell **you may have a child**, praise God, that's **paralysed**, I want you to know today that **God hears**, God will heal them. If you still believe. **You've got to believe that God is going to do it!**
> **There's no sickness, no sickness,**
> **no disease, that God can't heal.** Tell your neighbour that:
> **There's no sickness,** [Response: there's no sickness],
> **there's no disease,** [Response: there's no disease],
> **that God can't heal.** [Response: that God can't heal],
> **Oh, Alleluia! HE'LL DO IT, HE'LL DO IT,**
> **But you've got to believe it.**[81]

The style of the sermon encourages its listeners to visualise their sick loved ones, a powerful, yet potentially dangerous device. The emphasis upon the healing of loved ones being dependent on the faith of his listeners can load helpless relatives with further feelings of guilt if there is no recovery. Having seen a healed love one on the screen of the imagination, it would be easy to feel personally responsible if restoration does not take place.

The loudness of the verbal responses from his immediate audience indicates the power of this style of responsive preaching within a discursive community used to this approach. For those not familiar with this style of discourse, the sounds could easily become off-putting and prevent meaningful communication. On many other occasions Gregg Thomas uses this kind of language as a tool for psychological healing. He aims to heal the 'whole man' and to help liberate his listeners from past hurts.[82] The miraculous is therefore not explicitly routinised or domesticated by Thomas, but it is made accessible through a style of discourse that can be both pictorial, employing evocative compressed images such as 'dive in the pool', and coercive phrases such as: 'you've got to believe it!'

In another radio sermon he attempts to encourage his listeners to be 'transparent', to admit they are hurting and accept the 'healing balm of Gilead ... that's just God's anointing being poured on the wounds'.[83] The rich tone of his voice and his 'homiletical musicality'[84] add to the imaginative picture of healing oil, the balm of Gilead,[85] being poured on to wounds. Whilst this is not explicit representational pictorial language Gregg Thomas's broadcasts represent an important strand in radio preaching: the musical and impressionistic word-artist. Rather than attempting to create precise oral pictorial representations, Thomas tends to use language that can create a mood or atmosphere.

As these radio broadcasts are simply edited versions of different Sunday morning services, his listeners are effectively overhearing a dialogue between the preacher and a primarily black congregation. Thomas seems to stand within the Black homiletical tradition and appears to employ what Henry Mitchell controversially describes as 'Black language'.[86] Certainly his radio preaching draws effectively upon the 'lingua Franca of the Black ghetto, full of subtle shadings of sound and significance, cadences and color'.[87]

Thomas intersperses his sentences with phrases such as 'praise God' and 'hallelujah'. On hearing, 'you may have a child, praise God, that's paralysed', it would be perfectly possible for an outsider to his discursive community to interpret these exclamations as theological affirmations of sickness, rather than the verbal punctuation marks that they are.

Listening to the 'hum' or response from his immediate audience it appears that he does, in the words of Evans Crawford, 'beguile [some of] his listeners because it [his discourse] is familiar'.[88] Thomas also appears to establish a 'rapport and influence with them [his immediate listeners], without their being conscious of the fact that the preacher has deliberately chosen this language as the most appropriate to the task of meaningful communication'.[89] As with the 'country boys', many elements of his preaching are 'insider friendly', and because of this they are liable to exclude listeners who are from outside the speaker's discursive community.

The Radio Prophet

Pastor Craig E. Soaries of Atlanta, Georgia, represents a more outspoken and uncompromising strand among the city radio preachers. He is pastor of a small local independent church called The Victory House, which attracts 50 to 60 people every week. Pastor Soaries sees himself as a prophet who is prepared to be the 'laughing stock of America' in order to allow the 'voice of God' to come 'through his mouth':[90]

> I am a prophet. I don't go around calling myself... Prophet Soaries, but I have come to accept the fact that I am a voice. God's called me to be a voice crying in the wilderness of moral degradation in America. I've accepted it, and I never dreamed I'd be one, and here I am.[91]

This 'voice' leaves his invisible audience, whom he claims to love, in little doubt about his diagnosis of the current American condition. 'America is in crisis'.[92] In his eyes he has been 'called', and therefore has no choice but to put the spotlight on the nature of America's 'moral degradation'.[93]

In his radio preaching he characterises the moral degradation in aggressively graphic terms. For Pastor Soaries, sexual deviation will lead to souls being 'damned to everlasting burning hell',[94] and to the fall of America.[95] Corruption and greed in high places are also 'killing America'.[96] At times, his prophetic message of doom echoes the less sophisticated language of some of the 'country boys'. His use of pictorial language is reinforced both by metonymy[97] and by provocative, at times almost offensive, challenges to his listeners. 'Dare to be politically **in**correct!'[98] might be an appropriate epitaph for this 'prophet'. Behind his uncompromising message is a confidence, bordering on arrogance, in his own abilities as a preacher: 'Preaching is my life. I was born to preach.'[99] He admits that he ignores many of the 'homiletical and hermeneutical rules', even though he knows '*all* the formal styles of preaching'.[100] His fifteen years of radio experience have left him overconfident in his ability to communicate: he shouts at the microphone, for example, in a way that often precipitates 'popping'.[101] In other words, his aggressive style makes him difficult to listen to, and sometimes hard to hear clearly.

He is at his most pictorial when drawing upon biblical imagery. His style reflects a desire to 'deal with real life issues today': 'I'm not just here to tell you about Peter, James, or John, or Daniel in the lions' den, but I want to talk to you about your den, that you're in.'[102] This is one of Pastor Soaries' characteristic hermeneutical leaps. As well as using modern images to caricature modernity, he manipulates biblical imagery to support his own position.[103] This can be seen clearly when he identifies himself with the prophetic tradition when he argues against lesbianism in the local university. He claims: 'I'm standing with Daniel. I'm standing with John the Baptist who had his head cut off.'[104] Soaries' stance might be viewed as an example of what Martin Riesebrodt perceives as 'radical patriarchalism'[105] or 'patriarchal moralism'.[106] Riesebrodt notes that at the centre of 'the fundamentalist critique of society is the moral decay which is regarded as the result of the turn away from the divine law'.[107]

Behind Soaries' preaching lies a real anger at the signs of 'moral decay', which in his eyes are a 'result of the turn away from the divine law'. His rage with the way the current American political leadership has allowed the 'country to go down the drain' colours much of his radio preaching. His passion is channelled into both a desire to 'touch' his listeners, and a strong visual sense of his audience:

> I want to come straight out of the radio into their living room, into the car, and I see myself sitting right in the room with them, talking with them ... the people are so real to me, it's like I can even see some of them.[108]

Pastor Soaries dreams of expanding his empire via satellite 'across the world'. It remains to be seen how the vision of this 'prophet' will be fulfilled.

Soaries is a broadcaster who claims to vitalise some of his listeners, but who rarely appears to transfer that skill into using *representational* pictorial language that could connect with a listener from outside his own discursive community. In a similar way to Gregg Thomas he draws upon a considerable amount of biblical imagery which he attempts to integrate with autobiographical imagery. The result is a fusion of primary personal pictorial language with secondary biblical pictorial language. He becomes the prophet who stands with John the Baptist who 'had his head chopped off', though he has yet to share John the Baptist's fate. In contrast to Gregg Thomas he often uses this 'integrated' pictorial language as a way of asserting his own identity as a prophet and the outspoken leader of a small local church. Combine his microphone-popping style with the frequent articulation of his extreme conservative views, and it is probable that the approach and content of his broadcasts will distance him from listeners who are not part of his discursive and faith community.

Conclusion

We have considered the broadcast talk of rural and urban American radio preachers. The pictorial language that radio preachers such as Curtis Stoops employ is so drenched in biblical terms that while it may be familiar to listeners immersed in scriptural language, it will sound alien to listeners not 'versed in the word'. Biblical pictorial language is often combined with autobiographical discourse. This is sometimes expressed in exclusivist or highly coded terms. As a teaching and evangelistic device it will probably fail to draw or hold listeners. Certain extreme para-linguistic factors, such as the blowing style of the 'apocalyptic' preachers or the 'verbal athleticism' of Toby Powers, will distract attention from the message itself. A more audience-centred discourse, one that takes greater account of the listener and how a diverse radio audience might decode a verbal or non-verbal message, has a better chance of connecting speaker and listener. By failing to recognise this part of the communication equation speakers can build a barrier between themselves and those outside their small discursive communities.

There is a rich seam of insights that preachers can gain from encounter with American religious radio broadcasters, found in the Appalachian mountains, the Atlanta suburbs, and the New Orleans vicinity. First, we cannot assume that pictorial language will necessarily act as a bridge between our listeners and ourselves. Secondly, pictorial language can perform a range of functions, some of which simply reinforce the exclusive nature of preaching. Thirdly, verbal idiosyncrasies, such as 'wind sucking' or 'hahing' at the end of a phrase, may be a sign of divine agency for those within a particular faith community, but for those outside, they will probably be at best intriguing and at worst distracting or even antagonising. The responsibility for taking the initiative and stepping into the listener's world, and thereby anticipating the most appropriate form of discourse for effective communication, lies with the preacher. Fourthly, and following on from this observation, there is clearly a danger of forming an exclusive discursive ghetto, which is comfortable with 'the language of Zion', but fails to engage in translation for outsiders.

As a balance to these critical points we should acknowledge some positive insights from this small selection of American radio preachers, for example, Gregg Thomas's attempt to connect biblical imagery with contemporary experiences. Add to this the musicality of his speech and the result is 'religious programming that pounds and pulsates, frequently lacking clarity and logic, but never lacking zeal and animation'. Howard Dorgan comments that 'it is the type of broadcasting that the fastidious would avoid with the quick turn of a dial, the push of a button'.[109] Nevertheless, it is a useful reminder for restrained Western preachers that properly harnessed energy, passion and liveliness in the pulpit can attract listeners' attention.

Part of the appeal and fascination of American radio preaching remains its directness, its cultural specificity and its adherence to particular, at times extraordinary, discursive traditions. Even as we determine why it is that so many radio preachers fail to communicate beyond the bounds of their discursive ghettos, we should not ignore their passion and enthusiasm, nor the way in which they build up their own communities of faith. The passion and energy of a preacher such as Gregg Thomas would be far more likely to meet the expectations of a multi-racial Pentecostal congregation in an American or British inner city, than the restrained Radio 4 tones of Tilby or the Oxbridge sounding wartime broadcast lectures of C. S. Lewis.

The pictorial language employed by preachers such as Craig

Soaries and his fellow apocalyptic radio preachers illustrates how these broadcasters are involved in a form of 'cultural criticism'.[110] Drawing upon contemporary, historical, personal and biblical images, they select much from 'the secular world to vilify', they declare that 'world polluted and uninhabitable', and they identify 'a life that is more worthy of pursuing'.[111] Preachers may radically disagree with the theology and social attitudes portrayed, but at least at times these broadcasters attempt to move beyond purely biblical imagery and narratives.

Some of the radio preachers considered in this chapter act, to borrow an image used by Dietrich Bonhoeffer, 'like a sealed train travelling through foreign territory'.[112] Their studios may not literally be locked, but they certainly seem to consider themselves to be 'travelling through foreign territory', broadcasting in an alien land.[113] During the Second World War, in *Letters and Papers from Prison,*[114] Bonhoeffer pointed to growing secularisation and the importance of speaking about God in terms intelligible to a secular society. His approach stands in sharp contrast to many of the radio preachers analysed in this chapter. These radio preachers rely on biblical images and are unwilling to employ secular discourse to speak of God. Though they show familiarity with biblical imagery, they are distant in their talk about the divine.[115]

One explanation for their use of biblical and autobiographical pictorial language is that through such speech they can distance themselves from America's corruption. The exclusivist nature of much of their discourse allows them to maintain their distinctive identity in the face of America being 'taken over by homosexuals and secular humanists'.[116] As members of what Steve Bruce describes as 'sectarian sub-cultures',[117] the exclusivist styles of speech that many radio preachers employ allow them to assert their independence from an America they perceive to be in a state of moral decline, and to define their identities over and against the prevailing culture. This may help them to assert what they see as the distinctive Christian character of both themselves and a particular faith community. But such articulation can become a proclamation of superiority over the people amongst whom the preacher lives, or simply reinforce the use of insider discourse amongst the preacher's listeners. Biblical pictorial language, in such a case, has become an obstacle to real communication.

To argue that radio preachers are 'simply anti-modern' or are producing a 'counter-discourse to the discourse of modernity' misses 'the extensive degree to which they are also modern'.[118] Many of the radio preachers considered may have criticised aspects of what is often described as 'late-modernity',[119] but they happily employ the broadcasting tools of modernity.[120] Yet they often do so to draw listeners back to a former golden age, into a sectarian subculture, rather than point them forwards to a new territory. They would echo one of the most widely syndicated radio preaching voices, the late Dr J. Vernon McGee,[121] when he vividly reminisces, without a breath, about the golden days of faith:

> America needs to return to the day when Grandpa took the team out of the field in the early afternoon on Wednesday in order to hitch them to the old spring wagon into which Grandma put all the children after she washed their faces shining clean and they drove off to the prayer meeting at the little white church at the cross-roads underneath the oak trees where everyone believed the Bible.[122]

Many of the radio preachers considered here yearn nostalgically to return to those imagined halcyon days. The prayer meeting at the 'little white church' under the oak trees epitomises this idealised and almost certainly misleading view of past faith. Ironically, this time was also free of radio masts or TV aerials overshadowing the church. Radio preachers are themselves at a 'cross-roads' in America. Many are choosing the route that leads them safely back to their own communities of discourse. From there, they continue to look back longingly to an imaginary past where everyone 'believed the Bible'. In this protected discursive community they talk only to those who speak the same language, occasionally they shout in idiosyncratic style over the battlements where few outsiders listen to their cultural criticisms. Many radio preachers continue to make emphatic statements in the highly coded language of Zion and fail to translate their message into terms that would be accessible for outsiders.

It would be disastrous for preachers to follow in the footsteps of radio preachers who remain in, or are retreating into, the safety of their own discursive communities. Proclamatory discourse from the pulpit that excludes, whether in style and content, will not lead listeners back to a 'golden age'; it is more likely to turn them away. In contrast, I will turn in the third part of the book to explore the practical and theological arguments which support a move towards translation and embodied engagement with the listener. To do this we will first look at the work of a Jamaican 'radio bishop' now based in New York.

Notes

1. Garrison Keillor, [Radio Programme] *Garrison Keillor's Radio Preachers*, BBC Radio 4, 10 August 1994, Jolyon Mitchell, producer. (Hereafter referred to as: Keillor 1994.)
2. See Dorgan 1993, 2–3.
3. Ward 1994, 245.
4. Radio preachers may be the poor cousins within the 'Electronic Church', but they generally also support one party in what 'Martin Marty has called the "two party system of American Protestantism".' Their side, like their richer relatives in television, is usually 'oriented toward conservatism rather than modernism, evangelism rather than social action, and independence rather than ecumenism'. Hoover, 1990a, 233.
5. Sweet 1993, 57. Geoffrey Hodgson also approaches the subject historically and argues that: 'The vast majority of religious broadcasting in the United States came to be controlled by evangelicals.' Hodgson 1996, 173.
6. According to Tom Long, 'Radioland' for the radio preachers is like a 'big revival tent'. Long, Interview 21 March 1994.
7. Lineberry, Interview 21 March 1994.
8. 'FM radio, religious recordings, and programme time sales – conspired to turn evangelical radio into a religious ghetto.' Schultze 1990, 175.
9. See Jim Pennington's 'Christian Radio: Breaking Out of the Gospel Ghetto', in *Christianity Today*, 1979, 32.
10. Schultze 1990, 72.
11. Ward 1994, 53. For a more critical reading of religious radio see: Moore 1994, 231–5 (liberal protestants and radio) and 245–7 (evangelicals and radio).

12. Ward 1933 represents an early and the only extensive biography of this 'pioneer radio preacher'. According to Sweet, 'There is a desperate need to understand Charles E. Coughlin'. Sweet 1993, 60.
13. Sweet 1993, 59–60. Father Charles E. Coughlin garnered a radio audience of over 45 million, whilst Charles Fuller's 'Old Fashioned Revival Hour' broadcast in the 1940s had an estimated audience of over 20 million. See also Schultze 1990.
14. Lewis 1991, 238. 'Often implying anti-Semitism, he [Coughlin] denounced international bankers, blaming them for the depression and suggesting, "Democracy is over".'
15. Ward 1994, 56, cites Fuller himself: 'Some people say I reach 20 million people, I don't know.'
16. Ibid., 55–6. A number of factors have contributed to the decline of religious radio audiences. These include the fragmentation of the market, the segmenting of audiences, the advent of television and alternative forms of mass communication, and the 'secularisation of parts of the audience'.
17. See Kennedy 1994, 42. 'Christian radio has mushroomed to the extent that it is now the third most-common format on the dial, behind country and adult contemporary. The National Religious Broadcasters Association says 1,600 stations – one in ten – have a Christian format ... the regular core audience is between 3.5 million and 4 million.'
18. Ward 1994. See: 'Religious Broadcasting Statistical Summary: 1972–1994'. 359.
19. Ibid., 359. It is important to read these statistics of growth in religious radio in the context of the widespread growth of radio stations in the USA. In 1994 the total number of radio stations in the USA was 11,608 compared to 5,537 in 1965. See Black and Bryant 1995, 269.
20. Based in New Orleans, asked to remain anonymous. Off the record Interview, April 1994.
21. Craddock, Interview, 1 April 1994.
22. Duvall, director and writer, *The Apostle*, 1997. Duvall also played the preacher.
23. According to Thomas Lindlof there is 'no one set of speech-text conventions that all analysts follow', see Lindlof 1995, 211–12 and Stromberg 1990, 53, 55. I have been selective in my use of prosodic and general speech notations. Gumperz provides a useful introductory note on prosodic conventions, Gumperz 1982, xi. Finnegan cites a system used in transcribing a 'Baptist sermon which alternates between chant and sequences of lines in relative

repose', Finnegan 1992, 205. My notation system has been adapted from a range of sources. See especially Finnegan 1992, 205–6, Lindlof 1995, 212, and Scannell 1991, vi.

24. See Coulthard 1992, 35–49. Coulthard notes that 'paralinguistic phenomena in general and intonation in particular are areas of language patterning which have received little attention from linguists'.
25. Dorgan 1993.
26. Ibid., 121.
27. Ibid., 21.
28. Ibid., 21.
29. Gallimore, Interview 24 March 1994.
30. The three active categories of preachers: 'Singing', 'Athletic' and 'Blowing' reflect but one characteristic of their speaking. Gaffney's three categories for Islamic preachers provides an interesting parallel with the work of radio preachers: 'i) Preacher as the Affirmation of Traditional Authority, ii) Preacher as Advocate of Religiously Inspired Modernity, iii) Preacher as Apologist for the Ideology of Islamic Fundamentalism.' Gaffney 1994. I would suggest that many of the preachers considered in this chapter 'affirm traditional authority', defend the 'ideology' of Christian 'Fundamentalism', but mostly act as critics of parts of 'religiously inspired modernity'.
31. The Curtis Stoops story is told more extensively in Mitchell 1994, 20.
32. Stoops, Interview 24 March 1994.
33. Ammerman 1994, 149.
34. Stoops, untitled sermon 1993.
35. Dorgan 1993, 21.
36. Ibid., 204. Dorgan perceives that one of the common threads within his four case studies is that 'missions – or the sense thereof – have arisen out of a bout of personal troubles. In each instance the individual or individuals adopted the respective spiritual path after a period of personal disturbances – some physical, some psychological – with alcohol figuring in all four stories'.
37. Stoops, untitled sermon 1993.
38. Dorgan 1993, 21.
39. Stoops, untitled sermon 1993.
40. Schultze cites radio critic Jim Pennington who after listening to one religious station made this observation. See Pennington, 'Christian Radio: Breaking Out of the Gospel Ghetto,' in *Christianity Today*, 29 June 1979, 32.

41. Stoops, untitled sermon 1993.
42. Ibid.
43. Ibid. This entire passage could be in bold as it is almost all at shouting level, but in order to distinguish the different levels I have graded each word.
44. Romans 12:2: 'Do not be conformed to this world, but be transformed by the renewal of your mind' (RSV).
45. John 10:4, 14 and 16 appear to have been amalgamated, confused or paraphrased. The same appears to be true of his handling of Romans 10:14, 15 and 17.
46. Stoops, untitled sermon 1993.
47. See Romans 10:17: 'So faith comes from what is heard, and what is heard comes by the preaching of Christ' (RSV).
48. Finnegan 1992, 98–100. Finnegan makes a series of useful classifications of audiences. These include: a) primary versus secondary, b) integral versus accidental, c) homogeneous versus heterogeneous, and d) mass or impersonal versus personal.
49. Stoops, Interview 24 March 1994.
50. Finnegan 1992. Finnegan also highlights how boundaries between speech, chant and song are often 'multi-faceted and relative'. 140. In other words distinctions between categories can be more complex than at first sight.
51. Stoops, untitled sermon 1993.
52. See Jeremiah 20:9 'There is in my heart as it were a burning fire shut up in my bones' (RSV).
53. Graham 1987. Borrowing words from Graham's fascinating study, it is possible to argue that Curtis Stoops's 'vocal word conveys with peculiar force a sense of spontaneity, participation, or personal involvement for the individual and the group through the emotional, sensual impact . . . of texts read or recited aloud'. 157.
54. Keillor 1994. In 1994, Toby Powers had a fifteen-minute-long programme every Tuesday and Thursday on WGMI – 'Serving West Georgia and East Alabama'.
55. Powers, Interview 5 April 1995.
56. This clip has been played to six different groups of ten people or more of mixed age, nationality and background. Invariably they have displayed genuine surprise at the volume, pitch and pace of Powers's delivery.
57. Keillor 1994.
58. Carpenter 1983, 371–2. 'William A. Sunday (1862–1935) was the nation's most successful revivalist in an era when urban mass revivalism flourished.' 371.

59. Keillor 1994.
60. For example 'up-front' and 'in-your-face' were terms used by Michael Green, then the controller of Radio 4, at a briefing at BBC Manchester, Autumn, 1993.
61. Goffman 1981, 241.
62. Brother Clarence Brown's message 'How will Jesus Come?' broadcast on WGTH. Neither Brother Brown nor staff at the station knew the precise date. Spring 1994 was thought to be the most likely.
63. Also in 'How will Jesus Come?' message, undated tape.
64. Winnifred Garner, recorded sermon 1994.
65. Dorgan 1993, 61. Dorgan focuses in this section on Appalachian Holiness-Pentecostal preaching. He argues that its 'delivery is dominated by a high-volume, rapidly paced, but prosaic and emotionally explosive, exhortation that features a constant repetition of certain end-of-sentence exclamations (''Praise God!'' ''Amen!'' ''Hallelujah!'' ''Glory!'' ''Oh, Lord Jesus!'' ''Save us Lord!'' ''Praise his Name!'')'. 61.
66. 1 Corinthians 3:2: 'I fed you with milk, not solid food; for you were not ready for it;' (RSV).
67. Hebrews 5:12ff. 'You need milk, not solid food; for every one who lives on milk is unskilled in the word of righteousness, for he is a child. But solid food is for the mature, for those who have their faculties trained by practice to distinguish good from evil.' (RSV)
68. This was a common theme of the relatively well-known deceased radio preacher, Dr J. Vernon McGee of Pasadena, California, in his *Thru the Bible* Radio series.
69. Vernon Williams, Keillor 1994.
70. Ibid. In 1994, Vernon Williams was broadcasting every Sunday morning 'The Open Door Broadcast' on WGMI in Bremen, Georgia.
71. Keillor 1994.
72. Long, Interview 1994.
73. Goffman 1981, 241.
74. Ibid., 241.
75. See also McKay 1997. McKay cites the radio broadcasting of Alistair Cooke and Gerald Priestland: 'Both mastered the short talk, and the art of holding the listener's attention from start to finish.' 27.
76. This assertion is supported by listening statistics. See, for example, Schultze 1990, 172.
77. Thomas, Interview 1994.
78. From broadcast on 8 April 1995 on WSHO -AM 800 in New Orleans.

79. Mitchell 1990a, 87.
80. Thomas, Interview 9 April 1994.
81. Gregg Thomas, 'Jesus will use you to bring forth miracles', sermon used for broadcast on WSHO, on tape from the Christian Faith Temple Family Worship Centre, New Orleans, 20 February 1994.
82. Thomas, Interview 1994.
83. Keillor 1994.
84. Crawford 1995. See Chapter 1 on 'Homiletical Musicality' where Crawford outlines his 'musical understanding of how sermons are *heard* and the oral responses they awaken in listeners'. 17. See also Spenser 1987, and 1990 for a more developed use of the term 'homiletical musicality' in relation to the West African roots of this aspect of the black preaching tradition.
85. Jeremiah 8:22: 'Is there no balm in Gilead? Is there no physician?' Jeremiah 46:11: 'Go up to Gilead, and take balm.'
86. Mitchell 1990a, 82.
87. Ibid., 82.
88. See Crawford 1995, and especially Chapter 1.
89. Mitchell 1990a, 82.
90. Soaries, Interview 1994.
91. Ibid.
92. Ibid.
93. Ibid.
94. Soaries, 'Political Incorrectness', a radio message for Love WAEC AM 86, Atlanta, Georgia, 3 April 1994.
95. Soaries, like Dr J. Vernon McGee, believes that America is going exactly the same way ancient Rome went. (See Soaries, Interview 1994.)
96. Soaries, Interview 1994.
97. 'I see freedom of worship and freedom of expression under severe attack from Washington.' Soaries, Interview 1994. For more on Metonymy see Lakoff and Johnson 1980, Chapter 8: 'Metonymy', 35–40.
98. Soaries, 'Political Incorrectness', a radio message for Love WAEC AM 86, Atlanta, Georgia, 3 April 1994. He goes on to assert that you should be 'politically incorrect so you can be right with God'. Political incorrectness in this instance means taking a stand against Lesbian and Bisexual Movements. For him there is nothing complex in these issues: 'it is wrong, it is wrong'.
99. Soaries, Interview 1994.
100. Ibid.
101. This is a technical, descriptive term applied to 'mic-blasting',

which is normally caused by 'vocal breathiness' close to the microphone. McLeish 1988, 240.

102. Soaries, Interview 1994.
103. Wuthnow and Lawson 1994, 42. 'It [fundamentalism] does not simply respond to modernity; it caricatures modernity.'
104. Soaries clearly identifies himself with John the Baptist who told a 'politician of that day that he could not have his brother's wife'. Soaries, Interview 1994.
105. Riesebrodt 1993 (1990), 196.
106. Ibid., 178.
107. Ibid., 178–9.
108. Soaries, Interview 1994.
109. Dorgan 1993, 71.
110. Wuthnow and Lawson 1994, 41.
111. Ibid., 41.
112. 'Like a sealed train travelling through foreign territory the Church goes on its way through the world.' Bonhoeffer 1959 (1937), 251.
113. For a contrasting approach to this theme see Hauerwas and Willimon 1990.
114. Bonhoeffer 1971 (1951).
115. For an intriguing parallel with the discourse of TV evangelists see Thompson 1996, 88–99. Thompson's chapter highlights the inherent tension within certain TV evangelists' discourse, between on the one hand familiarity with the divine and on the other distance from the divine. 99. As argued above, such familiarity and distance can also be identified in the work of radio preachers such as Curtis Stoops and the country preachers.
116. Bruce 1996, 142.
117. Ibid., 141–2. Bruce memorably invites his readers to: 'Imagine a fundamentalist Baptist family in a small city in Virginia' who live in a cocooned world, where 'They know a lot about the world outside but that knowledge is passed through a very strong ideological prism. They know what is wrong with the rest of America: it has been taken over by homosexuals and secular humanists.'
118. Ibid., 41.
119. Thompson 1995, 8–9. Thompson alludes to his 'dissatisfaction' with much of the talk about post-modernity and post-modernism. He is not persuaded we have entered into a new age.
120. Bendroth 1996, 74ff.
121. In 1988 Dr J. Vernon McGee's *Thru the Bible* was syndicated to over 496 national religious broadcasting stations. This made it the second most widely syndicated daily religious programme. See

Schultze 1990, 175 (original source was 'Top NRB Daily Religious Programs', in *Religious Broadcasting*, April 1988, 8, 14). Interestingly, only James Dobson's more magazine style programme *Focus on the Family*, was to be found on more stations.

122. J. Vernon McGee, *Thru the Bible*, Isaiah 1:4–18, broadcast on WBGW, 24 March 1994. He is quoting from an editorial from the *Wall Street Journal* at the time of the depression.

PART III

Translation and Embodiment

CHAPTER 8

The Translated Word

Bishop E. Don Taylor (Episcopalian Area Bishop of New York) is a rare example of a religious radio broadcaster who simultaneously had both American and British audiences. He stands at some distance from the voices of the 'country boys' and the 'city prophets' or the wartime talks of the 'radio academic' and Radio Padre analysed in previous chapters. His distinctiveness merits close attention for he is a broadcaster who has attempted to translate his message into verbal forms that engage his listeners' visual and aural imaginations. Born in Jamaica, his unique radio ministry lasted for five years in the Virgin Islands, before he was invited to become one of the four assistant bishops of New York City in April 1994.

In the Virgin Islands Bishop Taylor was affectionately known in some circles as 'the radio bishop'. After leaving high school in Kingston, Jamaica, he went at eighteen years old to be a junior announcer at Radio Jamaica and Rediffusion. He 'developed a flair and love for broadcasting' at this early stage. He has also studied radio and broadcasting in Canada, learning from the practices of CBC (Canadian Broadcasting Corporation). His approach to broadcasting is characterised by sensitivity to his audience, his context and his medium.

This sensitivity is expressed by the way in which he paints familiar word pictures. His own description of the pictures he constructed whilst in the Virgin Islands is illuminating:

> The blue sea, all these islands are lapped by the Caribbean Sea. Everybody is within visual distance of the sea, so to talk about the blue of the sea and the sunlight sparkling on the waters, and the boats plying up and down the shores, and the fishermen pulling in

> their nets, is to talk the language that people understand, because they are *living with it every day* ... Donkeys walking down the hillsides. Women carrying baskets over their heads. The music, the thing people do when they are walking to the market. They sing among themselves. If you can break into song yourself, people will join in.[1]

One of Bishop Taylor's strengths is this use of word-pictures that resonate with his audience's everyday experience. These are not static portraits. The shore is lapped, the boats ply, the fishermen pull in their nets, the donkeys walk and the women carry: he constructs pictures with movement. He also portrays these scenes in multi-colour: the blue sea sparkles, for example. They not only appeal to the visual imagination, but also to the aural imagination as he introduces music to evoke sound memories. He clearly wishes both to understand his audience and to involve them on a number of different levels. He sings, they join in. He paints pictures, they imagine. It is as if he is attempting to engage at least two of his listeners' senses and so enable them to interact more fully with what he is saying.

Beneath the surface of such word-pictures lies a theology of broadcasting, a pastoral concern and a desire to translate his message into terms accessible to his listeners.

> I recognise that broadcasting is as much an instrument in the hands of God, as pulpit, as lectern, as altar, as chalice, as bread, as wine.[2]

This is a striking statement from an Anglo-Catholic bishop.[3] The emphasis upon wine, bread, chalice and altar is to be expected from a priest with a high view of the Eucharist. The inclusion of the pulpit and the lectern reflects a 'bifocal' attitude towards the preached Word and the celebrated sacrament.[4] Most surprising is his understanding that broadcasting 'as much as' various sacraments can be an 'instrument in the hands of God'. This may be hyperbole, but whilst Taylor does not go so far as to claim that broadcasting is a channel of grace, he is hinting at such an understanding of God's agency or involvement in this communicative act. Taylor alludes here to a belief in the possibility of God communicating through a range of senses: beyond being heard and seen, the elements of bread and wine are also felt and tasted.

On the basis of his belief that broadcasting has the potential to be a 'tool of God', it is not surprising that Bishop Taylor argues: 'If the Church is to communicate the gospel effectively it needs to learn some of the normal modern techniques of communication.'[5] This belief has intensified as he has grown older. He put his conviction into practice in the Virgin Islands, during the last five years of an eight-year bishopric, by producing a variety of programmes for one of the local radio stations. His main programme was a weekly Sunday morning show called *The Bishop Speaks.* Fifteen minutes of an hour-long programme were made up of his sermon. The remainder consisted of a largely traditional Anglican matins service. *The Bishop Speaks* was broadcast from WAVI, a radio station owned by a prominent Episcopalian, who allowed his bishop to use the station at no charge. The programme was initiated partly in answer to pastoral needs created by having a church of some 45,000 members scattered over ninety-nine islands. Small fishing communities or hoteliers living on tiny islands were not easily accessible, so this was an attempt to reach even the most isolated islanders. In Bishop Taylor's eyes *The Bishop Speaks* had additional pastoral effects: it unified the diocese, it enabled him to go beyond his own denomination and it even enhanced his image as bishop.[6]

The bishop admits it was a 'one man show'. Nevertheless, he attempted to try to 'broaden the base' so it 'was deeply rooted in the culture and lifestyle of the people'. In order to do this Bishop Taylor brought in local music, with reggae beat, as well as recording some of the music from local churches and Scripture readings from local schools. His aims were to vary the content as well as to make listeners from different islands feel that they had a stake in the programme. Birthday requests and local announcements encouraged audience ownership. Bishop Taylor kept his 'eyes and ears open' for current local incidents that would be relevant to his audience. His receptiveness to appropriate visual images was balanced by his awareness that 'language can become so picturesque and overbearing' that it 'destroys the message',[7] in communication theory terms, the encoding of the message can become too elaborate for it to be decoded appropriately.

The bishop's theology of broadcasting and his pastoral concern meant that he wished to translate his message into terms that his audience could receive and understand. This process of 'translation', or 'transference', can be described as pictorially updating biblical stories, in other words 'dynamic equivalence'.[8] He would tell the story of Jesus feeding the five thousand, for example, by setting it not 'out in the wilderness', but out in one of the local parks. Instead of the disciples, the local sanitation department might collect the remaining litter.[9] This example of translation is rooted in his pastoral concern to make such stories accessible to his audience in the Virgin Islands.

'Radio taught me to be deeply sensitive to the nature of the audience.' Like the Radio Padre some fifty years earlier, Taylor believes that the more you know your audience, the more you are able to communicate with them. He paints verbal pictures that are easily recognisable to his audience. This is part of his process of building a 'rapport' with his listeners, in the belief that the more you enter into their experiences, the more likely they are to enter into what you are saying. He sees communication as a two-way interactive principle so he enlivens what is primarily a one-way medium and engages his listeners more effectively.

The medium of radio is in Bishop Taylor's 'bloodstream'. He now aims to set up a station for the metropolitan diocese of New York. It will be fascinating to observe how he adapts his language and translates the biblical stories for the 'sea of people' who live among towering skyscrapers and yellow cabs. In the Virgin Islands the novelty of having a bishop broadcast a personal weekly show appears, given the positive feedback the bishop received, to have caught the imagination of the islanders. Whether it will be so successful in media-saturated New York remains an open question.

We have identified three strands behind Bishop Taylor's broadcast talk. His theology of broadcasting, his pastoral concern for his parishioners and his desire to translate his message into an accessible discourse which will engage his listeners' imaginations. He demonstrates a sensitivity to his audience, his context and the language appropriate for his medium that parallels the work of broadcasters such as Lionel Blue or Ed

Murrow. He claims that his speaking style has been shaped by the radio medium. In a way which also echoes the inner ear's role of translating 'sound vibrations into nerve pulses',[10] Taylor attempts to translate words into pictures, so that his listeners can interact more fully with the messages he communicates.

As an effective translator into pictorial discourse, Taylor stands with radio broadcasters we considered above such as Blue or Tilby. Preachers can learn from his enthusiasm for interacting with his listeners, and also from the way he translates biblical stories into forms of speech more likely to engage his audience. He moves beyond simple visual language, to discourse which will engage the other senses. But how far is it appropriate for preachers to *translate* their message into contemporary, multi-sensory, language?

Distinctive Discourse

I am advocating a 'dynamic equivalence' model for translating the message into forms more accessible for listeners.[11] There are those who reject such a translation model in preaching as merely a kind of 'linguistic accommodation' which undermines the distinctive nature of Christian discourse. One critic is William Willimon, professor of Christian Ministry at Duke Divinity School, Durham, North Carolina.

In his aptly titled book *Peculiar Speech*, Willimon is adamant that: 'we preachers need not be embarrassed by the distinctiveness of our speech'.[12] He claims that 'we preach within a distinctive universe of discourse. We talk funny.'[13] He claims the reason for this is that preaching is 'distinctive baptismal speech'.[14] Willimon argues that because preaching usually takes place in a distinctive baptised or being baptised community, it should maintain its 'peculiar' nature. If preachers are true to their baptismal vows a 'distinctive identity' will develop from 'this distinctive community of discourse'.[15] He asserts:

> Unfortunately, most of the theology I learned in seminary was in the translation mode. Take this biblical image and translate it into something more palatable ... In more liberal speech, talk tiptoes around the outrage of Christian discourse and ends up as an

> innocuous, though urbane, affirmation of the ruling order ... By the time most of us finish qualifying the scandal of Christian speech, very little can be said by the preacher that can't be heard elsewhere.[16]

His assumption is that translation will dilute, undermine, or even eclipse the scandalous nature of Christian speech. Clearly uneasy with the 'translation mode' of preaching, Willimon writes: 'I am troubled by preaching that is captured by the hermeneutics of translation, as if the Gospel can be transposed into some other idiom that is somehow superior to the gospel.'[17]

He extends his argument in a chapter on 'Preaching to Pagans', where he challenges those who suggest that:

> In a dangerously divided world, wouldn't our time as preachers be better spent in the search for some common universal, linguistic denominator rather than in the cultivation of the distinctiveness of Christian discourse?[18]

Willimon rejects the search for a 'common, universal' form of discourse[19] and instead he advocates the 'cultivation of the distinctiveness of Christian discourse'. He rejects the argument that: 'Our task as preachers, if we want to be heard by those in the world, is to adjust our parochial, "in house" ecclesial speech to the talk of the "wider world".'[20] He makes the point that preachers who break out of their own 'in house' discursive community, have simply 'moved into another' discursive group.[21]

In answer to the question of how the 'particular truths' of 'the baptismal community' should 'be proclaimed in a public world that does not share those truths', Willimon points out that the early Christians maintained their linguistic integrity. They did this by moving out from their original cultural context without being 'linguistically assimilated' into the Roman status quo. This does not mean, however, a complete rejection of new forms of speech. He cites, for example, the early Christian 'communicators' who 'readily used the Greek language that was available to them': 'they did not accept the cosmology, the world which Greek language conventionally described. The language was seized and used for a very different message in order to construe for the hearers a very different world.'[22] Whilst he rejects translation that dilutes the message, he nevertheless accepts an appropriation model for Christian speech: 'The language was seized and used for a very different message.'

In summary, Willimon appears to be arguing against a 'translation model' of preaching because it softens or distorts the original message. In his eyes 'the task of preaching is to teach what would not be known before it is announced, to cultivate those insights, means of describing, and vocabulary with which Christians describe the world'.[23] Throughout *Peculiar Speech* he argues that preachers should preserve the distinctive nature of Christian discourse. He is obviously not arguing against all kinds of translation, otherwise he would have to preach in Aramaic and Greek. But for Willimon, translating the form and content of the message into more culturally acceptable terms is exactly how to undermine its unique character.

The Translation Principle

Willimon's argument is vulnerable at a number of points. First, he treats translation as a single form. He does not offer a clear definition of what he means by the 'hermeneutics of translation'. By contrast, Alasdair MacIntyre identifies two 'distinct species of translation, translation by same-saying and translation by linguistic innovation'.[24] George Steiner outlines how, since the seventeenth century, the theory of translation has often been divided into three classes:

> The first comprises strict literalism, the word-by-word matching of the interlingual dictionary ... The second is the great central area of 'translation' by means of faithful but autonomous restatement. The translator closely reproduces the original but composes a text which is natural to his own tongue ... The third class is that of imitation, recreation, variation, interpretative parallel. It covers a large, diffuse area, extending from transpositions of the original into a more accessible idiom all the way to the freest, perhaps only allusive or parodistic echoes.[25]

Willimon's understanding of translation in *Peculiar Speech* is too narrow.

This leads us to the second point. Willimon implies that certain translation modes of communication will lead preachers to compromise, to dilute or even to corrupt their message in order to make it 'more palatable'. For Willimon, to allow contemporary thought forms or experience to dictate your message is to corrupt it.[26] This is not necessarily the case. He fails to see that 'linguistic innovation' does not necessarily mean dilution or corruption of the message. For instance, C. S. Lewis frequently translated his orthodox message into pictorial language in his radio talks. Consider this example from his radio talk on 'Eros':

> Rather like a garden, a garden is a glorious thing full of life, and giving us life; but you must not trust your garden to weed itself, or anything of that sort, it hasn't got that kind of goodness. A garden left to nature will soon not be a garden. It's the same with our passions. They also are life giving. But when God planted that garden of our passions he set a man [sic] over it to dress it, and set the man under himself.[27]

This form of translation into pictorial analogy probably makes Lewis's message more accessible, but not necessarily 'any more palatable'.

Thirdly, Willimon seriously underestimates the historical importance of translation for the foundation and growth of the Christian church. He does not do justice in his text to what Andrew Walls describes as 'the translation principle'.[28] Christianity is in a constant state of dynamic translation, and has been since its earliest days.[29] Think, for example, of the move from Aramaic spoken by Jesus to the *koine* Greek of the New Testament Gospels.[30] There never was, to our knowledge, an Aramaic text of the gospel.[31] 'Early Christianity was', according to Walls, 'touched by the translation principle. Not even Jewish Palestine could be culturally and linguistically sealed off from the Hellenistic world; and the very words of Jesus come to us in Greek dress.'[32] So when Willimon denies that 'the Gospel can be transposed into some other idiom that is somehow superior to the gospel' he underestimates the extent to which the gospel, as expressed in the New Testament, had already taken on a new idiom immediately after its birth. Christianity's willingness to translate and adapt itself to new cultural contexts was and is an important factor in its growth.[33]

Fourthly, Willimon fails to do justice to the implications of an incarnational theology for understanding the importance of translation. 'Christian faith rests on a divine act of translation: "the Word became flesh, and dwelt among us" (John 1:14).'[34] Walls develops the point more explicitly: 'Incarnation is translation. When God in Christ became man, Divinity was translated into humanity'.[35] In support of this, we can adapt two christologically significant Pauline phrases without misrepresenting the general sense of each claim. Jesus 'the sinless one was *translated* into sin in order that we might become the goodness of God';[36] or Jesus was 'rich' but '*translated* himself into poverty for your sake to make you rich out of his poverty'.[37] Most tellingly, for the current discussion, Walls asserts that, 'the first divine act of translation into humanity thus gives rise to a constant succession of new translations'.[38]

Willimon's theoretical understanding of the 'hermeneutics of translation' for preaching is too narrow, unnecessarily negative, lacking in historical perspective and appears weak in its theological foundations. As a preacher, however, Willimon displays a tension in his own sermons between faithfully holding on to distinctive Christian discourse and translating his message into accessible terms for his listeners in an American university chapel.[39] He may not acknowledge it, but in parts of his sermons Willimon himself employs a 'translation mode'. For example, in a sermon based on Philippians 3:17–21, entitled 'Be Imitators of Me', Willimon translates this issue of imitation into talking about how he handles his homiletics class. He actively discourages imitation of himself as the tutor. He even admits: 'Translated into honest English, this means: I want to get through this class without taking responsibility for you.'[40]

Undoubtedly, Willimon's book provides a salutary warning for preachers who seek to employ a translation mode of preaching. Consider the pressure on *Thought for the Day* contributors to offer moral homilies without mentioning God. Whether in Nazi Germany, Apartheid South Africa, or the

Consumerist West, preachers have always faced and continue to face the seductive temptation of translating their messages to fit the *Zeitgeist* or the ruling ideologies of their age. Christian preachers, however, stand in the tradition of a Galilean storyteller who frequently translated his message into accessible pictorial language and parables, not in order to affirm the status quo, but to challenge his listeners to 'a radical *metanoia*, a U-turn of the mind'.[41] There is a crucial distinction between translation and modification, contemporary clarification and faint-hearted reductionism.

Lesslie Newbigin's argument in *Foolishness to the Greeks* is pertinent at this point.[42] He argues that Christian communication across cultural frontiers should first be in the 'language of the receptor culture', and secondly challenge listeners and even call 'into question that way of understanding embodied by the language it uses'.[43] The challenge for preachers speaking in an audio-visual culture, therefore, is to speak in terms that can be understood, but to do so in such a way that the distinctive Christian story is not compromised. Newbigin warns against, on the one hand, speaking in such a way that your listeners will not understand the nature of your message, and on the other hand, speaking in terms so familiar to the receptor culture that the message will simply be 'absorbed into the existing world view'.[44]

In preaching there is an inevitable tension between accessible and distinctive discourse. Preachers can learn from the way broadcasters such as Tilby or Taylor translated their theological insights into the language of their listeners, whilst insisting on retaining their integrity as distinctive Christian speakers. As we have seen, some American radio preachers have retained their distinctive discursive styles, but have failed to translate their message into terms accessible to those outside their own discursive communities.

Acts of translation, we have argued, lie at the heart of Christian theology. One of the theological foundations for speaking visually is an understanding of the importance of translation. Indeed, it is not only appropriate but also crucial for preachers to be involved in translation. This does not mean literally taking on the job of translating from the Greek or the

Hebrew texts into modern English.[45] It refers rather to the role of drawing together the world of the biblical text and the world of the listener. The examples cited from radio broadcasting have illustrated ways in which preachers can bridge these two worlds through the skilled use of pictorial language. By making appropriate pictures with words the preacher can become a mediating and interpreting translator.

Towards a Renewed Form of Orality

The skills involved in translation are complex. It not only requires the ability to select contemporary images, metaphors and stories that will bridge the gulf between a secularised public and the world of the ancient biblical text. It also requires the ability to translate what is written and literary into forms of speech that can be heard and understood with ease.

Potential preachers were, and still are, trained in reading, writing and the often 'silent' world of textuality,[46] rather than being encouraged to develop skills for working in an oral culture. Fred Craddock believes they need to give attention to 'increasing their capacities for "oralizing"'.[47] To put it another way, preachers need to develop the skill of translating ideas that are often rooted in written texts, into oral communication. This is a skill which is exemplified in the work of the best of the religious radio broadcasters.

There are pragmatic questions about translation that cannot be ignored. Just as linguistic translators need to know both their own language and their receptor's language intimately, a preacher, seeking to translate the often challenging and disturbing message of a biblical text into contemporary and engaging discourse in a way that reclaims the original's force and insight, needs to know the world of the text and the world of the listeners. In particular, if preachers are to be heard today they need to understand the kind of speech which their listeners are accustomed to hearing and they need to develop tools for translating their own discourse into forms which will engage their audience's attention. Preachers need to develop a renewed form of orality.

One prolific author who has made a bold attempt to plot the main stages in the evolution or transformation of orality, is the Jesuit scholar Walter Ong. He outlines his understanding of the evolution of orality in *The Presence of the Word*,[48] where he identifies a number of 'stages of the word'. First, there is the unrecorded word – oral culture; secondly, the denatured word – alphabet and print dominated culture; thirdly, the electronic word – which could be termed as an audio-visual culture. In a later work Ong subdivides stage two, so that he separates manuscript and print culture,[49] and thereby creates a fourfold model of orality.[50] Farrell remarks this is a 'working hypothesis' still 'open to further elaboration'.[51] As such, Ong's evolutionary pattern of orality should be viewed not as 'water-tight' categories,[52] but for our purposes, a useful interpretative tool for reflecting on the discourse of religious radio broadcasters and contemporary preachers.

First, the unrecorded word – oral culture. In *The Presence of the Word*, Ong gives a number of examples of what he believes characterises communication within an oral culture. He notes that performers often employ repetition, formulaic and other mnemonic devices to assist the memorisation of epic stories. The use of arresting visual images is one such device. 'Oral singers are likely to favor striking visual imagery'[53] not 'merely because these are aesthetically pleasing but also because they serve as storage and recall devices – the ocular equivalents of verbal formulas'.[54] It is clear from Ong's analysis of oral culture that pictorial language is by no means a new aspect of orality.

The subcultures reflected by the rural and urban American radio preachers discussed earlier appear to retain many of the characteristics of primary orality. Most of their radio broadcasts are extemporaneous instead of relying upon a written script, and they draw upon formulaic speech forms, which involve frequent repetitions of certain phrases, exclamations, or particular words.[55]

Ong does not see oral culture, however, surviving in its purest form today. In *Orality and Literacy* (1982), he maintains that:

> Today primary oral culture in the strict sense hardly exists, since every culture knows of writing and has experience of its effects. Still,

> to varying degrees many cultures and subcultures, even in a high-technology ambience, preserve much of the mind-set of primary orality.[56]

The 'country boys' and 'city prophets' considered in the previous chapter represent subcultures that have preserved 'much of the mind-set of primary orality'. Those who are immersed in a silent, literary culture should bear in mind how many of these radio preachers are more closely connected to a primary oral culture. This insight may temper an overly negative judgement. Verbal idiosyncrasies and extremisms may be products of a discursive community that defines itself through a distinctive style of talk rather than through speech constrained by close adherence to a script.[57]

Ong identifies the second stage of the word as the 'denatured word – alphabet and print',[58] highlighting the link between seeing and articulating. He underlines how reading relies on a visual act, seeing the text. In other words, Ong argues that the shift from 'oral to written speech' is 'essentially a shift from sound to visual space'.[59] This was obviously not an instantaneous transformation.[60] In Ong's scheme, it was printing that led to the dominance of sight, and the 'denaturing' of the word.

Ong observes a number of characteristics of the 'denatured word'. In order to highlight the permanence of writing compared to the fleeting nature of the spoken word[61] he cites the familiar proverb: '*Verba volant, scripta manent* – words fly away, what is written stays put.'[62] For Ong, 'writing and print isolate',[63] whilst orality builds community. This point about isolation echoes an earlier suggestion in *The Presence of the Word* that: 'a typographic culture, because it is strongly visualist, isolates the individual from the tribe even in much of his verbal activity, mutes and minimizes interpersonal communication, and elaborates the visual in all its aspects...'[64] Ong believes that these characteristics of writing, the isolating and visualist tendencies, have had a considerable impact. He asserts that 'more than any other single invention, writing has transformed human consciousness'.[65] The strong implication is that it has also transformed orality.

Early religious radio broadcasts such as those of C. S. Lewis reflect some of the characteristics of a speaker born out of a print dominated culture. This is not an entirely surprising conclusion, as Lewis was an English don and prolific writer. From his childhood he was immersed in stories and images from the typographic culture of written texts. Ong argues that the advent of writing and then printing ensured that for the literate, articulation became increasingly closely linked with seeing words on the page. Unlike the extemporaneous radio preachers, Lewis always read aloud from a closely typed script, and appears very rarely, if ever, to have wandered away from it.

Lewis, of course, lectured and tutored in Oxford, and conversed in local pubs, but as an academic he spent a considerable part of his life 'silently and isolatedly' reading and writing. For some speakers, this would have been a distinct disadvantage, but Lewis's own understanding of writing novels may have eased his transition into broadcasting. Consider, for example, his advice to writers:

> Avoid all epithets which are merely emotional. It is no use *telling* us that something was 'mysterious' or 'loathsome' or 'awe-inspiring' or 'voluptuous'. Do you think your readers will believe you just because you say? You must go quite a different way to work. By direct description, by metaphor and simile, by secretly evoking powerful associations, by offering right stimuli to our nerves, and by the very beat and vowel-melody and length and brevity of your sentences, you must bring it about that we, we readers, not you exclaim, 'how mysterious!' or 'loathsome' or whatever it is. Let me taste for myself and you'll have no need to *tell* me how I should react to the flavour.[66]

Replace the word 'reader' with 'listener' and this becomes pertinent advice for broadcasters and preachers. Lewis's own radio broadcasts demonstrate many of these characteristics. Remember his 'enemy occupied territory' metaphor, his 'fleet of ships' analogy, and his story about a 'mask'.[67] Lewis's broadcasts reflect an attempt to break free from the isolated world of reading and writing, to create oral pictures that would engage all the senses of his listeners, and persuade his audience of the reasonableness of Christianity.

Nevertheless, whilst Lewis tried to sound spontaneous, we can detect at times that he is reading a carefully refined script. His broadcast orality relies upon the printed word. He is constrained by his own textuality. As Robin Meyers argues: 'preaching must recognize the difference between the eye and the ear, and its language must be both rich and sparse'.[68] At times Lewis's broadcasts are so linguistically rich with concepts, so tightly argued, that unless we read his text we can lose the flow of his argument.

In many ways C. S. Lewis serves as a good example of a literary scholar and radio broadcaster who attempts to straddle the divide between what Ong describes as the typographic word, and his final stage of orality: the electronic word.[69] Ong believes that we have 'entered into the electronic age, where a new oralism served by technology reigns'.[70] In Ong's eyes these technological developments have led to a 'renewed' or 'secondary orality'.[71]

Ong defines secondary orality in a number of ways. One of his most favoured approaches is to make a clear distinction between primary and secondary orality. In *Orality and Literacy*, for example, he explains:

> I style the orality of a culture totally untouched by any knowledge of writing or print, 'primary orality'. It is 'primary' by contrast with the 'secondary orality' of present-day high-technology culture, in which a new orality is sustained by telephone, radio, television, and other electronic devices that depend for their existence and functioning on writing and print.[72]

Ong perceives secondary orality as a 'breakthrough to a new kind of orality'.[73] The 'new kind of orality' may have similarities with primary orality, but the advent of electronic communication has not heralded the simple return to an oral culture:

> This new orality has striking resemblances to the old in its participatory mystique, its fostering of a communal sense, its concentration on the present moment, and even in its use of formulas. But it is essentially a more deliberate and self-conscious orality, based permanently on the use of writing and print, which are essential for the manufacture and operation of the equipment and for its use as well.[74]

Apart from time constraints, one of the reasons for a less spontaneous approach in speech radio is that the scripts are normally the product of one person writing alone, with a limited amount of help from the producer on duty. 'Secondary orality', according to Ong 'is founded on – though it departs from – the individualized introversion of the age of writing' and 'print'.[75] It is this reliance upon print, which sets primary and secondary orality apart. It also distinguishes the scriptless American radio preacher from the text-based *Thought for the Day* contributor. Roger Silverstone provides a clarification: 'What distinguishes secondary orality from primary orality is its continuing dependence on the analytical and technical and narrative skills that in turn depend on print. Secondary orality is a displaced orality.'[76]

Preachers who seek to learn from religious radio broadcasters like Tilby and Blue should bear in mind that they are listening to 'displaced orality', in other words speech that depends on print. Ong explores the implications of this 'displaced orality' more fully in *Interfaces of the Word* (1977):

> At one end of the continuum are the electronic sound media ... Here we are in the world of secondary orality, as it may be called, superficially identical with that of primary orality but in depth utterly contrary, planned and self-conscious where primary orality is unplanned and unselfconscious, totally dependent on writing and print for its existence.[77]

This is a more nuanced interpretation of how 'secondary orality' can give the appearance of spontaneity, but in reality relies upon print. It resonates with the work of Lionel Blue who successfully creates the illusion of spontaneity, whilst actually relying on a script. It is clear that Ong frequently contrasts 'primary and secondary orality' as a way of illuminating both his meaning and some of the characteristics of secondary orality:

> Secondary orality is both remarkably like and remarkably unlike primary orality. Like primary orality, secondary orality has generated a strong group sense, for listening to spoken words forms hearers into a group, a true audience, just as reading written or printed texts turns individuals in on themselves. But secondary orality generates a sense for groups immeasurably larger than those of primary oral culture – McLuhan's global village.[78]

Ong believes therefore that this 'strong group sense' is a further characteristic of secondary orality: the development of electronic communication has minimised, even shattered the traditional barriers of space and time.

He argues that electronic communication has changed the nature of public speech. 'On television [and radio] we use public address to reach millions of persons, but to reach each one as though we were having a face-to-face conversation with him or her. Our public speaking is private speaking now.'[79] Many of the rural American radio preachers considered earlier do not follow this pattern. They often speak or shout as if they were speaking to a large group of hundreds. By contrast, Lionel Blue is a broadcaster who, as we saw, recognises the importance of recreating an intimate face-to-face conversation.

Coming full circle to a point made in the first part of this book, the 'new electronic oral media' have radically altered the nature of public discourse. The marks of this shift to a new kind of orality include: 'spontaneity'[80] and 'conversational casualness',[81] but a spontaneity and casualness that are carefully constructed. For 'unlike early tribal orality, this present new orality is possible only through heavy reliance on visual constructs'.[82] The concept of 'visual constructs' can be approached from two different perspectives. On the one hand, the form of speaking is determined by whether the speaker is seeing a text, reading a script or viewing a teleprompter. On the other hand, the style and content of speech is also influenced by the way in which the speaker visualises the audience and the listening community.

Seeing, both literal and imagined, therefore continues to have a significant impact upon orality. Whilst drawing on words and hearing, this transformed orality relies heavily on pictures and sight. It thus points towards the need for a developed understanding and use of what we could describe as a pictorial secondary orality, both in homiletics and in religious broadcasting. Speakers need to acknowledge the shift into secondary orality, but also to recognise listeners' reliance upon seeing and imagining visual constructs.

From Pictorial to Experiential Orality

The term 'pictorial secondary orality' implies a variety of activities: visualising absent audiences as Craig Soaries did, visualising appropriate aspects of the biblical text as Angela Tilby does, making use of both impressionistic and representational pictorial language as C. S. Lewis did. As argued in the first part of this book, a new language has also developed in the last decade in homiletics, underlining the importance of 'making movies with words'.[83]

As radio bishop Don Taylor argues, however, the danger of relying entirely upon pictorial language is that it might lead to what Ong describes as the 'insatiable hunt for striking visual presentation, "the speaking picture".'[84] Appeals to the visual may create immediate impact, but used alone they will probably not sufficiently engage the imagination or inform the mind. Even pictorial language, another form of 'the speaking picture', may fail to communicate. One way of overcoming this potential deficiency is to extend the concept of 'pictorial secondary orality' to an 'experiential secondary orality', which recognises the role not only of sight, but of all five senses in the communication process. This will help engage the 'whole' listener, appealing not only to the visual but also to the tactile, olfactory, gustatory and auditory imaginations.

C. S. Lewis recognised this wider role of imaginative engagement when he argued for the importance of verbally 'offering the right stimuli to our nerves' and stimulating the taste buds through a sensitive use of language.[85] Above all he saw the importance of the imagination in freeing, informing, enlightening and persuading the intellect. At its best the picture was not instead of but part of the argument.

So we can extend the concept of 'pictorial orality' to a more multi-sensory approach to speaking. James Jones is a good example of a radio broadcaster who appeals multi-sensorially to listeners. A portrayal of his garden nestling 'in the shade of the Humber Bridge' is balanced by a description of his barbecue: 'We strew herbs on to the charcoals, an incense to create the smell of being in the South of France.'[86] This approach is by no means restricted to religious broadcasters. BBC correspondent Fergal Keane, for example, in one of many memorable broadcasts, describes savouring the smell of freshly baked bread in his Grandmother's house in Cork.[87]

Smell can evoke memories and emotions, distinct for each

person. The olfactory nerve connects with the part of the brain, the limbic system, which deals with emotions and feelings. So it is not surprising that particular smells can bring back specific memories. Helen Keller confides that: 'Even as I think of smells, my nose is full of scents that start awake sweet memories of summers gone and ripening fields far away.'[88] Needless to say, the same smell will evoke a different feeling in different people. There is clearly biblical precedent for appealing verbally to the sense of smell. The sensuous love poem, *Song of Solomon* reeks of perfumes, spices and unguents. 'My nard gave forth its fragrance' (1:12), 'the scent of your garments is like the scent of Lebanon' (4:11), 'his cheeks are like beds of spices yielding fragrance' (5:13).

In a communicative context where listeners' senses are bombarded from all sides and from a range of sources, if preachers are to be heard they need to move on from simply speaking visually to speaking experientially.[89] This involves not just sight but the full range of senses, and it involves enlisting the imagination in a way that can engage not just the intellect, but the whole person, emotions and will as well as mind. Ong's study on *Hopkins, the Self, and God* is relevant at this point as he discusses how Ignatius' *Spiritual Exercises* encourages the use of the five senses in the imagination. First, imagining people and their contexts visually, secondly, hearing in the imagination what they might say, thirdly, savouring the 'smell of the infinite fragrance', fourthly, tasting 'the infinite sweetness of the divinity'[90] and finally, developing an imaginative sense of touch.[91] Beyond such poetic language lies the reminder that words can imaginatively stimulate the five senses. In crude terms this could be described as verbal 'sense appeal'.[92] If we have listeners who for whatever reason are deprived of one or more of the senses, how much more important it is to be multi-sensory.[93]

The experiential language considered here does not represent a return to tribal orality. It is a more complex phenomenon, heralding the rediscovery of a form of speech which moves beyond pure pictorial orality to a multi-sensory and thus experiential orality. Since language can evoke the whole range of the senses, preachers need to recognise and develop an experiential form of discourse. The possibility of rediscovering such a language becomes the topic for the next chapter.

Notes

1. Example from his radio broadcasting cited in a recorded interview between Jolyon Mitchell and Bishop Taylor, 20 August 1995. The italics are mine. (Hereafter: Taylor, Interview 1995.)
2. Taylor, Interview 1995.
3. See Martini 1994, 84, for support of this view. Cardinal Martini argues: 'The mass media, in the variety of languages they use (words, images, sound, gesture, resonance, emotion, etc.) are potential tents in which the Word does not disdain to dwell; they are the hem of his garment through which saving power can flow.'
4. Coggan 1987. The former Archbishop of Canterbury advocates a bifocal understanding of the means of grace. '... the Living God comes to us both in the Sacrament of the Body and Blood of Christ and in the sacrament of the Word ...' 24.
5. Taylor, Interview 1995.
6. Ibid. This concern for enhancing 'his own image as bishop' raises the issue of motivation. A cynical interpretation would be that this programme was a vehicle for his self-promotion. Such a view does not, however, explain the inclusive style of the programmes, and his stated emphasis on being a 'channel' through his broadcasting.
7. Ibid.
8. Taylor attempts to capture the meaning and spirit of the original story, without 'being bound to its linguistic structure'. Whilst Taylor is obviously not engaged in translating from the Greek or Hebrew his method does have interesting parallels with Nida and Taber's four priorities for biblical translation: '1) Contextual consistency has priority over verbal consistency (or word-for-word concordance). 2) Dynamic equivalence has priority over formal correspondence. 3) The aural heard form of language has priority over the written form. 4) Forms that are used by and acceptable to the audience for which a translation is intended have priorities over forms that may be traditionally more prestigious.' Nida and Taber 1969, 14.
9. Radio preaching example cited in Taylor, Interview 1995.
10. Talbot-Smith 1995 (1990). These 'small electrical pulses' are conveyed to the brain by 'separate nerves'. 15–16.
11. I have appropriated Nida's term 'dynamic equivalence' for my own argument as a way of clarifying the model of translation that I am employing. Nida defines 'dynamic equivalence' as a 'translation in which the message of the original text has been so transported into

the receptor language that the response of the receptor is essentially like that of the original receptors'. Nida and Taber 1969, 202. The result of dynamic equivalence translation is far more than 'mere correct communication of information' as people will 'feel as well as understand what is said'. 25. See also Nida's earlier book, 1964. See also Eric North 1974, 'As Nida developed and popularised it, dynamic equivalence translation captures the meaning and spirit of the original without being bound to its linguistic structure (formal correspondence).' xii.

12. Willimon 1992, 8. See also Willimon 1994.
13. Ibid., 6.
14. Ibid., 9.
15. Ibid., 6.
16. Ibid., 9.
17. Ibid., 16.
18. Ibid., 76. He also implies strong disagreement with those who argue 'that the best hope for Christian preachers is to find some sort of religious *Esperanto,* a culturally approved common mode of discourse, a metalanguage that frees us from the linguistic bind imposed on us by having to work with pre-second-century Hebrew and Greek texts ...'
19. For a brief discussion of such a 'common language' or 'lingua franca', see Ford 1995, 154. Ford relates this to 'the supercession of religious language by a variety of scientific and professional languages, and the secularisation of political rhetoric'.
20. Ibid., 77.
21. Ibid., 79. See also Yoder 1984, Chapter 2. Willimon also uses Yoder to support his case.
22. Ford 1995, 80.
23. Ibid., 114. 'We must learn Christianity, even as we learn a foreign language.'
24. MacIntyre 1988, 372. MacIntyre also identifies a number of problems about translatability. Most relevant for the current discussion and for preachers is his consideration of 'situations in which the task of translation is from the language of one community whose language-in-use is expressive of and presupposes a particular system of well-defined beliefs into the different language of another such community with beliefs which in some key areas are strongly incompatible with those of the first community'. 379. See also the discussion of translation in Chapter 10 of this book.
25. Steiner 1992, 266.
26. See, for example, Willimon's critique of those who attempt to

translate the gospel into subjectivised garb and urge 'subordination of the authoritative text to the critical hermeneutics of the experience of the oppressed'. Willimon 1992, 16.

27. Lewis, *Four Talks on Love: Storge, Philia, Eros, Agape,* 1970, Tape 3.
28. Walls 1996, see especially Chapter 3: 'The Translation Principle in Christian History'.
29. See also Sanneh 1989. Sanneh asserts that: 'Even if in practice Christians wish to stop the translation process, claiming their form of it as final and exclusive, they have not been able to suppress it for all time.' 47.
30. Sanneh 1989 argues that 'ancient Greek, without any claim to being the native or working language of Jesus and the close circle of apostles, became the preponderant medium of religious discourse. The original Aramaic and Hebraic languages, which formed the basis of Jesus' preaching, became a minor undercarriage, making a halting intrusion in the generally smooth progress of the new discourse.' 31.
31. Walker 1996, 22.
32. Walls 1996, 32.
33. See Neill 1964, passim, and Sanneh 1989, 9–129.
34. Walls 1996, 26.
35. Ibid., 27.
36. 2 Corinthians 5:21 (adapted from the Jerusalem Bible). It would also be possible to use the term 'translate' in the RSV translation without undermining the sense: 'For our sake he *translated* (made) him to be sin who knew no sin, so that in him we might become the righteousness of God.'
37. 2 Corinthians 8:9 (adapted from the Jerusalem Bible). Whilst it would be possible to make a similar adaptation from Philippians 2:5–7, to: Jesus, though 'in very nature God' *translated* himself into the 'very nature of a servant', it would skirt too many complex and controversial exegetical difficulties with this particular passage.
38. Walls 1996, 27.
39. See Hauerwas and Willimon 1992. This tension can be detected in all ten of Willimon's sermons in this text, but see especially: 'Living Sacrifice' 29–37. and 'Be Imitators of Me' 43–50.
40. Ibid., 45.
41. Newbigin 1986, 6.
42. Hauerwas and Willimon 1992, 87–8. Willimon cites Newbigin with approval. Whilst Willimon does not acknowledge it, this represents a further qualification to his original argument concerning translation.

43. Newbigin 1986, 5–6. His third principle for Christian communication across cultural frontiers, is that it should rely not on human persuasiveness, but on God for its ultimate effectiveness.
44. Ibid., 7. Newbigin describes the two dangers in these terms: 'On the one hand, he may simply fail to communicate: he uses the words of the language, but in such a way that he sounds like a foreigner; his message is heard as the babblings of a man who really has nothing to say. Or, on the other hand, he may so far succeed in talking the language of his hearers that he is accepted all too easily as a familiar character – a moralist calling for greater purity of conduct ... In the attempt to be "relevant" one may fall into syncretism, and in the effort to avoid syncretism one may become irrelevant.' 7. See also Dawn's discussion of translation. She believes that preaching 'requires a careful dialectical balance in order to use the language of faith, but in a way that is accessible to people without falling into the ideological language of political agendas.' Dawn 1995, 231.
45. See, for example, Baker 1987. See especially Wolf, 176–95. See also Steiner 1992. '*After Babel* postulates that translation is formally and pragmatically implicit in *every* act of communication, in the emission and reception of every mode of meaning, be it in the widest semiotic sense or in more specifically verbal exchanges. To understand is to decipher. To hear significance is to translate.' xii.
46. Craddock 1985. He argues that 'much of the educational process today is silent ... in many cases, an excessively large amount of seminary education will consist of listening to lectures, reading, taking notes, writing papers, and sitting for exams, all in silence'. 21.
47. Ibid., 20.
48. Ong 1967. See especially Chapter 2, 'Transformations of the Word', 17–110. This is the first book of a trilogy that explores wide-ranging issues related to communication. See also Ong 1971 and 1977.
49. Ong 1977 makes a clear distinction between the two parts within this stage of 'alphabet and print'. Implicit to many of the arguments in this text is his belief that the manuscript or chirographic culture is distinctive, but not entirely separate from the print or typographic culture. See, for example, Chapter 1: 'Transformations of the Word and Alienation', and his discussions of 'closure and print' in section three, where in Chapter 9 he explores death and life in the text of the book: 'Like writing, print is related to death, although the relationship is not exactly the same. It is even more definitive.' 239.

50. This emerged from his trilogy written 'in the middle period of his scholarly career'. Farrell 1991, 35.
51. Ibid., 35. 'The four stages of culture identified by Ong – primary oral culture, manuscript culture, print culture, and secondary oral culture – are working hypotheses that take into account certain critical data, and yet they are open to further elaboration.' The weakness of this summary is that it underplays Ong's qualifications to his own argument. In *The Presence of the Word*, for example, he discusses certain 'complications' to and 'overlappings' within his scheme. See Ong 1967, 53: 'The movement through the sequence of media is of course not merely a matter of successive reorganisations of the sensorium.'
52. For a useful summary and adaptation of Ong's hypothesis see Soukup 1996, 55–66.
53. Ong 1967, 25. He cites Homer's 'rosy-fingered dawn' or 'wine-dark sea' as examples of often-repeated formulae by epic singers.
54. Ibid., 25. 'The oral-aural singer has a vocabulary of metrical phrases, fragments of verse, a huge store of verbal equipment prefabricated to fit into his verse structure, and often slightly malleable.' Ong goes on to suggest that the world of the 'unrecorded word' is one in which memory plays a more important role than our own 'world'. This manifested itself in the 'older oral-aural society' where encyclopædism had to be a matter of poetry, combined with the other great oral-aural speech form, oratory, which in turn was largely poetic.' 35.
55. For example, Curtis Stoops's repetition of 'that world of', Toby Powers's frequent use of 'good' and 'good for us to be here', and the 'blowing' apocalyptic radio preachers' regular 'hahing' illustrate the repetitive strain within this remarkable American oral tradition. It is important, however, to bear in mind that many of these preachers also draw extensively upon the written text of the Bible. (See Chapter 7 of this book.)
56. Ong 1982, 11.
57. Ong argues that 'oral cultures create and sustain certain specifically polemic and anxiety structures in the psyche, which are curiously calmed or at least repressed and relocated in cultures where knowledge is stored in the quiescence of writing and print'. Ong 1996a, 14. This fascinating insight may partly explain the violent polemic expressed by some American radio preachers and the sharp contrast this makes with the restrained broadcasts of Tilby and Lewis.
58. Ong 1967, 35–53. In this discussion I am following Ong's earlier

threefold, as opposed to his later four-fold, model of the evolution of orality. For an overview of Ong's work see: Farrell 1991, 25–43.

59. Ong 1982, 117.
60. Ong believes that 'eventually': 'print replaced the lingering hearing-dominance in the world of thought and expression with the sight-dominance which had its beginnings with writing but could not flourish with the support of writing alone'. Ong 1982, 121.
61. Contrast this view with an example Ong uses on at least two separate occasions. He refers to the way Ambrose of Milan in his *Commentary on St Luke* (iv.5) 'speaks out of the old oral tradition' and adds, 'Sight is often deceived, hearing serves as guarantee.' Ong 1967, 52–3. See also Ong 1982, 119.
62. Ong 1967, 42.
63. Ong 1982, 74.
64. Ong 1967, 283.
65. Ong 1982, 78.
66. Lewis 1960a, 219. Earlier Lewis explores the way phrases can communicate emotion. He cites *Prometheus Unbound* and how the author makes 'me imagine a boat rushing over waves, which are also identified with sounds. After that he need do no more; my emotion will follow of itself. Poetry most often communicates emotions, not directly, but by creating imaginatively the grounds for those emotions.' 216.
67. See Chapter 5 of this book.
68. Meyers 1993, 76.
69. Ong's title for this section is 'Electronics and the Sensorium Today', Ong 1967, 87–110.
70. Ibid., 286.
71. Ibid., 103.
72. Ong 1982, 11.
73. Ong 1967, 259.
74. Ong 1982, 136.
75. Ong 1971, 285.
76. Silverstone 1991, 148.
77. Ong 1977, 298.
78. Ibid., 136.
79. Ibid., 90.
80. Ong believes that: 'The new oral electronic media – most notably radio and television – tend to promote spontaneity, the unrehearsed reaction of interviewee and audience.' Ong 1996a, 18.
81. Ong argues that: 'radio and, more particularly, television demand a discursive and even a conversational casualness where they have

occasion to present theology . . . The conversational casualness is a mark of orality, but *orality of a new kind*, unlike the primary orality, which trafficked in the formality and the formulas discouraged by electronic oralism.' Ibid., 19.

82. Ibid., 260.
83. Wilson 1995, 267, and see also 183 and 255. He suggests for example on 264: 'In a small way we again become movie directors.'
84. Ong 1977, 131–2.
85. Lewis 1960a, 219.
86. James Jones, *Thought for the Day*, Radio 4, 16 August 1996.
87. Keane, 1996, 16.
88. Ackerman 1996 (1990), 3. She cites Keller on smell: 'Smell is a potent wizard that transports us across thousands of miles and all the years we have lived. The odors of fruits waft me to my southern home, to my childhood frolics in the peach orchard. Other odors, instantaneous and fleeting, cause my heart to dilate joyously or contract with remembered grief.'
89. In short, they should use words to appeal verbally to sight, hearing, touch, taste and smell. For two writers who agree see Adams 1982, especially Chapter 14, 'Sense Appeal' and David Day 1998, 30–1.
90. The Psalmist puts it succinctly: 'Taste and see that the Lord is good.' (Psalm 34:8) One interpretation of this text is that it means: Taste and by tasting, know (see) that the Lord is good.
91. Ong, 1986, 71. See also *The Spiritual Exercises of St. Ignatius Loyola* c.1522–3.
92. Adams 1982, see especially: Chapter 14 on 'Sense Appeal'.
93. This consideration has far-reaching consequences for preachers determined to include all members of the congregation, whatever their strongest sense; for example, having a sign translator or using Braille text.

CHAPTER 9

The Embodied Word

One thinker who has called for the discovery of a new language, or perhaps more accurately a new way of using language, is Jacques Ellul. A French sociologist and theologian, deeply influenced by Karl Barth, he was passionately interested in language and communication throughout his long career until his death in 1994 at the age of eighty-two. Two themes related to this concerned him, first 'the devaluation of spoken and written language in an image-centred mass media', secondly, 'the centrality of the word of God in the Judeo-Christian tradition'.[1]

As early as the 1940s Ellul had already perceived a breakdown of communication, and this led him to call for the development of a new language which might re-establish connections between people. He was not advocating the development of an Esperanto style language. Instead, he appears to use this 'new language' motif as a provocative metaphor to increase 'awareness' of the disintegration of language, the isolation of individuals and the importance of developing a 'personal' communication based on trust. So in *The Presence of the Kingdom* (1947) he argues that Christian intellectuals need to 'discover a new language' which will help humankind 'understand one another, in spite of publicity' and so 'abandon their despairing solitude'.[2] Unfortunately, Ellul does not go into detail about the nature of this new language. He does, however, in a way reminiscent of religious radio broadcasters such as Wright, Blue and Taylor, underline the importance of this language being able to aid connection and contact among humans.[3]

For Ellul the creation of a new language is a vital task. Towards the end of the book he writes:

> We need *a new form of communication* between human beings, in order that the relations between them, distorted by the conditions of life, by class feeling, by prejudice, may, by a renewal of their intelligence, be recreated upon a personal and living plane.[4]

This cry for a new form of communication is all the more urgent when read parallel with a later text by Ellul, *Hope in Time of Abandonment* (1973).[5] In this text he devotes a section to the 'Death of the Word', and briefly considers 'the disintegration of language'. He develops this theme more explicitly in *The Humiliation of the Word* (1981). In this text we find his most systematic exploration of the relationship between word and image.

Word Humiliated?

According to Ellul, we inhabit a new communicative environment, where we are bombarded by a host of electronic images. This not only leads to the disintegration of language and isolation from others, but it also changes what we see. Ellul's third chapter of *The Humiliation of the Word* is entitled 'Sight Triumphant'. He argues that what we see and what our ancestors saw are radically different. For our ancestors the natural world was humankind's primary image. By contrast today we are overwhelmed by a 'proliferation of artificial images ... A universe of images surrounds us: photos, films, television, advertising, billboards, road-signs, illustrations etc.'[6]

The regular and intense bombardment builds a 'screen' or 'circle' of artificial images 'placed between me and my world'. The result is that synthetic images may appear more real than that which we can see for ourselves.[7]

> Our eyes' function has been extraordinarily expanded. Our brain is constantly receiving the impact of imaginary sights and no longer of reality. Today we can no longer live without the reference and diversion provided by images. For a large proportion of our lives we live as mere spectators.[8]

In Ellul's opinion the ubiquity of artificially constructed images has serious implications. It creates a 'substitute reality',[9] a 'magic lantern universe',[10] which 'gums up our thinking'.[11] Immediate and transitory images created by the mass media have replaced in our minds careful thought mediated through a rigorous use of language. Images act like 'lightning, attacking us from all directions'.[12] The result of such an 'image explosion' is that the mass media 'surrounds us with images. The multiplication of visual techniques has produced this invasion of our eyes and thoughts by images.'[13] According to Ellul, invasion has led to domination: 'Images captivate our attention, fascinating us and filling us with hallucinations, so that we abandon everything.'[14]

As a consequence, in Ellul's distinctive terminology, sight may be triumphant but the word, representing language, has been humiliated:

> The word is greatly mutilated, cadaverous, and almost dead, but we must become conscious of what this means: our whole civilization is loathed along with the word. The word signals our civilization's possible death and provides the channel through which the poison can get in.[15]

This apocalyptic and strongly anthropomorphic language testifies to Ellul's fear that the word is 'humiliated, crushed, and meaningless'.[16] He claims that the invasion of images has led to our living in a 'wasteland of empty verbiage'.[17] There is now a 'contempt for language'[18] and a 'hatred of the word'.[19]

Not only have technologically constructed artificial images devalued language and speech, but this has been theologically disastrous. In the Bible, claims Ellul, everything points back to the word:

> 'The Word was made flesh' also means since the Word of God was incarnate, what is visible is forever excluded. The *invisible* God came as *word*. He cannot be recognised by sight. Nothing about Jesus indicates divinity in a visual way.[20]

For Ellul, 'seeing a photograph of Jesus would not prove anything more and would add nothing to his words'.[21]

He goes further, arguing that: 'In reality, the biblical revelation is radically opposed to everything visual ... The only possible relationship with God is based on the word, and nothing else. This is because the biblical God speaks, and does nothing else.'[22] He believes it is impossible to apprehend God through sight. Ellul cites Romans 10: '"Faith comes by hearing", says Paul (Rom. 10:17, JE). It comes by hearing exclusively, and absolutely never from what one sees ... Sight is utterly excluded from the faith relationship.'[23] Ellul is not arguing that 'the word is good and that sight is evil',[24] nor, so he states, does he mean 'that hearing and the word are *superior* to sight and image'.[25] He is, however, asserting the primacy of the word in God's communication:

> God's revelation is conveyed by the human word – by the word and nothing else. Action, miracles, and works only accompany and authenticate the word as demonstrations and accessories. Without the word they are nothing. Only the word can convey the word of God, the sole means God used to reveal himself to us.[26]

Ellul's work shows considerable reliance upon the Swiss theologian Karl Barth.[27] 'It is essential', according to Fasching, to see Ellul 'as carrying forward the tradition of dialectical theology associated with Karl Barth'.[28] Ellul's theological method is dialectical in the sense that he sees the image and word in 'opposition'.[29] For example, he entitles his fifth chapter in *The Humiliation of the Word* 'The Religious Conflict between Image and Word', a theme that runs throughout the text. The word 'is in fundamental opposition to the image'.[30] This conflict between word and image cannot be reconciled till the 'end of time'.[31] 'Thus the long-awaited reconciliation of image and word and of truth and reality is certain, but we must not try to manufacture it with our techniques and metaphysics here and now.'[32] On the basis of this belief in the 'certainty' of the eschatological reconciliation between word and image, he believes that we should now begin living 'its reality as a promise'.[33]

According to Ellul one way of 'saving the word' is by using 'understandable language' and 'open language'. He draws support for 'comprehensible language' from the teaching of Jesus, who 'speaks everyone's language' and had a 'determination to use reasonable language'.[34] He also asserts that Jesus 'avoids hermetic language, double meanings and elliptical expressions. Parables are rather a means of conveying meaning.'[35]

One interpreter argues that Ellul is urging a recovery of the 'love of language', so that it is 'saved from being reduced to technical manipulative communication'.[36] '*Open* language', he stresses, 'permits a continual adventure', and works against the tendency of language to become 'ideologically closed'.[37] Such accessible and open language has the potential to bring freedom and a foretaste of the reconciliation of word and image.

Regenerating Discourse

What are we to make of Ellul's arguments? He expresses them categorically and in an uncompromising fashion. Rarely are they supported by detailed empirical evidence. Recent data gathered by communication scholars have challenged some of Ellul's more extreme assertions.[38] Michael Real, for example, believes that: 'as a generalist, he [Ellul] sometimes lacks familiarity with specialised studies, opinions muscle aside evidence, and unfounded generalizations result about the role and effect of a particular individual medium or research method.'[39] Contrary to Ellul's suggestion discussed above, audiences are more sophisticated and more selective than to 'abandon everything' because of the image explosion.

Ellul is better seen as using hortative devices to startle us, awaken us from our critical slumbers, to make us think critically about our media dominated society and the way we understand the Christian story. There is some truth in his claim that our age is dominated by the electronic image. The power of modern 'image and spin doctors' and their carefully constructed pictures or sound-bites point to persuasion, manipulation and impression taking the place of careful argument and assessed evidence. A picture of the Queen next to McDonald's is preferred to a considered discussion of the role of the monarchy. Images, however, can be both powerful and useful. A picture of a starving or traumatised child can move us to compassion and action in a way words often do not. But this points to the dangers as well as the dominance of the image. The intention of the image-maker is often concealed. Language alone can help us to lay bare the image-maker's motives and investigate what is an appropriate response. It is the vital tool for making sense of the images that permeate our imaginative space.

Ellul's warnings about the invasive force of images in our society are apposite, if rather pessimistic. A more judicious judgement would be that we need image and word, not either/or, but both/and. Ellul claims that 'in the audiovisual realm the image is king. The word, practically useless, is in any case a serf, not an equal.'[40] This need not be the case. Words still have a powerful role to play in our society. The cumulative evidence of this book supports that assertion. We began by showing how a renewed concern with visual language, spoken words and the development of the imagination in the field of homiletics has generated increased confidence in the future of preaching as public oral discourse. We next perused evidence of the way in which talk radio has survived the potential crisis heralded by television and has created the opportunities for word-artists to flourish. The case studies provided examples of how conversational pictorial language has been used as a bridging device by a range of broadcasters, and also how certain oral idiosyncrasies, insider discourse and passionate enthusiasm could become either a bridge or a barrier between listener and speaker. In the case of the latter, not images but language has created the problems. In short, the range and diversity of orality discussed in the various parts of this book demonstrate that the word has by no means been vanquished by the image. We 'live and move and have our being' in an audio-visual culture, where both words and images are vying for attention. A theology of experiential orality that engages all the senses must recognise this fact.

A similar critique can be made of Ellul's claims about the disintegration of language in our image-saturated environment. Certainly its misuse and decay can create barriers rather than aid communication. Ellul is prescient in his reference to the isolation of the individual and the breakdown of communication in the midst of informational overload. It is, for example, a surprising failure of the Internet, the ultimate in instant linguistic world-wide communication between people, that its frequent use should, according to recent research, in some cases increase loneliness and depression and lead to a decline in interaction between family and immediate friends.[41]

Disembodied communication, where the speaker or sender is not physically present, is in some senses an incomplete communicative event. Colin Morris makes a similar point:

> The mechanisation of the message in whatever form – through literature, radio or television – results in speech without speaker, voice without presence, contact without personal engagement. It precludes that embarrassing tap on the shoulder as the hearer responds to our words with the demand: 'Prove it!'[42]

Wittgenstein is illuminating here. He argued that natural language does not exist in isolation. It becomes intelligible and gets its meaning only when it is seen as embedded in particular forms of life. He states that 'practice gives the words their sense'.[43] If we choose to inhabit depersonalised or brutalised forms of life it is inevitable the language we use and its inherent values will be similarly debased. Words of compassion and sensitivity cannot just be bolted on as a desirable extra to any lifestyle regardless.

We therefore need a much deeper analysis than Ellul offers if we are to have a regenerated language; an analysis that examines the presuppositions, values and structures of the actual forms of life we inhabit, what Wittgenstein calls its 'deep grammar'.[44] To refer only to images without distinction is to remain on the surface and to defeat the legitimate criticisms that the Christian preacher might make of our age. One imperative for preaching is to offer an alternative Christian world, one that is open to human habitation.

Embodied Discourse

This leads us directly to Ellul's contention that 'God's revelation is conveyed by the human word – by the word and nothing else'. This echoes Barth's belief that 'the God of the Bible is not "somewhere else", but is given only in, with and under the text itself'.[45] Stated so baldly this may seem too exclusive for modern pluralist ears but its general importance for preachers is not to be underestimated. Unless the preacher is able to get the biblical text to speak for itself, he or she is liable to lapse into an unproductive reductionism. But this raises a vital question. How is the preacher to get the text to speak for itself?

At this point it is worth drawing attention to a Johannine source:

> That which was from the beginning, which we have heard, which we have seen with our eyes, which we have looked upon and touched with our hands, concerning the word of life – the life was made manifest, and we saw it . . .[46]

Notice the sensory nature of the verbs: heard, seen, looked upon and touched. This appeal to the senses may have been a way of refuting the Gnostic heresy that Jesus was not really human. But it also reflects how the revelation of 'the word of life' was perceived by at least one group of early Christians as a multi-sensory experience.

This is a point supported by French theologian and broadcaster, Gérard Heinz. In 'God's revelation is not by words alone',[47] he suggests that 'God reveals himself plurisensorially to the world through word and image'. [48] He clarifies this point by admitting that 'God "speaks" mainly verbally',[49] but that the 'Biblical word cannot be reduced to exclusively verbal expression, but is a vivid and active reality. It is simultaneously verbal word, image, vision, sign, dream, mysterious encounter, feeling of presence etc.'[50] Heinz cites a range of biblical examples to support his argument. These include: Isaiah in the temple seeing the 'Lord sitting upon a throne, high and lifted up',[51] and Ezekiel seeing visions[52] and then being commanded literally to eat the scroll of lamentation which tastes of honey.[53] He also cites 1 John 1:1,[54] arguing that 'Revelation culminates as such in the incarnation which is also the highest degree of plurisensoriality.'[55] Heinz offers an important counter-argument to Ellul's belief that 'biblically everything leads back to the word' and that 'the biblical revelation is radically opposed to everything visual'. In the words of Martin Marty, Ellul 'despises compromise',[56] and this tendency clearly influences his defence of God's revelation through the word.

Neither is it desirable to dispense with all images. Sometimes the preacher's task is not to replace images with words but to adapt or exchange an inappropriate image for a more appropriate one. Barry Overend, British Preacher of the Year 1995, refers in his prize-winning sermon to the familiar and evocative finger in the National Lottery advertisement. He transforms this image to illustrate his theme of God's love. He replaces the pointing finger with a 'beckoning hand' and to the phrase 'It could be you' he adds 'It shall be you'. [57] As well as transforming the image, he extends the discourse.

Ellul's preoccupation with defending the spoken and heard word, at the expense of the other senses, leaves a muted version or rather a colourless form of Christianity. Such a view has little room for the God of Genesis 1 who saw that creation was good,[58] or the Lord of Genesis 8 who smelt the burnt offerings on the altar, or the God of Exodus who used the visual symbols of a burning bush or pillar of smoke as signposts for his people, or the God of John's Gospel who sent the Word to become visible, tangible flesh. Ellul deals with many of these strands in the biblical literature in a myopic fashion; in particular, he does little justice to the tradition that puts emphasis upon 'what we have seen with our eyes'.

In the synoptics Jesus heals the blind,[59] paints vivid word pictures,[60] and makes use of 'visual aids' such as children and fig trees.[61] In the Gospel of John, as Ellul himself admits,[62] sight is closely linked with belief and understanding.[63] Paul writes that the visible creation can reveal something of God's invisible nature,[64] and the resurrection appearances are foundational for his faith.[65] Even if the prologue of Hebrews begins with a reminder how 'God has spoken of old' and also how 'in these last days he has spoken to us by his Son', it continues with a graphic description of one who 'reflects the glory of God and bears the very stamp of his nature'.[66] God's revelation is not entirely limited to verbal communication.

This is not to suggest that either image or word can remove the mystery and otherness of God. To think this would be to lapse into idolatry. However clever our words, however evocative our images, we can never pretend to capture God. The divine always lies beyond our reach. 'We see through a glass darkly.'[67]

Consider the sacraments of the Eucharist and Baptism. They

have been described as visible words (*verba visibila*). Augustine famously argued that: 'The Word comes to the element; and so there is a sacrament, that is, a sort of visible word.'[68] As Jenson says:

> In speaking of 'visible' words, Augustine primarily contrasted the *invisible* word: God's own knowledge and intention of himself and his works, the inner reality of all that truth which God knows and is . . . God's inner truth comes to be spoken 'visibly', in ways accessible to our senses.[69]

A 'visible sign' need not appeal only to sight, it can appeal to all our senses. The Eucharist, which involves listening to the story of the last supper, seeing the bread broken, and tasting the bread and wine, is a multi-sensory experience. This sacrament engages the senses of hearing, sight, touch, taste and even smell. It therefore goes beyond the bounds of a simple verbal act of an 'acoustic community':[70] it is a more-than-verbal multi-sensory sign. Yet its mystery remains.

We need to include a multi-sensory perspective that recognises the role that more-than-verbal visible signs have to play in revelatory communication. This principle of embodiment is important for the development of a theology of a multi-sensory orality. Any attempt to connect with or speak to others in contemporary terms needs to be sensitive to our cultural context. Pierre Babin argues for the use of 'symbolic language', which he believes 'was Jesus' language' and 'is the dominant language of the media today'.[71] The case has been put here for a multi-sensory or experiential secondary orality, which draws upon this kind of pictorial language. Preachers employing such a form of communication need to be sensitive both to contemporary forms of orality and to the multi-sensory and embodied theological foundations of Christianity.

There is a sense in which words alone can never be enough.[72] The truism, 'actions speak louder than words', remains a vital reminder for preachers intent on improving their sermon's biblical prowess, theological perspicuity or verbal artistry. The speakers themselves are visual aids of what is being said. They are embodiments of the story.[73] The act of communication does not end when the preacher finishes the homily and steps out of the pulpit or from behind the lectern. Nor is it complete after the closing hymn, when the final blessing is given and the congregation departs. The embodiment of the word goes beyond the service itself. The way the speakers and the wider faith community listen, build relationships, forgive, include outsiders, counter injustice, spend their time and their money, communicates whether the word is authentically embodied.

We have identified three important procedures for developing a theological understanding of pictorial and multi-sensory orality: first, grasping the theological centrality of the 'translation principle', secondly, understanding the need for a renewed approach to orality, and thirdly, grappling with the multi-sensory revelation of God. We need to break out of the 'silent' print culture of the text, to a new kind of multi-sensory orality which has the potential to engage the listeners' imaginations and minds through an appeal to the whole range of their senses. As Robert Waznak argues:

> From the beginning, the Gospel was preached not in sacred languages but in the language of the people. Jesus spoke Aramaic, Paul used *koine* Greek, Origen chose not the stylized rhetoric of the academy but the familiar discourse of his culture. We too must proclaim the Gospel in our own day in words, images and forms that are called for by our video culture.[74]

Preachers have to engage not only with their distinctive historical roots, but also with their specific cultural context. For preachers in an audio-visual culture, speaking to easily distracted listeners, these practical implications emerge: Translate into accessible, pictorial and distinctive discourse. Oralise in conversational, 'spontaneous' and imaginative terms. Stimulate listeners with words not only pictorially, but also multi-sensorially, and thus experientially. If this is achieved, then an attempt to integrate the world and story of the text with the world and story of the listener may be successful.[75]

Notes

1. Fasching 1988a, 8.
2. Ellul 1951 (1997), 127.

3. Ibid., 127. This, he believes, is a task attempted not only by Christians: 'For the Christian intellectual this problem of language is the key-problem to contact with other men [sic]. Other people, too, have felt this need. Other people have sought for this language, but they have only ended up in a more hopeless solitude.' This reads like a selective view of history, especially when it is placed alongside Ellul's argument that there is a historical precedent for Christians to be successful with this creative linguistic act: 'Now at different times, in the course of Christian history, Christians have rediscovered a language.' Ibid., 128.
4. Ibid., 143.
5. Ellul 1973.
6. Ellul 1985 (1981), 114.
7. As he does in *The Presence of the Kingdom,* Ellul works with a model of the mass media as a highly powerful expression and instrument of what he has famously described as 'the technique'. For extensive discussion of the term 'technique', see his trilogy on this theme: Ellul 1964 (1954), 1980 (1977), 1990 (1988). Clifford Christians provides a helpful working definition: '*La technique* [the technique] is Ellul's term for the modern mind in which efficiency becomes a normative claim for all human activity, including the technological process.' Christians 1988, 7.
8. Ellul 1985 (1981), 126.
9. Ibid., 128.
10. Ibid., 221.
11. Ibid., 129. See also Ellul's earlier book discussing propaganda, 1973a (1962).
12. Ibid., 144. See also Fasching 1988a, 9. Fasching relates such views to Ellul's thoughts on 'media propaganda'. 'The constant flow of events portrayed through the media drowns the individual in a kaleidoscope of disconnected and uncoordinated imagery and information. Overwhelmed by the flood of sensory stimuli and disoriented by the constantly shifting geography of the hourly headlines, individuals are reduced to stereotyped gut reactions, shaped by societal propaganda.'
13. Ellul 1985 (1981), 148. Later he argues that the people have placed their confidence in the 'multiplication of artificial visual images'. The result is that 'thousands of changing images scatter my attention, provoking hallucination and hypnosis as I am submerged in them'. 192.
14. Ibid., 129. 'The image monopolizes: either you watch television or you do not, but you cannot watch television while writing letters or

doing dishes in the next room ... Through this process they divert us from lived reality.'

15. Ibid., 254.
16. Ibid., 254.
17. Ibid., 156.
18. Ibid., 162. See also Mengham 1995 for a more recent discussion on this theme.
19. Ibid., 172.
20. Ibid., 56. Ellul asserts: 'From beginning to end the bible only deals with the word.' 48.
21. Ibid., 84.
22. Ibid., 71.
23. Ibid., 80–1.
24. Ibid., 102. He continues: 'I simply insist that the word belongs to the order of truth and sight to the order of reality.'
25. Ibid., 230.
26. Ibid., 107.
27. See Bromiley 1981. 'It should be noted ... that for the most part only in the area of biblical exposition and dogmatics does Ellul lean heavily on Barth.' 47.
28. It is important to acknowledge, with Fasching, that Ellul himself emphasised that he has 'never been an unconditional "Barthian"'. Ellul 1976, 8.
29. See Ellul 1981, 291–308. Ellul also places in dialectical opposition 'reality' and 'truth', linking them with image and word respectively. Thus natural theology is critiqued by a logocentric revealed theology which resonates with the work of Barth. 'The Word is related only to Truth. The image is related only to reality.' Ellul 1985 (1981), 27. For Ellul the image can only deal with surface 'realities' and 'appearances', it is unable to communicate truth. The word, by contrast, 'alone has the capacity to enter the domain of the truth'. Fasching 1988a, 10.
30. Ellul 1985 (1981), 111. For Ellul this 'conflict between sight and word has to do with the ultimate value a society adopts for itself'. Ibid., 195.
31. Ibid., 184.
32. Ibid., 255.
33. Ibid., 259.
34. Ibid., 263.
35. Ibid., 263.
36. 'The love of language fosters clear and coherent communication, critical reflection and creative action.' Fasching 1988a, 10.

37. Ellul 1985 (1981), 263 and 264.
38. See Silverstone 1994 and Morley 1992. For example, it appears that many people do watch television while eating, washing up or even writing homework. Ellul's argument that the image (represented by the television in this case) necessarily monopolises needs to be qualified.
39. Real 1981, 124.
40. Ellul 1985 (1981), 218.
41. Mark Tran, 'Loneliness of Virtual Living', *The Guardian,* 31 August 1998, 1.
42. Morris letter to Jolyon Mitchell, 25 August 1998.
43. Wittgenstein 1980, 85. See also Malcolm 1993.
44. See Wittgenstein, 1968 (1953), Part 1, Section 664, 168e.
45. Helpfully discussed in Brueggeman 1997b, 19. See Barth 1957, 43–5.
46. 1 John 1:1–2 (RSV).
47. Heinz 1981a, 34–8. Heinz has worked for Radio France and FR3 and as a television producer for FR3's Third Channel. See also Heinz 1981b.
48. Heinz 1981a, 35.
49. Ibid., 35.
50. Ibid., 36.
51. Isaiah 6:1.
52. Ezekiel 1:15: 'I saw a wheel upon the earth . . .' (NIV)
53. Ezekiel 3:1–3: 'Son of man, eat what is offered to you; eat this scroll, and go, speak to the House of Israel . . . Then I ate it; and it was in my mouth as sweet as honey.' (NIV)
54. He adds part of v. 3: 'What we have seen and heard we declare to you so that we together may share in a common life.' Ibid., 36.
55. Ibid., 36.
56. Marty 1981, 10. 'Ellul invites the reader into the web of anti-technique thought and despises compromise.'
57. Broadcast on *Morning Worship,* BBC Radio 4, 5 November 1995. For full sermon see: Gledhill 1996, 152–5.
58. Even if these references were used metaphorically of God, they remain significant images of God's relation to creation.
59. Mark 10:46–52.
60. See, for example, Mark 4 (Matthew 13 and Luke 8).
61. Mark 10:13–16 (see also Matthew 19 and Luke 18). The fig tree episode can be found in Mark 11:20–25 (Matthew 21).
62. Ellul 1985 (1981), 242–54. Ellul considers the Gospel of John in great detail. He admits that: 'the verb "see" recurs continually

(more than 100 times) and is undoubtedly one of the essential themes of this book'. 243.

63. John 9 is probably the most explicit example of this theme, which runs through much of the Gospel of John.
64. Romans 1:19ff.
65. 1 Corinthians 15:3ff.
66. Hebrews 1:1–3.
67. 1 Corinthians 13:12.
68. Augustine, *In Johannem*, 80, 3. See also Augustine's *On Christian Doctrine* for an extensive discussion of the relationship between signs and the senses of seeing and hearing. Augustine 1958 (c. 397 AD), 35ff.
69. Jenson 1978, 4. See also Greenhalgh and Russell 1987.
70. Storrar 1990, 118.
71. Babin 1991, 146.
72. Sue Page's *Away With Words* explores the theme of this paragraph in greater detail. Page 1998.
73. See Wells 1998, 73–7: 'Embodying the Story'.
74. Waznak 1996, 143.
75. This is often spoken of as building a bridge. For a critique of the 'Bridge Metaphor' see Quicke 1997, 9–21. Quicke argues: 'I believe that it is essential that we further develop the rather static, partial and apparently straightforward model of that bridge. It is not enough to visualise preaching as an arc which goes through 180 degrees with the Bible on one side, the listeners at the other side, and the preacher making the connection.' Instead he places the preacher and listeners in a 'dynamic cycle' which 'powers 360 degrees back to God'. 17.

CHAPTER 10

Talking Pictures

In the opening chapter we asked the question: How do you communicate orally and effectively in a society where a whole range of audio-visual stimuli competes for your congregation or audience's attention? From this question a line of argument has developed based upon explorations in a variety of fields: homiletics; radio history, theory and practice; music videos; British and American religious radio broadcasting; and communication theology. We have seen that preachers can learn both positively and negatively from the practices of religious radio broadcasters. By way of conclusion I will elucidate and develop some of these lessons.

Before clarifying these insights, let us briefly recapitulate the thrust of the argument to this point. Our rapidly evolving communicative environment has contributed to a crisis in preaching. In the midst of today's Babel of electronic audio-visual stimuli, the prognosis for preaching looks uncertain. We identified recent homiletical responses to this crisis. These included developing a multi-perspectival approach to movement in sermons, a conversational style of discourse and a form of speech that imaginatively engages all the senses. Whilst writers in homiletics have drawn upon the language and forms of television and film to make such points, the language and forms of radio have generally been ignored. This is surprising, since preaching has more obvious parallels with speech radio than with either film or television, for at the heart of both preaching and speech radio is the spoken word. It is such a lacuna that this book seeks to fill.

We focused next on the world of radio, and on speech radio

in particular. Radio has experienced a crisis. Yet, to many commentators' surprise, in spite of the emergence of television, it has not only survived, but also in many areas prospered. In the course of its renaissance, radio has seen a number of transformations in its form and content. Technological developments have changed radio from being a largely communal activity with listeners seated in family groups around the radio set, into a portable, individualistic and privatised activity. Radio broadcasters' ability to adapt to new forms of orality and discourse has contributed to radio's survival. More specifically, a significant weapon in the radio broadcaster's armoury has been the ability to fire the listeners' imagination with pictorial language. 'Radio is particularly evocative', writes Robert Runcie, 'since the absence of images gives space for listeners to form and develop their own.'[1] This remains, even today, in a televisually dominated culture, one of the enduring qualities of radio. Ronald Falconer, a highly experienced Scottish religious broadcaster, put the point well when he argued over twenty years ago that:

> In radio we make our own pictures; on television they are made for us by another ... Whatever the radio programme, whether drama, documentary or act of worship, we are in a more active state, mentally, than when we watch its television equivalent.[2]

Part of the power of pictorial language is its ability to engage the imagination, and so motivate the listener to collaborate 'as an active participant'.[3] Preaching which employs this approach and allows listeners to make their own pictures, has the potential to involve listeners in a more dynamic mental activity. By contrast watching the television or a film demands less 'active' imaginative participation.

To explore these claims and examine in detail the power of the spoken word, case studies of religious radio broadcasters were analysed in the second part of this book. On the basis of the large listening figure estimates for Lewis and Wright, it is clear that both broadcasters must have connected in some way with their listeners in the 1940s. With the help of radio, both strode beyond the boundaries of their own discursive communities. This was partly facilitated by their use of pictorial language. In different ways they employed a range of pictorial language: representational, impressionistic and metaphorical.

We saw that Blue and Tilby, religious broadcasters of the 1990s, similarly employ a range of pictorial language: representational, impressionistic and metaphorical. Like their broadcasting predecessors, they used pictorial language in differing but effective ways. First, they use it iconoclastically to counter stereotypes and misunderstandings. Secondly, they use it to aid in the critical interpretation of our world. Thirdly, they use it iconographically to try to make abstract theology accessible, to create alternative worlds, to add colour to their narrative, and thereby to engage the visual imagination of their listeners. At times they even use pictorial language multi-sensorially, something that has the potential to build a connection or bridge between the broadcasters' theologically informed world-views and many of the listeners' more secular modes of discourse.

These radio broadcasters' use of visual, active and concrete pictorial language is worth emulating by preachers seeking to learn from broadcasting practice. Of course pictorial language is not the only technique employed by Tilby and Blue. Rather it works in conjunction with other devices, such as storytelling, which they use as they attempt to develop their listeners' fields of discourse, realms of meaning, horizons of faith and range of actions.

Religious radio broadcasters may have widely differing aims and methods. We considered a sample of American radio preachers and saw how particular oral signals can become obstacles, even barriers, for listeners outside the speaker's own discursive community. A diverse range of primary source material showed how some preachers run the risk of becoming trapped within a discursive ghetto. Having said this, such radio preachers may also have positive insights to offer preachers, such as the possibilities and risks of using emotion in preaching, and of being liberated from formal styles of speaking.

What of the theological foundations for the overall argument? A theology of pictorial and experiential language must take seriously our transformed discursive situation and the Johannine understanding of the incarnation as the Word becoming flesh.[4] On the basis of a critical reading of the work of

Willimon, Ellul and Ong, and on the basis of further reflection on the empirical data in the earlier chapters, I argued that the theological principles of 'translation' and 'embodiment' are particularly significant for the purpose of this book. The Word 'translates' into flesh and is thus embodied.

Stanley Grenz argues that the task of Christ's disciples 'is to embody and articulate the never-changing encounter with the triune God'.[5] Notice how he links the words 'embody' and 'articulate'. A theology of pictorial and experiential language should seek to bring together embodiment and articulation. The nature of Christian discourse itself requires us to make the connection between practice and proclamation, between life and words.

Preachers are involved in a process of translation, articulation and embodiment.[6] Moreover, on the grounds that the Word was embodied in the person of Jesus Christ, it was suggested that God communicates not simply via the sense of hearing, but also through the other senses. If this is the case, then a multi-sensory approach to pictorial language would do more justice not only to the empirical data, but also to the theological foundations explored in the last part of the book.

We have teased out a number of nuanced issues which face preachers and which lie behind the question of how to communicate orally and effectively in a society where audio-visual stimuli compete for audiences' attention. First, how can preachers fulfil their calling and at the same time adapt to a rapidly evolving communicative environment? Secondly, how can preachers modify and translate their discourse, without compromising its content, so as to connect with their listeners? Thirdly, how can preachers inculturate their discourse in such a way that it has the potential to communicate in spite of the prevailing electronic audio-visual media? In seeking to answer these questions preachers clearly have much to learn from the ways in which religious radio broadcasters have attempted to adapt, translate and inculturate their messages in a multi-media age.

Can we go further? Does the data furnished by this book enable us to draw any more specific conclusions that could conceivably aid modern preachers in their task? Do the earlier discussions suggest, at least in general terms, ways in which the quality and effectiveness of preaching might be enhanced? Conclusions have to be drawn with some caution. Communicative situations are by their very nature subject to dynamic change and transformation. Nevertheless, on the basis of the previous chapters four single imperatives emerge: listen, picture, translate and edit.

Listen

The data strongly indicates the importance of preachers *listening* carefully to the cultural and communicative context outside their own discursive community, as well as to the biblical traditions, the concerns of their audience and the musicality of their speech. David Schlafer contends that: 'Listening is more fundamental than speaking in the activity of preaching, so the most important task for any preacher is to become a good listener.'[7] Certain religious broadcasters, such as some of the American radio preachers considered earlier, appear to be listening to the interpretation of biblical traditions only from within their own discursive communities. The result is a form of discourse that excludes outsiders. This limited listening leads to a closed discursive style, unlikely to succeed in holding listeners' attention.

Listening also involves being sensitive to the appropriateness and musicality of particular words. 'The sounds of the language', suggests Camery-Hoggart, 'can intensify the visual images that the reader [and listener] is able to construct'.[8] Robin Meyers speaks of shopping for words, hunting for the 'plumpest and ripest words, thumping' them against the 'ear and *listening* for the sound quality. What is soft or bruised' should be 'put back', and the discerning preacher should dig down, and 'find something fresher',[9] and therefore more resonant with their message. C. S. Lewis demonstrated this skill in a number of his wartime radio talks. For example, in the first of his *Four Talks on Love*,[10] he discusses *Storge*, which he translates as 'affection' – the humblest of the loves:

> To produce *storge* in public is like getting your household furniture

> out for a move. It was all right in its native place, but it looks tawdry out of doors. It lives with humble, undressed, private things: The thump of a drowsy dog's tail on the kitchen floor. The sound of a sewing machine. Easy laughter and easy tears on some shrewd and wrinkled old face. A toy left on the lawn . . . It's to our emotions what soft slippers, and an easy almost worn chair and worn out old clothes are to our body.[11]

Notice how a word like 'thump' acts onomatopoeically, and how Lewis refers to the particular 'sound of a sewing machine'. 'Tawdry', 'drowsy' and 'soft slippers' combine precision with sound quality. He appeals not only to the visual imagination, but also to the aural and tactile sensitivities, both by his choice of words and by his reference to commonly heard sounds and feelings. Preachers too would do well to listen to the music of the words they use and hear.

Similarly it is invaluable, if a little painful, to listen back critically to an audio recording of a sermon, a lecture or other form of our own public discourse. If preaching, have I allowed the text to surprise me? How have I communicated this surprise? Are there any distracting verbal or visual idiosyncrasies? How easy is it to follow? How far do my language and approach enable listeners to participate in a co-creative act of communication? What Shingler and Wieringa believe applies to radio broadcasters also applies to preachers: 'Repetition, sign-posting and simplicity can all be used to counter the listener's propensity toward confusion, inattention and forgetfulness.'[12]

We can go further than this, and listen in our imaginations to the sound environment of specific biblical texts. Consider, for example, such an approach to the story of the paralysed man being lowered through the roof in Mark 2:1–12. Assuming a critical and thoughtful reading of the text, a preacher could then imagine himself or herself to be radio reporter or producer.[13] Questions we could consider include: What sounds would my microphone pick up? Are there any background noises? Which voices stand out? What sounds do I hear as the roof is being opened? How loud are the grumbling scribes or the healing words of Jesus? How noisy is the crowd response to the healing? Is the paralytic silent as he walks out in front of the crowd? An imaginative leap into the soundscape of the text can provide speakers and listeners with fresh insights into well-known stories.

Such textual listening combined with careful listening to our communicative setting will prevent speakers retreating into 'the language and sounds of Zion'. Instead, in the words of Buttrick, preachers must 'search the language of human conversation and, once more, find images and metaphors to proclaim the gospel'.[14] This act of searching will begin with listening to the form and content of everyday spoken language. Lionel Blue, and in a different context Gregg Thomas, are good examples of broadcasters who listen attentively to everyday language and employ it. We find a strong precedence for such an approach in the roots of Christianity. Edward Markquart claims:

> If you could have tuned Jesus in on the radio, you would *not* have known he was a preacher by the sounds of his religious tones or by his phrasing of biblical clichés. His language was fresh, secular, and part of the world in which he lived.[15]

Listening to some of the radio preachers discussed and even to certain *Thought for the Day* contributors not considered in this book, it is hard to miss the distinctly 'religious drones' of their speech. By contrast broadcasters such as Tilby and Blue often demonstrate a 'fresh' form of discourse, rooted in careful listening. A renewed orality can contribute to an ideal speech situation where speakers have developed a fresh capacity to listen. Canon David Winter, a former head of BBC Religious Broadcasting, agrees: 'Good broadcasters are people who have their ears open all the while and are really noticing, their eyes are open to what's going on.'[16]

Compare, for example, *Papa Don't Preach*, Madonna's song discussed in Chapter 1, with *Swim*, a song released more recently on her *Ray of Light* album. 'While the churches burn their preachers,' she sings, 'We can't carry these sins on our back ... Let the water wash over you ... So that we can begin again ... Wash away all our sins.'[17] Listening carefully and critically to Madonna and other contemporary artists could provide a speaker with a starting point for exploring the theme of forgiveness. Likewise, oral communication can be enriched by the speaker being sensitive to theological questions raised in television programmes such as *Star Trek, The X-Files, Coronation Street* or *Friends.* Popular films, and in many contexts, the Internet, are increasingly common points of reference in a fragmented culture. I am not arguing that such audio-visual texts should set the agenda for the preacher. What I am suggesting, is that listening does not stop at the biblical text. This emphasis upon multi-faceted listening provides further support for those writers on homiletics who encourage preachers to 'exegete their congregations'[18] or 'listen carefully' to those who listen to them.[19] A model of ministry which sees listening to the biblical text as the only role of the preacher is seriously flawed. It is vital to listen not only to the text, but also to the community of faith and the communicative setting. Adopting this listening approach would help make preaching more effective and faithful.[20]

Picture

Connected to the first imperative, listen, is a second one: *picture.* Many of the broadcasters analysed in this book point towards the need to picture both the listeners' concerns and the scene or written text that is being evoked. Wright's graphic description of a lonely gunners' station or Lewis's memorable image of God landing in enemy occupied territory reflects an openness to contemporary scenes, and an attempt to engage their listeners' imagination. Lewis's references, cited above, to 'tawdry furniture' brought outside for a move, or a toy left on the lawn, are examples of vivid and homely verbal pictures, which many in his audience could identify with. Preachers can learn from these concrete, specific and topical word pictures.

Tilby frequently goes beyond homely images and attempts to draw her listeners into a new world:

> We start at 5.00am and find the first shot. Mark [Tully] has to ride by on his camel with the Greek Orthodox monastery of St Catherine in the background, and the light of the sun is beginning to gild the mountains. It's still almost dark, so we have to wait for light to hit

> the valley. The first sequence happens without trouble. Now we load the camera, the recorder, the lens boxes, and reflectors onto the camels, and begin the long haul mounted or on foot up to the steps leading to the final ascent. We soon get separated. I decide to walk. It's about half past seven and the most glorious golden light is tipping the edge of the camel path as the sun rises over the mountains. Every figure in our party is transfigured as they wind in and out of its beams. The Orthodox speak of the uncreated light of God, the vision that comes from the desert, and this is the nearest thing I have ever seen to that sheer, pure, beauty. The camera is in its box, securely tied to its camel. Why didn't I do the fullest possible recce of this journey at the right time of day? The glory is here and now and I'm missing it . . .[21]

This vivid story, like much of Tilby's pictorial language, has a great deal to teach preachers. I am struck by her ability to recreate a scene with word pictures. The 'glorious golden' light 'gilds' the mountains and 'tips the edge of the camel path'. Consider how this graphic description provides the foundations for a memorable story. Pictorial language is a central building block for transforming this scene from a two-dimensional diary entry into a three-dimensional portrayal. As mentioned above, preachers should note that Tilby employs other devices to bring the story to life: active verbs, short sentences balanced with longer phrases and first person direct speech: 'Why didn't I . . .?'

Tilby does not overdescribe. Her listeners are not told about the colour or smell of the camels, the size of the camera boxes or the shape of the mountains. She makes sparse use of adjectives, leaving room for her listeners to develop the scene in their own imaginations. As Buttrick argues: 'adjectives clutter oral language and prevent understanding'.[22] Nouns and verbs dominate the above extract. As Richard Eslinger claims, 'adjectives do not work the same way in literary and in homiletic contexts', and in preaching, 'the effective tools of coloration and description are [generally] nouns and verbs'.[23] Sparsity of description combined with reliance upon nouns and verbs will provide conditions conducive to listeners building the picture in their imaginations, and thereby taking a more active part in the communication process.[24]

Tilby's description of their early-morning ascent up Mount Sinai serves as a useful reminder both of these homiletical insights and of the lessons highlighted in the case studies. Other broadcasters such as Lionel Blue, Ronald Selby Wright and Garrison Keillor demonstrate different stylistic characteristics, which reflect their own personalities, and reveal an eye and an ear sensitive to what is happening around them. These qualities are also found in the broadcasting of journalists such as Ed Murrow, Richard Dimbleby and more recently, Alistair Cooke and Fergal Keane. Preachers can learn from their use of concrete, active and specific images. We can also learn from the ways in which pictorial language is used in a variety of fashions: metaphorically, illustratively or representationally. In the Sinai extract, pictorial language is integrated within a single narrative, is delivered in a conversational style of speech and functions parabolically.

Preachers need to develop a sensitive eye both for what they see around them and for what they 'see' in the text. For example, a preacher seeking to illuminate the Passion can draw not only from their own 'Good Friday' and 'Easter Sunday' experiences, but also upon the biblical imagery of the 'broken bread, the thirty silver coins, the roar of the crowd, the scourge, the crown of thorns, the Cross and the empty tomb at dawn'.[25] Similarly, the parables are rich in verbal imagery. Take a selection of Lukan parables. They graphically portray a man who builds his house on rock (Luke 6:48–9), a sower who broadcasts his seed (Luke 8:5–8), and a father who runs, embraces and kisses his profligate son (Luke 15:20). Active images are woven together imaginatively to create unforgettable stories. Preachers who employ pictorial language parabolically stand in the tradition of the Galilean storyteller. As Cardinal Martini argues, when Jesus 'wanted to reveal the mysteries of the Kingdom – realities beyond our inspection – he told parables and used the language of images'.[26] The parabolic word, the language of images and the deceptively simple imperative: 'picture', has a strong biblical precedent.

In the words of James Jones preachers need to describe situations 'visually' and:

> Describe what it feels like, what it looks like, and as you describe it so

people are seeing it in their mind's eye, and they are engaged, in the same way that Jesus told parables. I contrast the abstract concept and the concrete image ... we are forever reducing theology to abstract concepts and then we wonder why we don't communicate with people. What we've got to do is to rediscover the rabbinical way, which is to tell a story and describe a situation, and from that description people can then intuit and deduce the principle or the moral that you're wanting to explore.[27]

I am arguing for a rediscovery or renewal in a method of preaching which draws primarily not upon abstract concepts, but upon concrete pictorial language.[28] This theme runs through the text here like a silver thread. Many radio broadcasters consider it to be a significant tool. These discussions are a reminder to preachers to use pictorial language in their preaching.[29] As I suggested in the second chapter there are inevitably dangers with overusing such a tool.[30] Nevertheless, in a context where a scholar such as Jacques Ellul perceives 'sight to be triumphant', pictorial language may contribute towards an 'understandable language' and 'open language that is not stereotyped'.[31] For preachers this open form of dialogical language should widen to include multi-sensory discourse.

Translate

A further imperative for preachers should be added to listen and picture: *translate*. Public speech needs to be translated into accessible, conversational and vivid terms.[32] As indicated in the last chapter, there is considerable precedent for translation which both enlivens ancient forms of expression and transforms literary texts into oral speech:

The founders of Christianity used the languages and idioms of the people: not a sacred or holy language, nor a learned language, nor did they encourage an ecstatic language. The languages and idioms used by the Christians were those of the wide publics of their time and place. The Christians renewed those in various ways and modified their vocabularies, but there was no flight from the vernacular ... Jesus taught in the living dialect of his time, Aramaic,

> not in the language of the Scripture, Hebrew. The early Church had no hesitation in translating his words into Greek or into the language of whatever population was evangelized: Latin, Syriac, Coptic, etc.[33]

My argument stands in the tradition of those that renewed, modified, and translated their discourse for their listeners' benefit.[34] Likewise, preachers should be prepared to translate biblical terms or narratives into a modern pictorial or multi-sensory guise.[35]

A modern retelling of the parable of the good Samaritan provides a useful insight into how one form of translation could work in a sermon. For example, an Irish setting might make this tale more accessible, and renew some of its original force for the late 1990s. I will use Eugene Lowry's fivefold narrative structure for preaching.[36] First, 'upset the equilibrium': a British soldier lies in a pool of blood on a road into Belfast: he has been shot. Secondly, 'analyse the discrepancy': an Orange-Order Unionist on his way to the local peace talks approaches but then ignores him. A Catholic priest trips over him by mistake, and then darts to the other side of the road. Thirdly, 'disclose the clue to resolution': an IRA member in tattered old jeans kneels beside the soldier. She thinks of her own brother, shot by a British soldier. Fourthly, 'experience the gospel': she wipes the blood off his face, heaves him into her car, and takes him to the hospital. Finally, and perhaps most problematical in this interpretation, 'anticipate the consequences': a Protestant journalist writes up the story. His headline is: 'The Road to Peace'. This kind of attempt to translate a well-known parable into a contemporary form relies upon a tight narrative structure and aptly chosen pictorial language.

Equally important is sensitivity to the listeners' context. In the same way that the parable of the good Samaritan would have provoked different responses amongst Samaritan, Jewish and Gentile listeners, so this translation into an Irish setting would carry different meanings for members of the Orange Order, Sinn Fein or the British Army. The obvious, but easily overlooked, point is that the listeners' own situations will inevitably influence how they hear, interpret and respond to this story. It may be that for certain audiences, outside the Irish situation or after the Good Friday agreement, such a translation would not effectively replicate the original force of the parable. If this is the case, then listeners are more likely to step back and become mere spectators rather than participants in the parable. The result can be a simple nod of the head, rather than a transformed imagination, lifestyle or world-view. So one valuable goal for preachers is, by imaginative translation, to seek characterisations and settings that will resonate with their hearers and with the original impact of the narrative.[37] This form of translation is more likely to invite listeners to move beyond being observers to becoming actors in the drama being played out for them.

Such a retelling or translation would also be more effective if kept free of 'religious language'.[38] James Jones is another example of a broadcaster and preacher who sees the importance of translating his message into appropriate and visual terms: 'I'm very, very conscious of not using religious language. I am always alert to try and phrase something in language that is contemporary and fresh ... I try and speak in clean, crisp, vivid pictures.'[39]

One of my criticisms of some of the radio preachers discussed earlier is that they have not translated their message into a contemporary or accessible guise. They have failed to recognise the importance of moving beyond their own familiar discursive patterns and the terms that they view as appropriate for Christian discourse.[40] Amos Wilder believes that:

> early Christian speech favoured no particular language. We can extend this to say that it offers no precedents for what is sometimes spoken of as the 'language of Zion', that is, a particular vocabulary and imagery thought of as sacred or pious.[41]

Many of the radio preachers of Chapter 8 are trapped within the 'language of Zion'. Preachers can learn from this negative example and avoid sliding into linguistic ghettos. Instead the challenge is to speak in terms that will engage not simply core members of their congregations, but also fringe members and outsiders.[42]

It is not just a question of style. Translation is an interpretative and creative act, which involves more complex and substantive issues than merely communicative techniques. Undoubtedly imaginative preachers and religious broadcasters will use appropriate pictorial and multi-sensory language to enliven what they have to say, to translate it into more intelligible terms for those inhabiting pluralist worlds of discourse, and to undermine or challenge previously fixed opinions. But not any picture, any translation will do. An authentic bridge between the worlds of the sacred text and our contemporary society will have to be true to both.[43] The critiques by Willimon and Newbigin indicate the dangers of reductionism and attenuation of the Christian story. A whole area of further research opens up:[44] just what are the appropriate pictures, models and metaphors that will reliably do this bridging work in our audio-visual culture?

Edit

Alongside and related to our imperatives listen, picture and translate stands a fourth: *edit.* Tilby demonstrates clearly the effectiveness of ruthlessly editing any unnecessary or unclear section, expression or word. She shows in her final scripts how a good broadcast or sermon is improved by careful editing and by being 'economical with words'.[45] For preachers who rely on abbreviated notes or no notes at all, this imperative remains equally relevant. The gift of spontaneity can all too easily become the curse of self-indulgent meandering. Nowhere is there more truth in the adage: 'less is more'. David Coomes supports this assertion. He finds that most 'sermons go on too long' and have too many points.[46] Tilby's sparse but refined scripts and Blue's conversational but disciplined stories provide useful models. Their carefully crafted, yet apparently spontaneous broadcasting is a good example of what Ong describes as 'secondary orality'. There is much to learn from this form of discourse, which news reporters such as Ed Murrow and Richard Dimbleby, presenters such as Garrison Keillor and religious broadcasters such as Wright, Lewis, Tilby and Blue use. One way of communicating effectively is to edit the sermon script or outline so that it allows variations in pace, pitch, tone, images and the texture of the presentation.[47] The editing process can be time-consuming and painful, but it invariably leads to a vastly more effective result. Editing should not be so severe, however, that the apparently spontaneous and oral quality of the sermon is lost.[48] Think of it not as a piece of writing, but as a piece of oral communication.

The emphasis upon using pictorial or multi-sensory language does not mean that I am suggesting that all other forms of discourse should be edited out.[49] Like Lewis's broadcasts there is a place for critical reasoning, a 'Thought for the Week', in preaching. Just as there is a wide range of literary genres within the Bible,[50] and a wide range of genres within radio broadcasting,[51] so preachers should employ a range of preaching forms.[52] Preachers need to edit themselves so that they do not convey the impression through their habitual preaching style, structure or forms that Christianity is entirely built upon pictorial constructs and has no place for sustained arguments about complex issues.[53] In other words, preachers who are persuaded by the argument of *Visually Speaking* should still vary the structural form and linguistic content of their sermons so that an implicit theological message is not conveyed by the consistent use of one particular sermonic form or structure.

I have argued that my data show the importance of first, listening to the text, the audience, and the wider communicative context; secondly, creating word pictures; thirdly, engaging in the translation process; and fourthly, rigorously editing the discourse. This is not intended to be a comprehensive summation of all the lessons identified for preachers in this book. Others include: adapt to a new communicative environment, oralise in conversational speech, use stories rather than abstract concepts, verbally re-enact textual or personal experiences, recognise that in the Christian story words are not separate from actions. Living in faith, hope and love demands more than simply intellectual assent.

These lessons are all in the four imperatives: listen, picture, translate and edit. As I have shown, elements of the four imperatives may be found in recent homiletic literature.[54] This book has directed attention to these important insights in a new way by drawing on a largely untapped source: religious radio broadcasting. My contention is that preachers can learn both positive and negative lessons from the practice of radio broadcasters, especially in the art of painting pictures with words. Clearly some broadcasters are more successful at this than others. Our changing communicative context demands that we renew our oralising skills, re-emphasise the importance of using fresh and contemporary language and stories, and particularly, that we refine the art of making pictures with words.

If we re-form orality in this way we have the potential to engage not simply the visual imagination, but also the other imaginative senses.[55] We will speak in a way that appeals multi-sensorially not simply to the mind but to the entire person. The result is a form of orality which bridges the word–image divide; it invites the listener to participate more fully in the communication process, and thereby moves listeners away from being overwhelmed by the Babel of audio-visual stimuli, and towards the Pentecost experience of effective communication and transformed living.[56] This renewed form of orality reflects the translation principle and the embodiment principle, which lie at the very heart of Christianity.

Notes

1. Runcie 1986, 17.
2. Falconer 1977, 92.
3. Powell III 1995, 75.
4. Grenz 1996, 174.
5. Ibid., 174.
6. See Long 1988. In his fourth chapter, Long, a former radio announcer emphasises 'The Embodiment of Preaching'. He describes listening to Sunday morning worship on his car radio: 'What I heard almost drove me to the conclusion that services of worship should never, under any circumstances, be broadcast on the radio.' 79.
7. Schlafer 1992, 22. 'The speaking of a sermon arises from listening to all kinds of voices.' 23. See also Morris 1996, 104–8. He argues that: 'one of the essential qualifications of the true preacher, is the ability to listen as well as to speak; indeed, preaching is essentially a listening vocation'. 105.

8. Camery-Hoggart 1995, 137.
9. Meyers 1993, 75.
10. Lewis *Four Talks on Love,* 1970, Tape 1. These talks were recorded in London on 19 and 20 August 1958, and broadcast in parts of the USA. They were seen by certain bishops as too 'frank' for a general American audience. One of Lewis's biographers, George Sayer, was critical in his assessment of these talks: 'The recordings are not an impressive performance. For one thing they are spoken too fast. For another they sound like they are being read. There is little of the admirable broadcasting technique of years before, which made every listener feel personally addressed.' Sayer 1997 (1988), 388. Sayer's critique is fair up to a point. Lewis does, however, slow his delivery down and he attempts to include his listeners by using a number of accessible images in each of these four talks. Lewis used the radio script as a basis for a book: *The Four Loves,* 1960.
11. Ibid., Tape 1. Compare with Lewis 1960, 35–6.
12. Shingler and Wieringa 1998, 84.
13. Compare Wilson's 'movie-making' approach in *The Practice of Preaching,* 1995. He suggests that 'once a responsible, scholarly understanding of the text is assured, the preacher presents that understanding in highly visual and vital ways. Ask, "If I were to make a movie of this text, what decisions would I need to make" (e.g., Is it night? Is there a breeze? Who is present? What are people wearing? Is there something unusual? What sounds are there?) As in a movie, most of these items are background items, those that the camera merely notes in panning; central action and dialogue are what the camera seeks. A few of these incidental details need not distort the determined thrust of the biblical text. Rather, they are an important dimension of effective communication in a multimedia world.' 183.
14. Buttrick 1987, 194. He continues: 'What we cannot do is fall back on stock theological terminology to any great degree. Instead, in our age, we must speak in a language of common image and metaphor, but do so with theological wisdom.' In a more recent book Buttrick goes further, appealing to his readers: 'Let us once more paint pictures of God's future.' Buttrick 1998, 19.
15. Markquart 1985, 178.
16. Winter, Interview 14 September 1995.
17. Madonna 1998.
18. Tinsdale 1997, 56–90.
19. Greene 1997a, 290.

20. This point is also strongly supported by James Jones who explains that as a preacher he has learnt again the importance of 'listening' from doing *Thought for the Day*. 'I think every sermon ought to be a dialogue. The dialogical nature is that you are for ever hearing what people are hearing, and you're thinking "as I say this what will people be saying?" And so your next paragraph has to deal with their "Yes, but..." So there's a real dialogue. A monologue is where you have no consideration for the audience or congregation. A dialogue is where you are, in your imagination, in dialogue with the people. And I think that is also certainly true for *Thought*.' Jones, Interview 1997. For an interesting parallel to this argument see: 'From Monologue to Conversation', Chapter 2 of this book.
21. 'Lost but not forgotten', (final) episode 5 of *The Jesus Diary*, Radio 3, 2–6 December 1996, produced by Norman Winter, written and presented by Angela Tilby. Tilby introduces this story in an intriguing style: 'So I end with a parable of how the camera misses its shot. We were in the right place, at the right time, but we lost the moment. Nevertheless, it is something to know what we missed. The created light we can see, is only a glimmer of the uncreated light we can't see.' She concludes this section by admitting that she finished the day 'in grief for the lost shot of the train of camels caught in daylight'.
22. Buttrick 1987, 192. Buttrick identifies the importance of doing descriptive work without using 'an alarming number of adjectives'.
23. Eslinger 1996, 11. He states: 'multiplying descriptive adjectives within a sermon actually works against its intended purpose'.
24. Meyers writes: 'Our efforts in the pulpit must be more like courtroom sketches than photographs. Leaving the listener with lines to draw and profiles to be sketched is more than desirable – it is the objective.' Meyers 1993, 81.
25. Browne 1984 (1958), 86. 'The Christian religion can never be presented without imagery.' Note how Browne includes the aural sign of the 'roar of the crowd' in his 'imagery'.
26. Martini 1994, 101. 'All religious language is interwoven with symbols, metaphors and images.' See also Hughes and Kysar 1997, 54–73. They suggest: 'the most important reason imagery has become so vital for preaching is that pictorial language engages the imagination and evokes response.' 56.
27. Jones, Interview 1997. He continues: 'In 1 Corinthians 13, St Paul said: "Now we look through a glass darkly". In Greek there is no "darkly" at all: what the Greek says is "Now we see through a glass

or a mirror in images, in enigmas." The Greek word is "enigma": Now we see through enigma, parables, riddles ... the language of Heaven is certainly not abstract concepts. What we have are metaphors, similes, stories, and as communicators we have to rediscover that method.' This emphasis on the enigmatic or indirect nature of communication is echoed by Tinsley 1979, 398–404.

28. This could be summarised as: 'Show don't tell.' See Jacks 1996. 'Show more than you tell.' 72.
29. This reminder can be found in many recent homiletic text books, see, for example: Rueter 1997, especially Chapter 6: 'Making Homilies Visual'; and Chapter 7: 'Making Homilies Oral'. Rueter asserts: 'The [verbal] pictures help preacher and listener see how the theme and its supporting points fit our daily lives.' 63.
30. As Wilson argues: 'Preachers to whom images very readily come will often load their sermons with images. In the worst cases, competing images shift the focus to a new scene or example every sentence or two. Rather than the images serving the central idea of the sermon, the central idea is subverted into serving the images.' Wilson 1995, 254. See also Eslinger 1996, 9. 'Language that serves up images wholesale represents a pitfall, for it leaves little or no time for any single image to serve as a catalyst for conceptual understanding.' James Jones argues that the danger of using concrete images is 'a) that it can be limiting, b) it can be manipulative', Interview 1997.
31. Ellul 1985 (1981), 263. See also Weber 1993, 208. In his conclusion Weber argues that language for preaching should be visual, concrete and accessible.
32. See Day 1998 for a useful exercise for practising translation skills, 90–1.
33. Wilder 1971 (1964), 18–19.
34. Amos Wilder's words in 1964 sound strangely contemporary: 'We hear on all sides about the need for the modernisation of the Christian message, translation of the ancient ideas and images, rediscovery of effective media discourse.' Ibid., 1–2. The attention given to imaginative moves, dialogue, visual stories and plots in preaching represent a significant part of this 'modernisation' process in the field of homiletics in the 1990s. My contention is that pictorial and multi-sensory language can contribute to each of these processes.
35. Henry Mitchell goes further and argues that preachers have an 'obligation to translate all theological ideas into a folk-type

language.' Mitchell 1977, 96ff. See also Steimle's argument that Jesus spoke in the 'language of Canaan' and preachers should follow his example and speak in more 'secular' terms. Steimle, Niedenthal and Rice 1980, 166–7.

36. For Eugene Lowry's approach to sermon structuring see Lowry 1980. See also Chapter 2 of this book.
37. See Long 1989a, especially Chapter 6. Long's underlying argument is that preachers should seek not to copy the form of the parable, but rather seek to regenerate its original impact.
38. One qualification to this argument comes with Eslinger's comment that: 'one of the hermeneutic issues of this new day in preaching is the cost of *translating* an oral text of biblical narrative into a *visual* presentation of sermonic imagery'. See Eslinger 1996, 8. There is a 'cost' or potential pitfall in any act of translation.
39. Jones, Interview 1997.
40. One way of breaking free from over-familiar discursive patterns is by 'imaginative elaboration'. I have borrowed this phrase from Henry Mitchell. Mitchell 1990a, 63–6. He suggests that: 'there is a great need for more vivid but not less valid details, often not given in the Bible or anywhere else. These details help the hearer to be caught up in the experience being narrated, and, as a result, to understand better and be moved to change.' I would suggest that this proposal for 'imaginative elaboration' further supports the case being put forward for pictorial and multi-sensory discourse. This form of translation may lead to what Steiner terms as 'transfiguration', where the imaginative impact may even 'surpass that of the primary text'. Steiner 1984, 105.
41. Wilder 1971 (1964), 20.
42. The precedents for such an action, discussed in the previous chapter, can be supported by a consideration of the preaching of Paul. 'Carrying the strange categories of a Jewish apocalyptic gospel into Hellenistic culture, Paul had to make a decision about how to put the two together. He could have insisted that the culture stop speaking in Greek categories and begin immediately to speak the language of Zion, but this was not his choice ... What Paul did,' affirms Long, 'is to look at the Hellenistic culture through the lens of the gospel, through the frame of the kerygma, and to spot cross-resurrection places where God was at work and then to announce those to his Hellenistic hearers.' Long 1996, 97. Long draws upon the work of Patte 1984.
43. See Dingemans 1996. Dingemans describes 'bridges that connect our world with the world of the bible' as 'analogical bridges'. 45.

He continues: 'How can we bridge our feelings of the year 2000 with the experiences of two thousand years ago? ... Is not our modern, technical, communication-rich world too far remote from the primitive world, including the faith, of the bible?'. 46.

44. It would be an interesting research project, for example, to investigate what modes of translation of the biblical text are most appropriate for preachers or religious broadcasters to draw upon? John Dryden's belief that 'all translation' can be reduced to three categories would provide a useful set of alternatives for such a discussion. He describes the first form of translation as, 'that of metaphase, or turning an author word by word, and line by line, from one language into another ... The second way is that of paraphrase, or translation with latitude, where the author is kept in view by the translator, so as never to be lost, but his words are not so strictly followed as by his sense; and that too is admitted to be amplified, but not altered. The third way is that of imitation, where the translator (if now he has just lost that name) assumes the liberty, not only to vary from the words and sense, but to forsake them both as he sees occasion; and, taking only some general hints from the original, to run divisions on the ground-work, as he pleases.' Dryden 1808 (1680), 11–12.
45. Jones also puts great emphasis on being ruthless, and 'paring down' both *Thought for the Day* scripts and sermons. He admits that one of the things he has learnt from doing *Thought* as a preacher is 'to be economical with words'. I agree with his assertion that: 'Too many preachers are verbose and repetitive.' Jones, Interview 1997.
46. Coomes, Interview 1996. 'I'm not a great sermon-lover at all. I find most sermons, they go on too long, they've got one, two, three points, so there're several thoughts whereas it's best to have just one, developed, and usually they've got an agenda and they're just going to preach it every week in a different guise, whereas the best *Thoughts* are always tackling new things, always tackling them from an imaginative way, a clever way, and are sharp, to the point, and one thought.'
47. Variation of volume, pace and pitch can be heard taken to an extreme and distracting level in the broadcasts of Toby Powers. Repetition is one of the characteristics of an oral culture and is to be found in many of the broadcasts of the radio preachers discussed in Chapter 7. This can initially be mesmerising and then become tedious. For preachers this acts as a reminder of the importance of editing 'unnecessary sections'.

48. See Markquart 1985. Markquart emphasises the importance of developing 'living language' for sermons. 178–9.
49. It is important to re-emphasise a point made on a number of occasions in this book. Pictorial (and multi-sensory) language is but one device amongst a range of techniques employed by the experienced broadcasters considered in this text.
50. See Long 1989a. Long discusses *Preaching and the Literary Forms of the Bible.* Long 1989b.
51. It is important to re-emphasise a point made in Chapter 2 that speech radio is much more than simply 'the art of making pictures with words'. The different genres within speech radio draw on a variety of formats: call-ins, public debates, rolling news, dramas, magazine features, etc.
52. See Killinger 1994 (1985), 50–9. For other lists of different forms see also Craddock 1985, 177; and Long 1989b, 126–30. Long emphasises 'the importance of variety', and asserts that: 'As a matter of practical experience, preachers must guard against gravitating toward a narrow range of sermon patterns. As preachers, we tend to create sermon forms that match our own ways of listening and learning, and therefore we must self-consciously move beyond our own preferred patterns.' 130.
53. Nevertheless, arguments in the New Testament epistles are often supported or enhanced by a well-chosen image. David Schlafer points out how: 'an abstract definition of faith in the eleventh chapter of Hebrews, for example, is immediately fleshed out by a brief retelling of stories about Abel, Enoch, Noah, Abraham, and Sarah, Moses and others. The argument concludes with the breathtaking image in Hebrews 12 of the cloud of witnesses who support us as we run an arduous race.' Schlafer 1992, 64.
54. See, for example, Killinger 1994 (1985).
55. For example, Ed Murrow's evocative description of the 'drip, drip' of a splintered tin of peaches in blitz-damaged London can suggest an image, evoke a sound, and if the sharp edge of the metal and sweet smell of juice were added to the description it could provoke the senses of touch and smell as well. (See Chapter 3 of this book.)
56. This point finds support in Walter Brueggemann's interpretation of Acts 2: 'In Pentecost, when the ideal speech situation emerges, we are granted both ears to hear and tongues to speak.' This comment echoes Habermas's concept of the 'ideal speech situation', and illustrates Brueggemann's belief in 'the fresh capacity to listen' brought about through Pentecost. See Brueggemann 1982, 104.

Bibliography

Abramson, Albert. 1995. 'The Invention of Television', in *Television: An International History*. Anthony Smith, editor. Oxford: Oxford University Press.

Achtemeier, Elizabeth. 1980. *Creative Preaching*. Nashville, TN: Abingdon Press.

Achtemeier, Elizabeth. 1989. *Preaching from the Old Testament*. Louisville, KY: Westminster John Knox Press.

Achtemeier, Elizabeth. 1998. *Preaching Hard Texts from the Old Testament*. Peabody, MA: Hendrickson Publishers.

Achtemeier, Elizabeth. 1998. *Preaching from the Minor Prophets*. Grand Rapids, MI: Eerdmans.

Ackerman, Diane. 1996 (1990). *A Natural History of the Senses*. London: Phoenix.

Adam, Peter. 1996. *Speaking God's Words: A Practical Theology of Preaching*. Leicester: IVP.

Adams, Jay E. 1982. *Preaching With Purpose: The Urgent Task of Homiletics*. Grand Rapids, MI: Zondervan.

Allen, Ronald J. 1992. *Preaching the Topical Sermon*. Louisville, KY: John Knox Press.

Allen, Ronald J. 1995. *The Teaching Sermon*. Nashville, TN: Abingdon Press.

Allen, Ronald J., editor. 1998a. *Patterns of Preaching: A Sermon Sampler*. St Louis, MO: Chalice Press.

Allen, Ronald J. 1998b. *Interpreting the Gospel: An Introduction to Preaching*. St Louis, MO: Chalice Press.

Allen, Ronald J., Barbara S. Blaisdell and Scott B. Johnston.

1997. *Theology for Preaching: Authority, Truth and Knowledge of God in a Postmodern Ethos.* Nashville, TN: Abingdon Press.

Ammerman, Nancy T. 1994. 'Accounting for Christian Fundamentalisms: Social Dynamics and Rhetorical Strategies', in *Accounting for Fundamentalisms: The Dynamic Character of Movements.* Martin E. Marty and R. Scott Appleby, editors. Chicago, IL: University of Chicago Press.

Ang, Ien. 1990. 'The Nature of the Audience', in *Questioning the Media: A Critical Introduction.* John Downing, Ali Mohammadi and Annabelle Sreberny-Mohammadi, editors. London: Sage.

Angell, James W. 1995. *The Romance of Preaching.* Lima, OH: CSS Publishing Company.

Apple, Jacki. 1993. 'The Art of Radio', in *Radiotext(e).* Neil Strauss, editor. New York, NY: Semiotext(e).

Arnheim, Rudolph. 1936. *Radio.* London: Faber & Faber.

Arthur, Chris, editor. 1993. *Religion and the Media.* Cardiff: University of Wales Press.

Aufderheide, Pat. 1986. 'Music Videos: the Look of the Sound', in *Journal of Communication* 36, 57–78.

Augaitis, D., and D. Lander, editors. 1994. *Radio Rethink: art, sound and transmission.* Banff, Alberta: Walter Phillips Gallery.

Augustine. 1961 (c. AD 397). *Confessions.* Translated by R. S. Pine-Coffin. Harmondsworth: Penguin.

Babin, Pierre, with Mercedes Iannone. 1991. *The New Era in Religious Communication.* Minneapolis, MN: Fortress Press.

Bailey, Raymond, editor. 1992. *Hermeneutics for Preaching: Approaches to Contemporary Interpretations of Scripture.* Nashville, TN: Broadman Press.

Baker, Kenneth, editor. 1987. *The Making of a Contemporary Translation: New International Version.* London: Hodder & Stoughton.

Baldwin, Thomas F., D. Stevens McVoy and Charles Steinfield. 1996. *Convergence: Integrating Media, Information and Communication.* London: Sage.

Barnouw, Erik. 1966. *A Tower in Babel: A History of Broadcasting in the United States to 1993.* New York: Oxford University Press.

Barnouw, Erik. 1968. *The Golden Web: A History of Broadcasting in the United States, 1933–1953.* New York, NY: Oxford University Press.

Barnouw, Erik. 1970. *Tube of Plenty: The Evolution of American Television.* New York, NY: Oxford University Press.

Barrett, Andrew C. 1995. 'Public Policy and Radio – A Regulator's View', in *Radio: The Forgotten Medium.* Edward C. Pease and Everetter E. Dennis, editors. London: Transaction Publishers.

Barth, Karl. 1957 (1924). *The Word of God and the Word of Man.* New York, NY: Harper & Brothers.

Barth, Karl. 1963 (1961).*The Preaching of the Gospel.* Philadelphia, PA: Westminster.

Barth, Karl. 1975 (1932). *Church Dogmatics* I, 1. Edinburgh: T & T Clark.

Barth, Karl. 1991. *Homiletics.* Louisville, KY: Westminster: John Knox Press.

Bartlett, David L. 1999. *Between the Bible and the Church: New Methods for Biblical Preaching.* Nashville, TN: Abingdon Press.

Bartow, Charles L. 1980. *The Preaching Moment: A Guide to Sermon Delivery.* Nashville, TN: Abingdon Press.

Bartow, Charles L. 1997. *God's Human Speech: A Practical Theology of Proclamation.* Peabody, MA: Hendrickson Publishers.

Bausch, William J. 1985. *Storytelling: Imagination and Faith.* Mystic, CT: 23rd Public Press.

Beasley-Murray, George R. 1996. *Preaching the Gospel from the Gospels.* Revised edition. Peabody, MA: Hendrickson Publishers.

Bendroth, Margaret Lamberts. 1996. 'Fundamentalism and the Media, 1930–90', in D. A. Stout and J. M. Buddenbaum, *Religion and Mass Media, Audiences and Adaptations.* London: Sage.

Berger, Arthur Asa. 1991. *Media Analysis Techniques.* Revised Edition. London: Sage.

Berger, Arthur Asa. 1992. *Media Research Techniques.* London: Sage.

Berger, John. 1972. *Ways of Seeing.* London: BBC Books; Harmondsworth: Penguin.

Berger, Peter. 1970 (1969). *A Rumour of Angels.* London: Allen Lane–Penguin.

Bergmeier, Horst J. P., and Rainer E. Lotz. 1997. *Hitler's*

Airwaves: The Inside Story of Nazi Broadcasting and Propaganda Swing. New Haven, CT: Yale University Press.

Berland, Jody. 1993. 'Contradicting Media: Toward a Political Phenomenology of Listening', in *Radiotext(e).* Neill Strauss, editor. New York, NY: Semiotext(e).

Berry, Gordon L., and Joy Keiko Asamen. 1993. *Children and Television: Images in a Changing Sociocultural World.* London: Sage.

Best, E. 1988 (1978). *From Text to Sermon: Responsible Use of the New Testament in Preaching.* Second Edition. Edinburgh: T & T Clark.

Biernatzki, W. E. 1996. 'Recent Work on Information/Communication and Secondary Orality', in *Communication Research Trends* 16/3, 17–29.

Biernatzki, W. E. 1997. 'Radio', in *Communication Research Trends* 17/4, 3–29..

Black, James. 1977 (1924). *The Mystery of Preaching.* London: Marshall, Morgan & Scott.

Black, Jay, and Jennings Bryant. 1995 (1983). *Media: Introduction to Communication.* Fourth Edition. Dubuque, IA: Brown & Benchmark.

Black, Kathy. 1996. *A Healing Homiletic: Preaching and Disability.* Nashville, TN: Abingdon Press.

Black, Matthew, and William A. Smalley. 1974. *On Language, Culture, and Religion: in Honor of Eugene A. Nida.* The Hague: Mouton.

Blue, Lionel. 1985a (1979). *A Backdoor to Heaven: An Autobiography.* Revised Edition. London: Fount.

Blue, Lionel. 1985b. *Bright Blue: Rabbi Lionel Blue's Thoughts for the Day.* London: BBC Books.

Blue, Lionel. 1998. *My Affair with Christianity.* London: Hodder & Stoughton.

Bohren, Rudolf. 1963. *Preaching and Community.* Richmond, VA: John Knox Press.

Bond, Stephenson D. 1991. *Interactive Preaching.* St. Louis, MO: CBP Press.

Bonhoeffer, Dietrich. 1959 (1937). *The Cost of Discipleship.* London: SCM Press.

Bonhoeffer, Dietrich. 1971 (1951). *Letters and Papers from Prison.* London: SCM Press.

Bonhoeffer, Dietrich. 1991 (1975). *Wordly Preaching: Lectures on Homiletics.* New York, NY: Crossroad.

Boyer, Paul. 1992. *When Time Shall Be No More: Prophecy – Belief in American Culture.* Cambridge, MA: Harvard University Press.

Boys, Mary C. 1983. 'Parabolic Ways of Teaching', in *Biblical Theology Bulletin* 3/3, 82–9.

Brecht, Bertolt. 1993 (1932). 'The Radio as an Apparatus of Communication', in *Radiotext(e),* Neil Strauss, editor. New York: Semiotext(e). Also in *Brecht on Theatre: The Development of an Aesthetic.* Translated by John Willet, editor. 1978 (1958). London: Eyre Methuen. In the same volume see also Brecht's essay on 'An Example of Pedagogics'.

Brewer, Annie. 1993. *Talk Shows and Hosts on Radio.* Dearborn, MI: Whitefoord.

Briggs, Asa. 1993. 'Christ and the Media: Secularisation, Rationalism, and Sectarianism in the History of British Broadcasting, 1922–1976', in *Secularisation, Rationalism and Sectarianism: Essays in Honour of Bryan R. Wilson.* Eileen Barker, James Beckford and Karel Dobbelarre, editors. Oxford: Clarendon Press.

Briggs, Asa. 1995. *The History of Broadcasting in the United Kingdom* (Volumes I–V). London: Oxford University Press, 1995. (1961–1975).

Briggs, Asa. 1995. *The Birth of Broadcasting, 1896–1927 (Volume I).*

Briggs, Asa. 1995. *The Golden Age of Wireless, 1927–1939 (Volume II).*

Briggs, Asa. 1995. *The War of Words, 1939–1945 (Volume III).*

Briggs, Asa. 1995. *Sound and Vision, 1945–1955 (Volume IV).*

Briggs, Asa. 1995. *Competition, 1955–1974 (Volume V).*

Brindley, David. 1996. *Story, Song and Law: The Craft of Preaching in Today's Church.* Swindon: British and Foreign Bible Society.

Briscoe, Stuart D. 1994. *Fresh Air in the Pulpit: Challenges and Encouragement from a Seasoned Preacher.* Leicester: IVP.

Bromiley, Geoffrey W. 1981. 'Barth's Influence on Jacques Ellul', in *Jacques Ellul: Interpretative Essays.* Clifford Christians and Jay M. Van Hook, editors. Urbana, Chicago, IL and London: University of Illinois Press.

Brooks, Peter. 1983. *Communicating Conviction.* London: Epworth Press.

Brooks, Phillips. 1877. *Lectures on Preaching.* London: Allenson. Republished in 1989 as: *The Joy of Preaching.* Grand Rapids, MI: Kregel Publications.

Brooks, R. T. 1964. *Person to Person.* London: Epworth Press.

Brown, H. C., H. Gordon Clinard, Jesse J. Northcult, and Al Fasol. 1996. *Steps to the Sermon: An Eight-Step Plan for Preaching with Confidence.* Revised edition. Nashville, TN: Broadman and Holman.

Brown, Jack, and Milton Kahn. 1986. *Please Stand By: A History of Radio – Study Guide.* Harold Salisbury, editor. Cyprus, CA: Southern California Consortium; Chicago, IL: Nelson Hall.

Browne, R. E. C. 1984 (1958). *The Ministry of the Word.* London: SCM Press.

Bruce, Steve. 1995. *Religion in Modern Britain.* Oxford: Oxford University Press.

Bruce, Steve. 1996. *Religion in the Modern World.* Oxford University Press.

Brueggemann, Walter J. 1978. *The Prophetic Imagination.* Minneapolis, MN: Fortress Press.

Brueggemann, Walter J. 1982. *Genesis.* Atlanta, GA: John Knox Press.

Brueggemann, Walter J. 1986. *Hopeful Imagination: Prophetic Voices in Exile.* Minneapolis, MN: Fortress Press.

Brueggemann, Walter J. 1989. *Finally Comes the Poet: Daring Speech for Proclamation.* Minneapolis, MN: Fortress Press.

Brueggemann, Walter J. 1993. *The Bible and Postmodern Imagination: Texts Under Negotiation.* London: SCM Press.

Brueggemann, Walter J. 1995. 'Preaching as Reimagination', in *Theology Today* 52/2, 313–29.

Brueggemann, Walter J. 1997a. *Cadences of Home: Preaching among Exiles.* Louisville, KY: Westminster John Knox Press.

Brueggemann, Walter J. 1997b. *Theology of the Old Testament: Testimony, Dispute, Advocacy.* Minneapolis, MN: Fortress Press.

Bryman, Alan, and Robert G. Burgess, editors. 1994. *Analyzing Qualitative Data.* London: Routledge.

Buechner, Fred. 1977. *Telling the Truth, The Gospel as Tragedy, Comedy and Fairy Tale.* San Francisco, CA: Harper and Row.

Bultmann, Rudolf. 1958. *Jesus and the Word.* New York, NY: Charles Scribner's Sons.

Bultmann, Rudolf, *et al.* 1961 (1948). *Kerygma and Myth: A Theological Defense.* Revised Edition. Hans Werner Bartsch, editor. New York, NY: Harper and Row.

Burghardt, Walter J. 1987. *Preaching the Art and the Craft.* Mahwah, NJ: Paulist Press.

Burke, John, editor. 1983. *A New Look at Preaching.* Dublin: Veritas Publications.

Burnett, Ron. 1995. *Cultures of Vision: Images, Media and the Imaginary.* Bloomington and Indianapolis, IA: Indiana University Press.

Buttrick, D. 1987. *Homiletic: Moves and Structures.* Philadelphia, PA: Fortress Press.

Buttrick, D. 1992 (1988). *Preaching Jesus Christ: An Exercise in Homiletic Theology.* Minneapolis, MN: Fortress Press.

Buttrick, D. 1992. *The Mystery and the Passion: A Homiletical Reading of the Gospel Traditions.* Minneapolis, MN: Fortress Press.

Buttrick, D. 1993. 'Preaching to the "Faith" of America', in *Communication and Change in American Religious History.* Leonard I. Sweet, editor. Grand Rapids, MI: Eerdmans.

Buttrick, D. 1994a. 'On Doing Homiletics Today', in *Intersections: Post-Critical Studies in Preaching.* Richard L. Eslinger, editor. Grand Rapids, MI: Eerdmans.

Buttrick, D. 1994b. *A Captive Voice: The Liberation of Preaching.* Louisville, KY: Westminster John Knox Press.

Buttrick, D. 1996. 'Teaching Preaching in a New Century', in *Preaching on the Brink: The Future of Homiletics.* Martha J. Simmons, editor. Nashville, TN: Abingdon Press.

Buttrick, D. 1998. *Preaching the New and the Now.* Louisville, KY: Westminster John Knox Press.

Buttry, Daniel L. 1998. *First-Person Preaching: Bringing New Life to Biblical Stories.* Valley Forge, PA: Judson Press.

Camery-Hoggatt, Jerry. 1995. *Speaking of God: Reading and Preaching the Word of God.* Peabody, MA: Hendrickson Publishers.

Campbell, Charles L. 1997. *Preaching Jesus: New Directions for Homiletics in Hans Frei's Postliberal Theology.* Grand Rapids, MI: Erdmans.

Capon, Robert Farrar. 1998. *The Foolishness of Preaching: Proclaiming the Gospel against the Wisdom of the World.* Grand Rapids, MI: William B. Eerdmans.

Carpenter, Humphrey. 1997 (1978). *The Inklings: C. S. Lewis, J. R. R. Tolkein, Charles Williams and Their Friends.* London: HarperCollins.

Carpenter, Joel. 1983. 'Billy Sunday', in *Christianity in America: A Handbook.* Mark Knoll, *et al.*, editors. Grand Rapids, MI: Eerdmans.

Carpini, Michael X. Delli. 1995. 'Radio's Political Past', in *Radio: The Forgotten Medium.* Edward C. Pease and Everetter E. Dennis, editors. London: Transaction Publishers.

Carr, Wesley. 1990. *Ministry and the Media.* London: SPCK.

Carroll, John T., and James R. Carroll. 1996. *Preaching the Hard Sayings of Jesus.* Peabody, MA: Hendrickson Publishers.

Chapell, Bryan. 1992. *Using Illustrations to Preach with Power.* Grand Rapids, MI: Zondervan.

Chapell, Bryan. 1994. *Christ-Centred Preaching: Redeeming the Expository Sermon.* Grand Rapids, MI: Baker Book House.

Childers, Jana. 1998. *Performing the Word: Preaching as Theatre.* Nashville, TN: Abingdon Press.

Christians, Clifford. 1981. 'Ellul on Solution: An Alternative but No Prophecy', in *Jacques Ellul: Interpretative Essays.* Clifford Christians and Jay M. Van Hook, editors. Urbana, Chicago, IL and London: University of Illinois Press.

Christians, Clifford. 1988. 'Is Ellul Prophetic?', in 'Perspectives on Jacques Ellul', *Media Development.* 35/2, 6–7.

Christians, Clifford. 1997. 'Technology and Triadic Theories of Mediation', in *Rethinking Media, Religion, and Culture.* Stewart M. Hoover and Knut Lundby, editors. London: Sage.

Christopher, Joe R. 1981. *C.S. Lewis.* Boston, MA: Twayne Publishers.

Clark, Neville. 1991. *Preaching in Context.* Bury St Edmunds: Kevin Mayhew Ltd.

Clements, Roy. 1998. 'Expository preaching in a postmodern world', in *Cambridge Papers* 7/3.

Cleverley Ford, D. W. 1995. *Preaching What We Believe.* London: Mowbrays.

Clifford, Nigel. 1994. *Christian Preachers.* Bryntirion, Bridgend, Mid Glamorgan: Evangelical Press of Wales.

Coggan, Donald. 1964 (1945). *The Ministry of the Word.* Revised Edition. London: Lutterworth.

Coggan, Donald. 1996 (1987). *New Day for Preaching: The Sacrament of the Word.* London: SPCK.

Collins, Raymond F. 1996. *Preaching the Epistles.* New York, NY: Paulist Press.

Coomes, David. 1992. *Dorothy L. Sayers: A Careless Rage for Life.* Oxford: Lion Publishing.

Corneck, Graham. 1995. *Fieldwork Diary.* Unpublished project towards MTh at the University of Edinburgh.

Coulter, David. 1997. 'The Church of Scotland Chaplains in the Second World War'. Unpublished PhD Thesis, University of Edinburgh.

Coulthard, Malcolm. 1992. 'The Significance of Intonation in Discourse', in *Advances in Spoken Discourse Analysis.* Malcolm Coulthard, editor. London: Routledge.

Cox, James W. 1993 (1985). *Preaching: A Comprehensive Approach to the Design and Delivery of Sermons.* San Francisco, CA: HarperCollins.

Craddock, F. B. 1978. *Overhearing the Gospel.* Nashville, TN: Abingdon Press.

Craddock, F. B. 1979 (1971). *As One Without Authority.* Nashville, TN: Abingdon Press.

Craddock, F. B. 1985. *Preaching.* Nashville, TN: Abingdon Press.

Craddock, F. B. 1990. 'Inductive Preaching'. Unpublished paper for the Societas Homiletica, Stetson University, August 20–23.

Craft, Charles H. 1991. *Communication Theory for Christian Witness.* Maryknoll, NY: Orbis Books.

Craig, A. C. 1953. *Preaching in a Scientific Age.* London: SCM Press.

Crawford, Evans E., with Thomas H. Troeger. 1995. *The Hum: Call and Response in African American Preaching.* Nashville, TN: Abingdon Press.

Crisell, Andrew. 1994. *Understanding Radio.* Second Edition. London: Routledge.

Crowley, David, and Heyer, Paul. 1995 (1991). *Communication in History: Technology, Culture and Society.* Second Edition. New York, NY: Longmans, Green.

Cunningham, David S. 1990. *Faithful Persuasion: In Aid of a Rhetoric of Christian Theology.* Notre Dame, IN and London: University of Notre Dame Press.

Curran, James, and Michael Gurevitch, editors. 1991. *Mass Media and Society.* London: Edward Arnold.

Curran, James, and Jean Seaton. 1994. *Power Without Responsibility: The Press and Broadcasting in Britain.* Fourth Edition. London: Routledge.

Dahlgren, Peter. 1995. *Television and the Public Sphere: Citizenship, Democracy and the Media.* London: Sage.

Davie, Grace. 1994. *Religion in Britain since 1945: Believing Without Belonging.* Oxford: Basil Blackwell.

Davis, Ellen F. 1995. *Imagination Shaped: Old Testament Preaching in the Anglican Tradition.* Valley Forge, PA: Trinity Press International.

Davis, Henry Grady. 1958. *Design for Preaching.* Philadelphia, PA: Fortress Press.

Davis, Ken. 1991. *Secrets of Dynamic Communication.* Grand Rapids, MI: Zondervan.

Dawn, Marva J. 1995. *Reaching Out without Dumbing Down: A Theology of Worship for the Turn-of-the Century Culture.* Grand Rapids, MI: Eerdmans.

Day, David. 1998. *A Preaching Workbook.* London: SPCK.

Dayan, Daniel, and Elihu Katz. 1992. *Media Events.* Cambridge, MA: Harvard University Press.

De Clerck, Paul. 1992. 'In the Beginning was the Word', in *Studia Liturgica* 22/1, 1–16.

Demaray, Donald E. 1990. *Introduction to Homiletics.* Second Edition. Grand Rapids, MI: Baker Book House.

Denisoff, Serge R. 1988. *Inside MTV.* New Brunswick, NJ: Transaction Books.

Denzin, Norman K. 1995. *The Cinematic Society: The Voyeur's Gaze.* London: Sage.

Dillenberger, John. 1986. *A Theology of Artistic Sensibilities: The Visual Arts and the Church.* London: SCM Press.

Dillistone, F. W. 1956. *Christianity and Communication.* London: Collins.

Dimbleby, J. 1975. *A Biography.* London: Book Club Associates.

Dingemans, Gijsbert D. J. 1996. 'A Hearer in the Pew', in

Preaching as a Theological Task – World, Gospel, Scripture. Thomas G. Long and Edward Farley, editors. Louisville, KY: Westminster John Knox Press.

Dinwiddie, Melville. 1968. *Religion by Radio.* London: Allen & Unwin.

Ditingo, Vincent M. 1995. *The Remaking of Radio.* Boston, MA: Focal Press.

Donovan, Paul. 1997. *All Our Todays: Forty Years of Radio 4's 'Today' Programme.* London: Jonathan Cape.

Dorgan, Howard. 1993. *The Airwaves of Zion: Radio and Religion in Appalachia.* Knoxville, TN: University of Tennessee Press.

Dorsett, Lyle W. 1990. 'Researching C. S. Lewis', in *A Christian for all Christians.* Andrew Walker and James Patrick, editors. London: Hodder & Stoughton.

Dryden, John. 1808 (1680). 'Preface to the Translation of Ovid's Epistles', in *Works,* XII. W. Scott, editor. London: William Miller.

Ducey, Richard V. 1995. 'Riding Radio's Technological Wave', in *Radio: The Forgotten Medium.* Edward C. Pease and Everetter E. Dennis, editors. London: Transaction Publishers.

Duffett, Robert G. 1995. *A Relevant Word: Communicating the Gospel to Seekers.* Valley Forge, PA: Judson Press.

Duke, R. W. 1980. *The Sermon as God's Word: Theologies of Preaching.* Nashville, TN: Abingdon Press.

Dunning, John, 1976. *Tune in Yesterday: The Ultimate Encyclopaedia of Old-Time Radio: 1925–1976.* Englewood Cliffs, NJ: Prentice-Hall.

Durber, S., and H. Walton, editors. 1994. *Silence in Heaven: a book of women's preaching.* London: SCM.

Dyer, Richard, 1993. *The Matter of Images: Essays on Representations.* London: Routledge.

Dyson, F. 1994. 'The genealogy of the radio voice', in *Radio Rethink: art, sound and transmission.* D. Augaitis and D. Lander, editors. Canada: Walter Phillips Gallery.

Editorial. 1977. 'Preaching Today', in *Expository Times* 88: 237–8.

Edwards, Paul. 1994. *The Practical Preacher.* Collegeville, MN: Liturgical Press.

Eggold, Henry J. 1980. *Preaching is Dialogue: A Concise Introduction to Homiletics.* Grand Rapids, MI: Baker Book House.

Eilers, Franz-Josef. 1992. *Communication between Cultures: An Introduction to Intercultural Communication.* Manila, Philippines: Divine Word Publications.

Eilers, Franz-Josef. 1993. *Church and Social Communication.* Manila, Philippines: Logos Publications.

Eilers, Franz-Josef. 1994. *Communicating in Community: An Introduction to Social Communication.* Manila, Philippines: Divine Word Publications.

Eisenstein, Elizabeth L. 1993 (1983). *The Printing Revolution in Early Modern History.* Canto Edition. Cambridge: Cambridge University Press.

Eldridge, John. 1993. *Getting the Message: News, Truth and Power.* London: Routledge.

Eliade, M. 1987. *The Encyclopaedia of Religion,* VI. New York, NY: Macmillan.

Elley, Derek, editor. 1994. *Variety Movie Guide.* London: Hamlyn.

Ellul, Jacques. 1951 (1947). *The Presence of the Kingdom.* London: SCM Press.

Ellul, Jacques. 1964 (1954). *The Technological Society.* New York, NY: Knopf.

Ellul, Jacques. 1973a (1962). *Propaganda: The Formation of Men's Attitudes.* New York, NY: Random House.

Ellul, Jacques. 1973b (1972). *Hope in Time of Abandonment.* New York, NY: Seabury.

Ellul, Jacques. 1976. *The Ethics of Freedom.* Grand Rapids, MI: Eerdmans.

Ellul, Jacques. 1980 (1977). *The Technological System.* New York, NY: Continuum.

Ellul, Jacques. 1981. 'On Dialectic', in *Jacques Ellul: Interpretative Essays.* Clifford Christians and Jay M. Van Hook, editors. Urbana, Chicago, IL and London: University of Illinois Press.

Ellul, Jacques. 1985 (1981). *The Humiliation of the Word.* Grand Rapids, MI: Eerdmans.

Ellul, Jacques. 1988. 'Some thoughts on the responsibility of new communication media', in 'Perspectives on Jacques Ellul', *Media Development,* 35/2, 3–5.

Ellul, Jacques. 1990 (1988). *The Technological Bluff.* Grand Rapids, MI: Eerdmans.

Elvy, Peter. 1995. 'Broadcasting Evangelical Christianity: A Critical Comparison of Britain and Hungary, 1989–1993'. Unpublished PhD Thesis, University of Edinburgh.

Engelman, Ralph. 1996. *Public Radio and Television in America: A Political History.* London: Sage.

English, Donald. 1996. *An Evangelical Theology of Preaching.* Nashville, TN: Abingdon Press.

Eslinger, Richard L. 1987. *A New Hearing: Living Options in Homiletic Method.* Nashville, TN: Abingdon Press.

Eslinger, Richard L., editor. 1994. *Intersections: Post-Critical Studies in Preaching.* Grand Rapids, MI: Eerdmans.

Eslinger, Richard L. 1995. *Narrative and Imagination: Preaching the Worlds that Shape Us.* Minneapolis, MN: Fortress Press.

Eslinger, Richard L. 1996. *Pitfalls in Preaching.* Grand Rapids, MI: Eerdmans.

Evans, Elwyn. 1977. *Radio: A Guide to Broadcasting Techniques.* London: Barrie & Jenkins.

Fairclough, Norman. 1995. *Media Discourse.* London: Edward Arnold.

Falconer, Ronald. 1977. *Message, Media and Mission.* Edinburgh: The St Andrew Press.

Fasching, Darrell J. 1988a. 'The Liberating Paradox of the Word', in 'Perspectives on Jacques Ellul', *Media Development,* 35/2, 8–11.

Fasching, Darrell J. 1988b. *The Thought of Jacques Ellul: A Systematic Exposition.* Toronto Studies in Theology, 7. Lewiston, NY: Edwin Mellen Press.

Farrell, Thomas J. 1991. 'An Overview of Walter J. Ong's Work', in *Media, Consciousness, and Culture.* Bruce E. Gronbeck, *et al.,* editors. London: Sage.

Farris, Stephen. 1998. *Preaching That Matters: The Bible and Our Lives.* Louisville, KY: Westminster John Knox Press.

Feldman, Tony. 1997. *Introduction to Digital Media.* London: Routledge.

Finnegan, Ruth. 1992. *Oral Traditions and the Verbal Arts: A Guide to Research Practices.* London: Routledge.

Fiske, John. 1990. *Introduction to Communication Studies.* Second Edition. London: Routledge.

Fiske, John, and John Hartley. 1978. *Reading Television.* London and New York, NY: Methuen.

Flichy, Patrice. 1995. *Dynamics of Modern Communication: The Shaping and Impact of Communication Technologies.* London: Sage.

Foley, John Miles, editor. 1987. 'A Festschrift for Walter J. Ong', in *Oral Tradition* 2.

Foot, M. R. D., and J. M. Langley. 1979. *MI9.* London: Bodley Head.

Forbes, James. 1989. *The Holy Spirit and Preaching.* Nashville, TN: Abingdon Press.

Ford, David. 1995. 'Constructing a Public Theology', in *Dare We Speak of God in Public?* Frances Young, editor. London: Mowbrays.

Ford, David, editor. 1997. *The Modern Theologians: An introduction to Christian Theology in the twentieth century.* Second Edition. Oxford: Blackwell Publishers.

Fornatale, Peter, and Joshua E. Mills. 1980. *Radio in the Television Age.* Woodstock, NY: Overlook Press.

Frank, Anne, 1939–45. *The Diary of Anne Frank: The Critical Edition.* David Barnouw and Gerrold van der Stroom, editors. New York, NY: Doubleday. 1989 (1986).

Freire, Paulo. 1971. *Pedagogy of the Oppressed.* New York, NY: Herder & Herder.

Fuller, Reginald H. 1981. *The Use of the Bible in Preaching.* London: Bible Reading Fellowship.

Funk, Robert W. 1982. *Parables and Presence: Forms of the New Testament Tradition.* Philadelphia, PA: Fortress Press.

Fyall, Robert. 1997. *Preaching Old Testament Narrative.* Cambridge: Grove Books.

Gadamer, Hans-Georg. 1989 (1960). *Truth and Method.* Second Revised Edition. New York, NY: Continuum.

Gaffney, P. D. 1994. *The Prophet's Pulpit: Islamic Preaching in Contemporary Egypt.* Berkeley, CA and London: University of California Press.

Galli, Mark, and Craig Brian Larson. 1994. *Preaching that Connects: Using the Techniques of Journalists to Add Impact to Your Sermons.* Grand Rapids, MI: Zondervan.

Garmonsway, G. M., compiler. 1969. *The Penguin English Dictionary*. Second Edition. Harmondsworth: Penguin.

Garner, Ken. 1995. 'Reading RAJAR: Making Sense of Radio Ratings', in *Media Education Journal* 19, 'Festivals and Audiences Issue', Winter, 6–9.

Garrett, Graeme. 1980. '"My brother Esau is an Hairy Man": An encounter between Comedian and the Preacher', in *Scottish Journal of Theology* 33/3, 239–56.

Garrison, Webb B. 1960. *Creative Imagination in Preaching*. Nashville, TN: Abingdon Press.

Gauntlett, David. 1995. *Moving Experiences: Understanding Television's Influences and Effects*. Academia Research Monograph, 13. London: John Libbey.

Gay, Paul du, Stuart Hall, Linda Janes, Hugh Mackay and Keith Negus. 1997. *Doing Cultural Studies: The Story of the Sony Walkman*. London: Routledge.

Gilder, George. 1990. *Life After Television: The Coming Transformation of Media and American Life*. Revised Edition. New York, NY: W. W. Norton.

Gillard, Frank. 1964. *Sound Radio in the Television Age*. BBC Lunchtime Lectures, second series, no. 6.

Gilmore, Alec. 1996. *Preaching as Theatre*. London: SCM Press.

Girard, Bruce, editor. 1992. *A Passion for Radio: Radio Waves and Community*. Montreal and New York, NY: Black Rose Books.

Gledhill, Ruth, editor. 1995. *The Times Book of Best Sermons*. London: Cassell.

Gledhill, Ruth, editor. 1996. *The Times Best Sermons of 1996*. London: Cassell.

Gledhill, Ruth, editor. 1997. *The Times Best Sermons for 1998*. London: Cassell.

Gledhill, Ruth, editor. 1999. *The Fourth Times Book of Best Sermons*. London: Cassell.

Goddard, Andrew. 1995. 'Obituary: Jacques Ellul (1912–1994)' in *Studies in Christian Ethics*, 9/1, 140–53.

Goethals, Gregor. 1981. *The TV Ritual: Worship at the Video Altar*. Boston, MA: Beacon Press.

Goethals, Gregor. 1990. *The Electronic Golden Calf: Images,*

Religion and the Making of Meaning. Cambridge, MA: Cowley Publications.

Goffman, Erving. 1981. *Forms of Talk.* Philadelphia, PA: University of Pennsylvania Press.

Golby, Michael, Jane Greenwald and Ruth West, editors. 1975. *Curriculum Design.* London: Croom Helm.

Gonzalez, Justo L., and Catherine G. Gonzalez. 1980. *Liberation Preaching: The Pulpit and the Oppressed.* Nashville, TN: Abingdon Press.

Gowan, Donald E. 1981 (1980). *Reclaiming the Old Testament for the Christian Pulpit.* Edinburgh: T & T Clark.

Graddol, David, and Oliver Boyd-Barrett. 1993. *Media Texts: Authors and Readers.* Clevedon: Open University Press.

Graham, William. 1987. *Beyond the Written Word: Oral Aspects of Scripture in the History of Religion.* Cambridge: Cambridge University Press.

Green, Christopher, and David Jackman, editors. 1995. *When God's Voice is Heard: Essays on Preaching Presented to Dick Lucas.* Leicester: IVP.

Green, Garrett. 1989. *Imagining God: Theology and the Religious Imagination.* Grand Rapids, MI: Eerdmans.

Green, Roger L., and Walter Hooper. 1974. *C. S. Lewis: A Biography.* London: Collins.

Greene, Mark. 1997a. 'Is Anybody Listening?', in *Anvil* 14/4, 283–94.

Greene, Mark. 1997. *The Three-Eared Preacher: a feedback tool for busy ministers.* London: London Bible College, Open Learning Department.

Greenhalgh, John, and Elizabeth Russell. 1987. *Signs of Faith, Hope and Love: The Christian Sacraments Today.* San Francisco, CA: Collins.

Greidanus, Sidney. 1988. *The Modern Preacher and the Ancient Text: Interpreting and Preaching Biblical Literature.* Grand Rapids, MI: Eerdmans.

Grenz, Stanley J. 1996. *A Primer on Postmodernism.* Grand Rapids, MI: Eerdmans.

Griffin, William. 1988 (1986). *C. S. Lewis, The Authentic Voice.* London: Lion.

Gronbeck, Bruce E. 1991. 'The Rhetorical Studies Tradition

and Walter J. Ong: Oral-Literacy Theories of Mediation, Culture, and Consciousness', in *Media, Consciousness, and Culture.* Bruce E. Gronbeck, Thomas J. Farrell and Paul A. Soukup, editors. Newbury Park, CA: Sage.

Gumperz, J. 1972. 'The Speech Community', in *Language and Social Context.* Pier Paolo Giglioli, editor. Harmondsworth: Penguin.

Gumperz, J., editor, 1982. *Language and Social Identity.* Cambridge: Cambridge University Press.

Gushee, David P., and Robert H. Long. 1998. *A Bolder Pulpit: Reclaiming the Moral Dimension of Preaching.* Valley Forge, PA: Judson Press.

Habermas, Jürgen, 1989 (1962). *The Structural Transformation of the Public Sphere.* Cambridge: Polity Press.

Hall, Stuart. 1980. 'Encoding/Decoding', in *Culture, Media, Language.* S. Hall, D. Hobson, A. Lowe and P. Willis, editors. London: Hutchinson.

Hall, Thor. 1971. *The Future Shape of Preaching.* Philadelphia, PA: Fortress Press.

Hamelink, Cees J. 1996. 'Globalisation and Human Dignity: The Case of the Information Superhighway', in *Media Development* 43/1, 18–21.

Hanks, Joyce Main, compiler. 1984. *Jacques Ellul: A Comprehensive Bibliography.* Greenwich, CT: Jai Press.

Hargrave, Andrea. 1994. *Radio Audience Attitudes.* London: John Libbey.

Harries, R. 1984. 'Reflections on Religious Broadcasting', in *Kairos* 9, Easter.

Harris, James H. 1995. *Preaching Liberation.* Minneapolis, MN: Fortress Press.

Harrison, Mark. 1995. *Visions of Heaven and Hell.* London: Channel 4 Television.

Hart, Geoffrey. 1989. 'The Word and Sacrament', in *Churchman* 103/4, 294–304.

Harvey, David. 1989. *The Condition of Postmodernity: An Enquiry into the Origins of Cultural Change.* Oxford: Basil Blackwell.

Hastings, Adrian. 1987 (1986). *A History of English Christianity 1920–1985.* London: Fount.

Hatim, Basil, and Ian Mason. 1997. *The Translator as Communicator.* London: Routledge.

Hauerwas, Stanley, and William H. Willimon, 1990. *Resident Aliens: Life in the Christian Colony.* Nashville, TN: Abingdon Press.

Hauerwas, Stanley, and William H. Willimon. 1992. *Preaching to Strangers: Evangelism in Today's World.* Louisville, KY: Westminster John Knox Press.

Hayes, Brian. 1994. 'The Role of the Public Voice in Present-day Radio', in *Radio and Audience Attitudes.* Andrea Hargrave, editor. London: John Libbey.

Heath, R. B. 1969. *Radio and Television.* London: Hamish Hamilton.

Hebdige, Dick. 1988. *Hiding in the Light.* London: Routledge.

Heidegger, Martin. 1962. *Being and Time.* Oxford: Basil Blackwell.

Heinz, Gérard. 1981a. 'God's revelation is not by words alone', in *Media Development* 28/4, 34–8.

Heinz, Gérard. 1981b. *Radiodiffusion et Télévision: approches théologiques.* Strasbourg: University of Strasbourg PhD.

Hellwig, Monika K. 1987. 'Making Homilies for Our Times', in *Theology Today* 43, 561–8.

Henderson, David W. 1998. *Culture Shift: Communicating God's Truth to Our Changing World.* Grand Rapids, MI: Baker Book House.

Hethcock, William. 1995. 'The Sermon as an Educational Event', in *Scottish Episcopal Church Review* 4/1. Summer, 30–49.

Heyer, George S. 1980. *Signs of our Times.* Edinburgh: Handsel Press.

Hickman, Tom. 1995. *What did you do in the War, Auntie?: The BBC at War, 1939–45.* London: BBC Books.

Higdon, Lewis. 1995. *Simply Preaching.* Norwich: Canterbury Press.

Hilkert, Mary Catherine. 1998. *Naming Grace: Preaching and the Sacramental Imagination.* New York, NY: Continuum.

Hobsbawn, Eric. 1995 (1994). *Age of Extremes: The Short Twentieth Century 1914–1991.* London: Abacus.

Hodgson, Geoffrey. 1996. *The World Turned Right Side Up: A*

History of the Conservative Ascendancy in America. Boston, MA and New York, NY: Houghton Mifflin Company.

Hoefler, Richard Carl. n.d. *Creative Preaching and Oral Writing.* Lima, OH: CSS Publishing.

Hoekstra, Henk, and Marjeet Verbeek. 1994. 'Possibilities of Audiovisual Narrative for Moral Formation', in *Mass Media and the Moral Imagination.* Philip J. Rossi and Paul A. Soukup, editors. Kansas City, MO: Sheed & Ward.

Holbert, John C. 1991. *Preaching Old Testament: Proclamation and Narrative in the Hebrew Bible.* Nashville, TN: Abingdon Press.

Holland, DeWitte T. 1980. *The Preaching Tradition: A Brief History.* Nashville, TN: Abingdon Press.

Holloway, Richard. 1979. 'Preaching', in *Theology* 82, 404–12.

Holm, Jean, and John Bowker, editors. 1994. *Picturing God.* London: Pinter Publishers.

Hoover, Stewart M. 1982. *The Electronic Giant.* Elgin, IL: Brethren Press.

Hoover, Stewart M. 1990. 'The Meaning of Religious Television', in *American Evangelicals and the Mass Media.* Quentin J. Schultze, editor. Grand Rapids, MI: Zondervan.

Hoover, Stewart M. 1997. *Mass Media Religion: The Social Sources of the Electronic Church.* London: Sage.

Hoover, Stewart M., and Robert Abelman, 1990. *Religious Television: Controversies and Conclusions.* Norwood, NJ: Ablex.

Hoover, Stewart M., and Knut Lundby, editors. 1997. *Rethinking Media, Religion, and Culture.* London: Sage.

Horsfield, Peter. 1984. *Religious Television: The American Experience.* New York, NY: Longmans, Green.

Hughes, Robert G., and Robert Kysar. 1997. *Preaching Doctrine: For the Twenty-First Century.* Minneapolis, MN: Augsburg Fortress.

Hunt, Ernest E. 1982. *Sermon Struggles: Four Methods of Sermon Preparation.* New York, NY: Seabury.

Hunter, D. G., editor. 1989. *Preaching in the Patristic Age.* Mahwah, NJ: Paulist Press.

Hutcheon, Linda. 1994. *Irony's Edge: The Theory and Politics of Irony.* London: Routledge.

Hutchley, Ian. 1996. *Confrontation Talk. Arguments and Power on Talk Radio.* Mahwah, NJ: Lawrence Erlbaum Associates.

Hybels, Bill, Stuart Briscoe and Haddon Robinson. 1989. *Mastering Contemporary Preaching.* Leicester: IVP.

Inbody, Tyron, editor. 1990. *Changing Channels: The Church and the Television Revolution.* Dayton, OH: Whaleprints.

Ivanov, Vladimir. 1990. 'Iconography and Icon', in *Icons: Windows on Eternity.* Gennadios Limouris, compiler. Geneva: World Council of Churches.

Jabusch, W. F. 1980. *The Person in the Pulpit.* Nashville, TN: Abingdon Press.

Jacks, Robert G. 1995. *Getting the Word Across: Speech Communication for Pastors and Leaders.* Grand Rapids, MI: Eerdmans.

Jacks, Robert G. 1996. *Just Say the Word: Writing for the Ear.* Grand Rapids, MI: Eerdmans.

Jamieson, Kathleen Hall. 1988. *Eloquence in an Electronic Age: The Transformation of Political Speechmaking.* Oxford: Oxford University Press.

Jankowski, Nicholas W., and Fred Wester. 1991. 'The qualitative tradition in social science inquiry: contributions to mass communication research', in *A Handbook of Qualitative Methodologies for Mass Communications Research.* Klaus B. Jensen and Nicholas W. Jankowski, editors. London: Routledge.

Jenks, Chris. 1995. *Visual Culture.* London: Routledge.

Jensen, Joli. 1990. *Redeeming Modernity: Contradictions in Media Criticism.* London: Sage.

Jensen, Klaus Bruhn, and Nicholas W. Jankowski, editors. 1991. *A Handbook of Qualitative Methodologies for Mass Communication Research.* London: Routledge.

Jensen, Richard A. 1996. *Preaching Mark's Gospel: a narrative approach.* Lima, OH: CSS Publishing.

Jensen, Richard A. 1997. *Preaching Luke's Gospel: a narrative approach.* Lima, OH: CSS Publishing.

Jensen, Richard A. 1998. *Preaching Matthew's Gospel: a narrative approach.* Lima, OH: CSS Publishing.

Jenson, Robert W. 1978. *Visible Words: The Interpretation and Practice of Christian Sacraments.* Philadelphia, PA: Fortress Press.

Jeter Jr, Joseph R. 1998. *Crisis Preaching: Personal and Public.* Nashville, TN: Abingdon Press.

Johnston, Michael. 1998. *Engaging the Word.* Boston, MA: Cowley Publications.

Johnstone, Ronald L. 1971/72. 'Who Listens to Religious Radio Broadcasts Anymore?', in *Journal of Broadcasting* 16, 91–102.

Jones, G. W. 1968. 'Proclamation Is Dialogue – Not Monologue', in *Theology Today* 24, 509–11.

Jones, Nicholas, 1995. *Soundbites and Spin Doctors: How politicians manipulate the media – and vice versa.* London: Cassell.

Jones, Steven G., editor. 1995. *CyberSociety: Computer-Mediated Communication and Community.* London: Sage.

Keane, Fergal. 1996. *Letter to Daniel: Despatches from the Heart.* Harmondsworth: Penguin Books (with BBC Books).

Keck, Leander E. 1978. *The Bible in the Pulpit: The Renewal of Biblical Preaching.* Nashville, TN: Abingdon Press.

Keefe, Carolyn. 1974 (1971). 'On the Air', in *C. S. Lewis, Speaker and Teacher.* Carolyn Keefe, editor. London: Hodder & Stoughton.

Keillor, Garrison. 1992 (1991). *Radio Romance.* London: Faber & Faber.

Keillor, Garrison. 1994. *Garrison Keillor's Radio Preachers.* BBC Radio 4, 10 August. Jolyon Mitchell, producer.

Keith, Michael C., with Joseph Krause. 1993. *The Radio Station.* Third Edition. Boston, MA: Focal Press.

Kelly, John C. 1981. *A Philosophy of Communication.* London: Centre for the Study of Communication and Culture.

Kendrick, Alexander. 1969. *Prime Time: The Life of Edward R. Murrow.* Boston, MA: Little, Brown & Co.

Kennedy, George A. 1980. *Classical Rhetoric and Its Christian and Secular Tradition from Ancient to Modern Times.* Chapel Hill, NC: University of North Carolina Press.

Kennedy, George A., translator. 1991. Aristotle. *On Rhetoric: A Theory of Civic Discourse.* Oxford: Oxford University Press.

Kennedy, Rodney. 1993. *The Creative Power of Metaphor: A Rhetorical Homiletics.* Lanham, MD: University Press of America.

Kepel, Gilles. 1994. *The Revenge of God: The Resurgence of Islam, Christianity and Judaism in the Modern World.* Cambridge: Polity Press.

Khlebnikov, Velimir. 1993. 'The Radio of the Future', in *Radiotext(e).* Neill Strauss, editor. New York, NY: Semiotext(e).

Killinger, John. 1985. *Fundamentals of Preaching.* Philadelphia, PA: Fortress Press.

Killinger, John. 1995. *Preaching to a Church in Crisis, A Homiletic for the Last Days of the Mainline Church.* Lima, OH: CSS Publishing.

Killinger, John. 1999. *Preaching the New Millennium.* Nashville, TN: Abingdon Press.

Kinnard, Roy, and Tim Davis. 1992. *Divine Images: A History of Jesus on the Screen.* New York, NY: Citadel Press.

Kraft, Charles H. 1991. *Communication Theory for Christian Witness.* Revised Edition. New York, NY: Orbis Books.

Kuhn, Raymond. 1995. *The Media in France.* London: Routledge.

Lakoff, George, and Mark Johnson. 1980. *Metaphors We Live By.* Chicago, IL: University of Chicago Press.

Larsen, David L. 1995. *Telling the Old, Old Story: The Art of Narrative Preaching.* Wheaton, IL: Crossway.

Leach, J. 1997. *Responding to Preaching.* Cambridge: Grove Books.

Lee, Jung Young. 1997. *Korean Preaching: An Interpretation.* Nashville, TN: Abingdon Press.

Lee, Philip, editor. 1995. *The Democratization of Communication.* Cardiff: University of Wales Press.

Levy, Suzanne. 1995. 'Devoted to ''Auntie Beeb''', in *Radio: The Forgotten Medium,* Edward C. Pease and Everetter E. Dennis, editors. London: Transaction Publishers.

Lewis, C. S. 1936. *The Allegory of Love.* London: Oxford University Press.

Lewis, C. S. 1942. *Broadcast Talks.* London: Geoffrey Bles.

Lewis, C. S. 1943. *Christian Behaviour.* London: Geoffrey Bles.

Lewis, C. S. 1944. *Beyond Personality.* London: Geoffrey Bles.

Lewis, C. S. 1960a. *Studies in Words.* Cambridge: Cambridge University Press.

Lewis, C. S. 1960b. *The Four Loves.* London: Geoffrey Bles.

Lewis, C. S. 1966. *Of Other Worlds: Essays and Stories.* Walter Hooper, editor. London: Geoffey Bles.

Lewis, C. S. 1977 (1952). *Mere Christianity.* Glasgow: Fount.

Lewis, C. S. 1980a (1950). *The Lion, The Witch and The Wardrobe.* London: Fontana Lions.

Lewis, C. S. 1980b (1956). *The Last Battle.* London: Fontana Lions.

Lewis, C. S. 1984. *Mere Christianity.* An Anniversary Edition of the Three Books: *The Case for Christianity, Christian Behaviour* and *Beyond Personality,* with an introduction by Walter Hooper. New York, NY: Macmillan.

Lewis, C. S. 1988 (1966). *Letters of C. S. Lewis.* London: Fount. W. H. Lewis, editor (1966); Walter Hooper, reviser (1988).

Lewis, Peter M. 1996. 'Raiding the lost archives: early BBC programmes and the role of myth in BBC radio history'. Paper for *Hearing is Believing* conference, at University of Sunderland, 2 March.

Lewis, Peter M., and Jerry Booth. 1989. *The Invisible Medium: Public, Commercial and Community Radio.* London: Macmillan.

Lewis, Sinclair. 1927. *Elmer Gantry.* New York, NY: Harcourt, Brace and Company.

Lewis, Tom. 1991. *Empire of the Air: The Men Who Made Radio.* London: HarperCollins.

Liefeld, Walter J. 1995. *New Testament Exposition: From Text to Sermon.* Carlisle: Paternoster Press.

Limouris, Gennadios. 1990. 'The Microcosm and Macrocosm of the Icon: Theology, Spirituality and Worship in Colour', in *Icons: Windows on Eternity.* Gennadios Limouris, compiler. Geneva: World Council of Churches.

Lindbeck, G. 1984. *The Nature of Doctrine: Religion and Theology in a Post-Liberal Age.* Philadelphia, PA: Westminster.

Lindlof, Thomas R. 1995. *Qualitative Communication Research Methods.* London: Sage.

Lischer, Richard. 1987. *Theories of Preaching: Selected Readings in the Homiletical Tradition.* Durham, NC: Labyrinth Press.

Lischer, Richard. 1992. *A Theology of Preaching.* Revised Edition. Durham, NC: Labyrinth Press.

Lischer, Richard. 1995. *The Preacher King: Martin Luther King, Jr. and the Word that Moved America.* New York, NY: Oxford University Press.

Lister, Martin, editor. 1995. *The Photographic Image in Digital Culture.* London: Routledge.

Lloyd-Jones, Martin D. 1985. *Preaching and Preachers.* London: Hodder and Stoughton.

Loktev, Julia. 1993. 'Static Motion, or the Confessions of a Radio Driver', in *Radiotext(e).* Neill Strauss, editor. New York, NY: Semiotext(e).

Long, Thomas G. 1988. *The Senses of Preaching.* Atlanta, GA: John Knox Press.

Long, Thomas G. 1989a. *Preaching and the Literary Forms of the Bible.* Philadelphia, PA: Fortress Press.

Long, Thomas G. 1989b. *The Witness of Preaching.* Louisville, KY: John Knox Press.

Long, Thomas G. 1996. 'Learning to Speak of Sin', in *Preaching as a Theological Task: World, Gospel, Scripture.* Thomas G. Long and Edward Farley, editors, Louisville, KY: Westminster John Knox Press.

Long, Thomas G., and Cornelius Plantinga, Jr. 1994. *A Chorus of Witnesses.* Grand Rapids, MI: Eerdmans.

Long, Thomas G., and Edward Farley, editors. 1996. *Preaching as a Theological Task: World, Gospel, Scripture.* Louisville, KY: Westminster John Knox Press.

Lopez, Vigil José Ignacio. 1991. *Rebel Radio.* Willimantic, CT: Curbstone Press.

Lowery, Shearon A., and Melvin L. DeFleur. 1995. *Milestones in Mass Communication Research: Media Effects.* Third Edition. White Plains, NY: Longmans, Green.

Lowry, Eugene L. 1980. *The Homiletical Plot: The Sermon as Narrative Art Form.* Nashville, TN: Abingdon Press.

Lowry, Eugene L. 1985. *Doing Time in the Pulpit: The Relationship between Narrative and Preaching.* Nashville, TN: Abingdon Press.

Lowry, Eugene L. 1993. 'The Revolution of Sermonic Shape' in *Listening to the Word.* G. R. O'Day and Thomas G. Long, editors. Nashville, TN: Abingdon Press.

Lowry, Eugene L. 1997. *The Sermon: Dancing the Edge of Mystery.* Nashville, TN: Abingdon Press.

Lowry, Eugene L. 1998. *How to Preach a Parable: Designs for Narrative Sermons.* Nashville, TN: Abingdon Press.

Lyon, David. 1985. *The Steeple's Shadow.* London: SPCK.

Lyon, David. 1994. *Postmodernity.* Buckingham: Open University Press.

Lyotard, Jean-François. 1984. *The Postmodern Condition: A Report on Knowledge.* Manchester: Manchester University Press.

McClure, John S. 1991. *The Four Codes of Preaching.* Minneapolis, MN: Fortress Press.

McClure, John S. 1995. *The Roundtable Pulpit: Where Leadership and Preaching Meet.* Nashville, TN: Abingdon Press.

McClure, John S., editor. 1998. *Best Advice for Preaching.* Minneapolis, MN: Fortress Press.

McCurley, Foster R. 1996. *Wrestling with the Word: Christian Preaching from the Hebrew Bible.* Valley Forge, PA: Trinity Press International.

McDonald, J. I. H. 1996. 'The view from the ditch – and other angles. Interpreting the Parable of the Good Samaritan', in *Scottish Journal of Theology* 49/1, 21–37.

McDonnell, James and Frances Trampiets, editors. 1989. *Communicating Faith in a Technological Age.* Slough: St Paul Publications.

McElvaney, William K. 1989. *Preaching from Camelot to Covenant.* Nashville, TN: Abingdon Press.

McFague, Sallie. 1975. *Speaking in Parables: A Study in Metaphor and Theology.* Philadelphia, PA: Fortress Press.

McFague, Sallie. 1982. *Metaphorical Theology: Models of God in Religious Language.* Philadelphia, PA: Fortress Press.

McFague, Sallie. 1997. *Super, Natural Christians.* London: SCM Press.

MacIntyre, Alasdair. 1988. *Whose Justice? Which Rationality?* London: Gerald Duckworth.

McIntyre, Ian. 1993. *The Expense of Glory.* London: HarperCollins.

MacIntyre, John. 1987. *Faith, Theology and Imagination.* Edinburgh: Handsel Press.

McKay, Johnston. 1997. *This Small Pool.* The Mair Lectures, University of Glasgow, 1995. Glasgow: Trinity St Mungo Press.

McKenzie, Alyce M. 1996. *Preaching Proverbs: Wisdom for the Pulpit.* Louisville, KY: Westminster John Knox Press.

McKim, Donald K. 1994. *The Bible in Theology and Preaching: How Preachers Use Scripture.* Revised Edition. Nashville, TN: Abingdon Press.

McLaughlin, Raymond W. 1979. *The Ethics of Persuasive Preaching.* Grand Rapids, MI: Baker Book House.

McLeish, Robert. 1988. *The Technique of Radio Production: A*

Manual for Broadcasters. Second Edition. London and Boston, MA: Focal Press.

McLellan, Andrew R. C. 1997. *Preaching For These People.* London: Mowbray.

McLuhan, Marshall. 1962. *The Gutenberg Galaxy: The Making of Typographic Man.* London: Routledge.

McLuhan, Marshall. 1987 (1964). *Understanding Media: The Extensions of Man.* London: Ark.

McQuail, Denis. 1992. *Media Performance: Mass Communication and the Public Interest.* London: Sage.

McQuail, Denis. 1994. *Mass Communication Theory.* Third Edition. London: Sage.

McQuail, Denis, and Sven Windahl. 1993. *Communication Models: For the Study of Mass Communication.* Second Edition. New York, NY: Longmans, Green.

Mackey, J. P., editor. 1986. *Religious Imagination.* Edinburgh: Edinburgh University Press.

Malcolm, Norman. 1993. *Wittgenstein: A Religious Point of View.* Peter Winch, editor. London: Routledge.

Malise, Ruthven. 1991. *The Divine Supermarket: Shopping for God in America.* London: Vintage.

Marion, Jean-Luc. 1991 (1982). *God Without Being: Hors Texte.* Chicago, IL and London: University of Chicago Press.

Markquart, Edward F. 1985. *Quest for Better Preaching.* Minneapolis, MN: Augsburg.

Martini, Carlo Maria. 1994. *Communicating Christ to the World.* Kansas City, MO: Sheed & Ward.

Marty, Martin E. 1981. 'Introduction', in *Jacques Ellul: Interpretative Essays.* Clifford Christians and Jay M. Van Hook, editors. Chicago, IL: University of Illinois Press.

Marty, Martin E. 1984. *The Word, People Participating in Preaching.* Philadelphia, PA: Fortress Press.

Massey, J. E. 1980. *The Making of the Sermon: Order and Movement in Preaching.* Nashville, TN: Abingdon Press.

Matelski, Marilyn J. 1995a. 'Resilient Radio', in *Radio: The Forgotten Medium.* Edward C. Pease and Everetter E. Dennis, editors. London: Transaction Publishers.

Matelski, Marilyn J. 1995b. *Vatican Radio: Propagation by the Airwaves.* Westport, CT: Praeger.

Matheson, Peter. 1998. *Reformation Rhetoric.* Edinburgh: T & T Clark.

Melville, Herman. 1956 (1851). *Moby Dick.* New York, NY: Signet.

Mengham, Rod. 1995. *The Descent of Language.* London: Fontana.

Meyers, Robin R. 1993. *Ears to Hear: Preaching as Self-Persuasion.* Cleveland, OH: Pilgrim Press.

Middleton, Richard J., and Brian J. Walsh. 1995. *Truth is Stranger than it Used to Be: Biblical Faith in a Postmodern Age.* London: SPCK.

Milburn, Geoffrey, and Margaret Batty, editors. 1995. *Workaday Preachers: The Story of Methodist Local Preaching.* Peterborough: Methodist Publishing House.

Miles, Margaret R. 1985. *Image as Insight: Visual Understanding in Western Christianity and Secular Culture.* Boston, MA: Beacon Press.

Miles, Margaret R. 1996. *Seeing and Believing: Religion and Values in Movies.* Boston, MA: Beacon Press.

Miller, Calvin. 1995. *Marketplace Preaching: How to Return the Sermon to Where it Belongs.* Grand Rapids, MI: Baker Book House.

Miller, Charles E. 1992. *Ordained to Preach: A Theology and Practice of Preaching.* New York, NY: Alba House.

Miller, Spencer. 1935. 'Radio and Religion', in *Annals of the American Academy of Political and Social Science* 177, January, 135–40.

Mitchell, Ella Pearson. editor. 1985. *Those Preachin' Women: Sermons by Black Women Preachers.* Valley Forge, PA: Judson Press.

Mitchell, Ella Pearson, editor. 1988. *Those Preachin' Women.* (Volume 2). Valley Forge, PA: Judson Press.

Mitchell, Ella Pearson, editor. 1996. *Those Preachin' Women.* (Volume 3). Valley Forge, PA: Judson Press.

Mitchell, Ella Pearson, editor. 1991. *Woman: To Preach or Not to Preach.* Valley Forge, PA: Judson Press.

Mitchell, Henry H. 1977. *The Recovery of Preaching.* London: Hodder & Stoughton.

Mitchell, Henry H. 1990a. *Black Preaching: The Recovery of a Powerful Art.* Nashville, TN: Abingdon Press.

Mitchell, Henry H. 1990b. *Celebration and Experience in Preaching.* Nashville, TN: Abingdon Press.

Mitchell, Henry H., and Emil Thomas. 1994. *Preaching for Black Self-Esteem.* Nashville, TN: Abingdon Press.

Mitchell, Jolyon. 1994. 'Song of a Preacher Man', in *Ariel,* London: BBC Staff Magazine, 9 August.

Mitchell, Jolyon. 1996a. 'New Developments in Homiletics', in *Encounter With God.* Forrester, D. *et al.*, Edinburgh: T & T Clark, 93–101.

Mitchell, Jolyon. 1996b. *Imagining God in a Visual Culture.* Edinburgh: Theological Institute of Scottish Episcopal Church, Occasional Paper No. 5.

Mitchell, Jolyon. 1997a. 'Preaching in an Audio-Visual Culture', in *Anvil* 14/4, 262–72.

Mitchell, Jolyon. 1997b. 'Preaching Parables in a Media Age', in *The College of Preachers Fellowship Paper* 104, 3–7.

Mitchell, Jolyon. 1998. 'Rediscovering the Value of Radio in a Mass Media Culture', in *Muslim Education Quarterly* Volume 16, Number 1, 51–64.

Mitchell, Jolyon. 1999. 'Speaking Visually – using pictorial language', in *Speaking English* Volume 32, Number 1, 29–34.

Mitroff, Ian I., and Warren Bennis. 1993 (1989). *The Unreality Industry.* New York, NY: Oxford University Press.

Moeller, Pamela Ann. 1993. *A Kinesthetic Homiletic: Embodying Gospel in Preaching.* Minneapolis, MN: Fortress Press.

Moltmann, Jürgen. 1974. *The Crucified God.* London: SCM Press.

Montefiore, Hugh, editor. 1992. *The Gospel and Contemporary Culture.* London: Mowbrays.

Montgomery, John Warwick. 1977. 'Mass Communication and Scriptural Proclamation', in *Evangelical Quarterly* 49/1, 3–29.

Moore, R. Laurence. 1994. *Selling God: American Religion in the Marketplace of Culture.* Oxford and New York, NY: Oxford University Press.

Morgan, Michael and Nancy Signorielli. 1990. 'Cultivation Analysis: Conceptualization and Methodology', in *Cultivation Analysis: New Directions in Media Effects Research.* Nancy

Signorielli and Michael Morgan, editors. Newbury Park, CA: Sage.

Morris, Colin. 1990. *Starting from Scratch.* London: Epworth Press.

Morris, Colin. 1996. *Raising the Dead: The Art of the Preacher as Public Performer.* London: Fount.

Moyd, Olin P. 1995. *The Sacred Art: Preaching and Theology in the African American Tradition.* Valley Forge, PA: Judson Press.

Mulder, David P. 1996. *Narrative Preaching: stories from the pulpit.* St Louis, MO: Concordia Publishing House.

Murrow, Edward R. 1941. *This is London.* Elmer Davis, editor. New York, NY: Simon and Schuster.

Murrow, Edward R. 1993 (1945). 'Broadcast from Buchenwald', in *Radiotext(e).* Neill Strauss, editor. New York, NY: Semiotext(e), 152–4.

Murrow, Thomas M. 1956. *Worship and Preaching.* London: Epworth Press.

Myers, Doris. 1994. *C. S. Lewis in Context.* Kent, OH: Kent State University Press.

Nash, Tom. 1995. *The Christian Communicator's Handbook, A Guide to Help You Make the Message Plain.* Wheaton, IL: Victor Books.

Negrine, Ralph. 1994 (1989). *Politics and the Mass Media.* Second Edition. London: Routledge.

Neill, Stephen. 1964. *A History of Christian Missions.* Harmondsworth: Penguin.

Nelmes, Jill, editor. 1996. *An Introduction to Film Studies.* London: Routledge.

Newbigin, Lesslie. 1986. *Foolishness to the Greeks: The Gospel and Western Culture.* London: SPCK.

Newbigin, Lesslie. 1991. *Truth to Tell: The Gospel as Public Truth.* London: SPCK.

Nicasio, Lino Evora. 1993. *How to Preach so People will Listen.* Manila, Philippines: Logos Publications.

Nichols, Randall J. 1987. *The Restoring Word: Preaching as Pastoral Communication.* San Francisco, CA: Harper & Row.

Nida, Eugene A. 1964. *Toward a Science of Translating.* Leiden: E. J. Brill.

Nida, Eugene A., and Charles R. Taber. 1969. *The Theory and Practice of Translation.* Leiden: E. J. Brill.

Nightingale, Virginia. 1996. *Studying Audiences: The Shock of the Real.* London: Routledge.

Nolland, John. 1993. *Luke.* 3 volumes. Dallas, TX: Word Books.

Noren, Carol M. 1992. *The Woman in the Pulpit.* Nashville, TN: Abingdon Press.

Norrington, David C. 1996. *To Preach or Not to Preach.* Carlisle: Paternoster Press.

North, Eric. 1974. 'Eugene A. Nida: An Appreciation', in Matthew Black and William A. Smalley, editors. *On Language, Culture and Religion: in Honor of Eugene A. Nida.* The Hague: Mouton.

Novak, Michael. 1982. 'Television Shapes the Soul', in *Television: The Critical View.* Horace Newcomb, editor. Third Edition. Oxford: Oxford University Press.

O'Day, G. R. 1987. *The Word Disclosed: John's Story and Narrative Preaching.* St Louis, MO: CBP Press.

O'Day, G. R., and Thomas G. Long, editors. 1993. *Listening to the Word: Studies in Honor of Fred B. Craddock.* Nashville, TN: Abingdon Press.

Ong, Walter J. 1967. *The Presence of the Word: Some Prolegomena for Cultural and Religious History.* New Haven, CT: Yale University Press.

Ong, Walter J. 1971. *Rhetoric, Romance and Technology: Studies in the Interaction of Expression and Culture.* Ithaca, NY: Cornell University Press.

Ong, Walter J. 1977. *Interfaces of the Word: Studies in the Evolution of Consciousness and Culture.* Ithaca, NY: Cornell University Press.

Ong, Walter J. 1982. *Orality and Literacy: The Technologizing of the Word.* New York, NY: Routledge.

Ong, Walter J. 1986. *Hopkins, the Self, and God.* Toronto: University of Toronto Press.

Ong, Walter J. 1996a. 'Communications Media and the State of Theology', in *Media, Culture and Catholicism.* Paul Soukup, editor. Kansas City, MO: Sheed & Ward.

Ong, Walter J. 1996b. 'Information and/or Communication:

Interactions', in *Communication Research Trends* 16/3, 3–17.

Ong, Walter J. 1998. 'Writing: Ancient Origins with Modern Implications', in *Communication Research Trends* 18/2, 4–20.

Orwell, George. 1970 (1958). 'Poetry and the Microphone', in *George Orwell, The Collected Essays, Journalism and Letters: Volume 2.* Sonia Orwell and Ian Angus, editors. Harmondsworth: Penguin, 1970. Originally written Autumn 1943, and published as New Saxon Pamphlet, No. 3, March 1945.

Orwell, George. 1984. 'Inside the Whale', in *The Penguin Essays of George Orwell.* Harmondsworth: Penguin.

Osborn, Ronald E. 1999. *Folly of God: The Rise of Christian Preaching.* (Volume 1) St Louis, MO: Chalice Press.

O'Sullivan, Tim, John Hartley, Danny Saunders and John Fiske. 1983. *Key Concepts in Communication.* London and New York, NY: Routledge.

Padilla, C. René. 1981. 'God's Word and Man's Words (Preaching)', in *Evangelical Quarterly* 53, 216–26.

Page, Sue. 1998. *Away With Words: A training book on the whole spectrum of Christian communication.* London: SPCK.

Pagliari, Robert. 1993. *Fourteen Steps to Dynamic Preaching.* Liguori, St Louis, MO: Liguori Publications.

Patte, Daniel. 1984. *Preaching Paul.* Philadelphia, PA: Fortress Press.

Patton, Michael Quinn. 1980. *Qualitative Evaluation Methods.* London: Sage.

Patton, Michael Quinn. 1987. *How to Use Qualitative Methods In Evaluation.* London: Sage.

Pease, Edward C., and Everetter E. Dennis, editors. 1995 (1993). *Radio – The Forgotten Medium.* New Brunswick, NJ and London: Transaction Publishers.

Pelikan, Jaroslav. 1985. *Jesus Through the Centuries: His Place in the History of Culture.* Yale, CT: Yale University Press.

Peterson, Eugene H. 1985. 'Theological Table-Talk, First Language', in *Theology Today* 42, 211–14.

Phenix, P. H. 1975 (1964). 'Realms of Meaning', in *Curriculum Design.* Michael Golby, Jane Greenwald and Ruth West, editors. London: Croom Helm.

Pitt-Watson, I. 1978. *The Folly of Preaching.* Philadelphia, PA: Westminster Press.

Pitt-Watson, I. 1986. *A Primer for Preachers.* Grand Rapids, MI: Baker Book House.

Plou, Dafne Sabanes. 1996. *Global Communication: Is there a Place for Human Dignity?* Geneva: World Council of Churches.

Postman, Neil. 1985. *Amusing Ourselves to Death: Public Discourse in the Age of Show Business.* Harmondsworth: Penguin.

Powell III, Adam Clayton. 1995. 'You are What You Hear', in *Radio: The Forgotten Medium.* Edward C. Pease and Everetter E. Dennis, editors. London: Transaction Publishers.

Quicke, Michael. 1997. 'Preaching for the Next Millennium', in *The College of Preachers Fellowship Paper* 103, 9–21.

Rad, G. von. 1977. *Biblical Interpretations in Preaching.* Nashville, TN: Abingdon Press.

Rahner, K., editor. 1996. *The Renewal of Preaching.* Mahwah, NJ: Paulist Press.

Real, Michael R. 1981. 'Mass Communications and Propaganda in Technological Societies', in *Jacques Ellul: Interpretative Essays.* Clifford Christians and Jay M. Van Hook, editors. Urbana, Chicago, IL and London: University of Illinois Press.

Real, Michael R. 1996. *Exploring Media Culture: A Guide.* London: Sage.

Reid, Colin. 1987. *Action Stations: A History of Broadcasting House.* London: Robson Books.

Reid, Robert Stephen. 1995. 'Postmodernism and the Function of the New Homiletic in Post-Christendom Congregations', in *Homiletic* 20/2, Winter, 1–13.

Reierson, Gary B. 1988. *The Art in Preaching.* Lanham, MD: The University Press of America.

Reith, John. 1924. *Broadcast Over Britain.* London: Hodder & Stoughton.

Reymond, Bernard. 1993a. 'Preaching the New Media', in *Modern Churchman* New Series, Vol. XXXIV, No. 5, 19–29.

Reymond, Bernard. 1993b. 'Homiletics and Theology: Re-evaluating their Relationship', in *Modern Churchman* New Series, Vol. XXXIV, No. 5, 30–43.

Reynolds, Barbara. 1993. *Dorothy L. Sayers: Her Life and Soul.* London: Hodder & Stoughton.

Reynolds, Gillian. 1994. 'Radio Future', in *Radio and Audience Attitudes.* Andrea Hargrave, editor. London: John Libbey.

Rhoads, B. Eric. 1995. 'Looking Back at Radio's Future', in *Radio: The Forgotten Medium.* Edward C. Pease and Everetter E. Dennis, editors. London: Transaction Publishers.

Rice, Charles. 1983. 'Shaping Sermons by the interplay of Text and Metaphor', in *Preaching Biblically.* Don M. Wardlaw, editor. Philadelphia, PA: Westminster.

Ricoeur, Paul. 1991. 'Life in Quest of Narrative', in *On Paul Ricoeur: Narrative and Interpretation.* David Wood, editor. London: Routledge.

Riegert, Eduard R. 1990. *Imaginative Shock: Preaching and Metaphor.* Burlington, Ontario: Trinity Press.

Riesebrodt, Martin. 1993 (1990). *The Emergence of Modern Fundamentalism in the United States and Iran.* Berkeley, CA: University of California Press.

Robbins, Kevin. 1996. *Into the Image: Culture and Politics in the Field of Vision.* London: Routledge.

Robinson, Edward. 1993. *Icons of the Present: Some Reflections on Art, the Sacred and the Holy.* London: SCM Press.

Robinson, G., and J. Rundell, editors. 1994. *Rethinking Imagination: Culture and Creativity.* London: Routledge.

Robinson, Haddon W. 1990. *Biblical Preaching: The Development and Delivery of Expository Messages.* Grand Rapids, MI: Baker Book House.

Rogness, Michael. 1994. *Preaching to a TV Generation: The Sermon in the Electronic Age.* Lima, OH: CSS Publishing.

Rose, Lucy Atkinson. 1997. *Sharing the Word: Preaching in the Roundtable Church.* Louisville, KY: Westminster John Knox Press.

Rossi, Philip J., and Paul A. Soukup, editors. 1994. *Mass Media and the Moral Imagination.* Kansas City, MO: Sheed & Ward.

Rueter, Alvin C. 1997. *Making Good Preaching Better: A Step-by-Step Guide to Scripture-Based, People-Centred Preaching.* Collegeville, MN: Liturgical Press.

Runcie, Robert. 1986. *Religious Broadcasting Today.* Canterbury:

University of Kent. Centre for the Study of Religion and Society.

Runia, Klaas. 1983. *The Sermon Under Attack.* Exeter: Paternoster Press.

Rusling, Dawn C. 1995. *1996 – Who's Who in British Radio.* First Edition. Hull: Eurobroadcast Publications.

Rust, Eric C. 1982. *The Word and Words: Towards a Theology of Preaching.* Macon, GA: Mercer University Press.

Sacks, Jonathan. 1991. *The Persistence of Faith: Religion, Morality and Society in a Secular Age.* London: Weidenfeld & Nicolson.

Salmon, Bruce C. 1988. *Storytelling in preaching: A guide to the theory and practice.* Nashville, TN: Broadman Press.

Sangster, Edwin W. 1954. *The Craft of The Sermon.* London: Epworth.

Sanneh, Lamin. 1989. *Translating the Message: The Missionary on Culture.* Maryknoll, NY: Orbis Books.

Sarno, Ronald A. 1987. *Using Media in Religious Education.* Birmingham, AL: Religious Education Press.

Sayer, George. 1997 (1988). *Jack: A Life of C. S. Lewis.* London: Hodder & Stoughton.

Scannell, Paddy, editor. 1991. *Broadcast Talk.* London: Sage.

Scannell, Paddy. 1996. *Radio, Television and Modern Life.* Oxford: Basil Blackwell.

Scannell, Paddy, and David Cardiff. 1991. *A Social History of British Broadcasting. Volume 1: 1922–1939, Serving the Nation.* Oxford: Basil Blackwell.

Schafer, R. Murray. 1993. 'Radical Radio', in *Radiotext(e).* Neil Strauss, editor. New York, NY: Semiotext(e).

Schiffer, Michael Brian. 1991. *The Portable Radio in American Life.* Tucson, AZ: University of Arizona Press.

Schlafer, David J. 1992. *Surviving the Sermon: A Guide to Preaching for Those Who Have to Listen.* Boston, MA. Cowley Publications.

Schlafer, David J. 1995. *Your Way with God's Word: Discovering Your Distinctive Preaching Voice.* Boston, MA: Cowley.

Schlesinger, Philip. 1987 (1978). *Putting Reality Together.* Second Edition. London: Routledge.

Schultze, Quentin J. 1987. 'The Mythos of the Electronic

Church', in *Critical Studies in Mass Communication* 4, 245–61.

Schultze, Quentin J., editor. 1990. *American Evangelicals and the Mass Media: Perspectives on the Relationship Between American Evangelicals and the Mass Media.* Grand Rapids, MI: Zondervan.

Schultze, Quentin J., *et al.* 1991. *Dancing in the Dark.* Grand Rapids, MI: Eerdmans.

Schwartz, Tony. 1973. *The Responsive Chord: How Radio and TV Manipulate You . . .* New York, NY: Anchor.

Scott, Bernard Brandon. 1985. *The Word of God in Words: Reading and Preaching.* Philadelphia, PA: Fortress Press.

Seidman, I. E. 1991. *Interviewing As Qualitative Research.* New York, NY: Teachers College Press.

Seymour-Smith, Martin. 1976. *The English Sermon 1550 – 1650, an Anthology.* Cheadle: Carcanet Press.

Seymour-Ure, Colin. 1991. *The British Press and Broadcasting since 1945.* Oxford: Basil Blackwell.

Shayon, Robert Lewis. 1969. 'The Two Men who were Murrow', in *Columbian Journalism Review,* Autumn.

Shields, Rob, editor. 1996. *Cultures of Internet: Virtual Spaces, Real Histories, Living Bodies.* London: Sage.

Shingler, Martin and Cindy Wieringa. 1998. *On Air: Methods and Meanings of Radio.* London: Edward Arnold.

Siegfried, Regina, editor. 1993. *In the Company of Preachers.* Collegeville, MN: Liturgical Press.

Silverman, David. 1993. *Interpreting Qualitative Data. Methods for Analysing Talk, Text and Interaction.* London: Sage.

Silverstone, Roger. 1991. 'Television, Rhetoric, and the Return of the Unconscious in Secondary Oral Culture', in *Media, Consciousness, and Culture.* Bruce E. Gronbeck *et al.*, editors. Newbury Park, CA: Sage.

Simmons, Martha J., editor. 1996. *Preaching on the Brink: The Future of Homiletics.* Nashville, TN: Abingdon Press.

Simpson, Paul. 1993. *Language, Ideology and Point of View.* London: Routledge.

Sittler, Joseph. 1966. *The Anguish of Preaching.* Philadelphia, PA: Fortress Press.

Skudlarek, William. 1981. *The Word in Worship.* Nashville, TN: Abingdon Press.

Sleeth, Ronald E. 1986. *God's Word and Our Words.* Atlanta, GA: John Knox Press.

Smith, Christine. 1989. *Weaving the Sermon: Preaching in a Feminist Perspective.* Louisville, KY: John Knox Press.

Soskice, Janet Martin. 1987 (1985) *Metaphor and Religious Language.* Oxford: Clarendon Press.

Søgaard, Viggo. 1993. *Media in Church and Mission: Communicating the Gospel.* Pasadena, CA: William Carey Library.

Soukup, Paul A. editor. 1996. *Media, Culture and Catholicism.* Kansas City, MO: Sheed & Ward.

Spenser, Jon. 1987. *Sacred Symphony: the Chanted Sermon of the Black Preacher.* Westport, CT : Greenwood.

Spenser, Jon. 1990. *Protest and Praise: Sacred Music of Black Religion.* Minneapolis, MN: Fortress Press.

Sperber, A. M. 1986. *Murrow: His Life and Times.* New York, NY: Freundlich Books.

Sroka, Leonard A. 1994. *Stay Tuned: A Guide to Communion in the Age of Communication.* New York, NY: Alba House.

Steimle, Edmund A., Morris J. Niedenthal and Charles L. Rice. 1980. *Preaching the Story.* Philadelphia, PA: Fortress Press.

Steiner, George. 1984. *Antigones: The Antigone myth in Western literature, art and thought.* Oxford: Oxford University Press.

Steiner, George. 1992. *After Babel: Aspects of Language and Translation.* Second Edition. Oxford: Oxford University Press.

Stevenson, Nick. 1995. *Understanding Media Cultures: Social Theory and Mass Communication.* London: Sage.

Stewart, James S. 1946. *Heralds of God.* The Warrack Lectures (1943). London: Hodder & Stoughton.

Stewart, James S. 1996. *Walking With God.* Edited by Gordon Grant. Edinburgh: St Andrew Press.

Storrar, William. 1990. *Scottish Identity: A Christian Vision.* Edinburgh: Handsel Press.

Stott, John. 1982. *I Believe in Preaching.* London: Hodder & Stoughton.

Stott, William. 1986 (1973). *Documentary Expression and Thirties America.* Chicago, IL: Chicago University Press.

Stout, Daniel A., and Judith M. Buddenbaum, editors. 1996.

Religion and Mass Media: Audiences and Adaptations. London: Sage.

Stratford, T. 1998. *Interactive preaching: opening the word then listening.* Cambridge: Grove Books.

Strauss, Neil, editor. 1993. *Radiotext(e).* New York, NY: Semiotext(e).

Stromberg, Peter G. 1990. 'Ideological Language in the Transformation of Identity', in *American Anthropologist* 92/1, March.

Swain, Bernard. 1986. *Liberating Leadership: Practical Styles for Pastoral Ministry.* San Francisco, CA: Harper & Row.

Sweet, Leonard I., editor. 1993. *Communication and Change in American Religious History.* Grand Rapids, MI: Eerdmans.

Talbot-Smith, Michael. 1995 (1990). *Broadcast Sound Technology.* Second Edition. Oxford: Butterworth–Heinemann.

Tannen, Deborah. 1989. *Talking Voices: Repetition, Dialogue, and Imagery in Conversational Discourse.* Cambridge: Cambridge University Press.

Taylor, Barbara Brown. 1993. *The Preaching Life.* Boston, MA: Cowley Publications.

Taylor, Barbara Brown. 1997. *Bread of Angels.* Boston, MA: Cowley Publications.

Taylor, Barbara Brown. 1998a. *When God is Silent.* The 1997 Lyman Beecher Lectures on Preaching. Boston, MA: Cowley Publications.

Taylor, Barbara Brown. 1998b. *God in Pain: Teaching Sermons on Suffering.* Nashville, TN: Abingdon Press.

Tedlock, Denis. 1983. *The Spoken Word and the Work of Intepretation.* Philadelphia, PA: University of Pennsylvania Press.

Theissen, Gerd. 1995. *The Sign Language of Faith: Opportunities for Preaching Today.* London: SCM Press.

Thiselton, Anthony. 1980. *The Two Horizons.* Grand Rapids, MI: Eerdmans.

Thomas, Richard. 1994. *An Introduction to Church Communication.* Oxford: Lynx Communications.

Thompson, Jeremy. 1996. *Preaching as dialogue: is the sermon a sacred cow?* Cambridge: Grove Books.

Thompson, John B. 1995. *The Media and Modernity: A Social Theory of the Media.* Cambridge: Polity Press.

Thompson, John. 1996. 'Voice Genres: The Case of Televangelical Language', in *The Nature of Religious Language.* Stanley E. Porter, editor. Roehampton Institute, London Papers, 1. Sheffield: Sheffield Academic Press.

Thorn, Richard. 1996. 'Virtual Reality: A Sound Proposition?'. Paper for *Hearing is Believing* conference at University of Sunderland, 2 March.

Tillich, Paul. 1959. *A Theology of Culture.* London and New York, NY: Oxford University Press.

Tillich, Paul. 1998. *Against the Third Reich: Paul Tillich's Wartime Radio Broadcasts into Nazi Germany.* Ronald H. Stone and Matthew L. Weaver, editors. Louisville, KY: Westminster John Knox Press.

Tinsley, John. 1979. 'Communication, or "Tell it Slant"', in *Theology Today* 35/4, 398–404.

Tinsley, John. 1980. 'Tell it Slant', in *Theology* 83, 163–70.

Tisdale, Leonara Tubbs. 1997. *Preaching as Local Theology and Folk Art.* Minneapolis, MN: Fortress Press.

Tolson, Andrew. 1996. *Mediations: Text and Discourse in Media Studies.* London: Edward Arnold.

Torrance, Thomas F. 1994. *Preaching Christ Today: The Gospel and Scientific Thinking.* Grand Rapids, MI: Eerdmans.

Traber, Michael. 1993. 'Changes of Communication – Needs and Rights in Social Revolution', in *Communication and Democracy.* Slavko Splichal and Janet Wasko, editors. Norwood, NJ: Ablex.

Tracy, David. 1981. *The Analogical Imagination: Christian Theology and the Culture of Pluralism.* London: SCM Press.

Tracy, David. 1987. *Plurality and Ambiguity: Hermeneutics, Religion and Hope.* London: SCM Press.

Troeger, Thomas H. 1982. *Creating Fresh Images for Preaching.* Valley Forge, PA: Judson Press.

Troeger, Thomas H. 1990. *Imagining a Sermon.* Nashville, TN: Abingdon Press.

Troeger, Thomas H. 1992. *The Parable of Ten Preachers.* Nashville, TN: Abingdon Press.

Troeger, Thomas H. 1996. *Ten Strategies for Preaching in a Multi-Media Culture.* Nashville, TN: Abingdon Press.

Trollope, Joanna. 1991. *The Rector's Wife.* London: Bloomsbury.

Tugwell, Simon. 1991. *The Way of the Preacher.* London: Darton Longman & Todd.

Tully, Mark. 1996. *An Investigation into the Lives of Jesus: God, Jew, Rebel, The Hidden Jesus.* London: BBC Books.

Turner, Timothy A. 1995. *Preaching to Programmed People: Effective Communication in a Media-Saturated Society.* Grand Rapids, MI: Kregel.

Valle, Carlos A. 1996. 'Communication and Mission', in *Renewing Communication and Mission.* Carlos A. Valle, editor. London: World Association of Christian Communication.

Vanderburg, William H., editor. 1981. *Perspectives on Our Age: Jacques Ellul Speaks on His Life and Work.* New York, NY: Seabury.

Van Seters, Arthur, editor. 1988. *Preaching as a Social Act: Theology and Practice.* Nashville, TN: Abingdon Press.

Vibert, Simon. 1992. 'The Word in an Audio-Visual Age: Can we still preach the Gospel?' in *Churchman* 106/2, 147–58.

Vibert, Simon. 1993. *The Church in the Age of the TV Image: Dare we still preach?* Orthos 12. Northwich, Cheshire: Fellowship of Word and Spirit.

Virilio, Paul. 1994. *The Vision Machine.* London: British Film Institute; Indianapolis, IN: Indiana University Press.

Walker, Andrew. 1996. *Telling the Story: Gospel, Mission and Culture.* London: SPCK.

Wallace, James. 1995. *Imaginal Preaching: An Archetypal Perspective.* New York, NY: Paulist Press.

Walls, Andrew F. 1996. *The Missionary Movement in Christian History: Studies in the Transmission of Faith.* Edinburgh: T & T Clark.

Walsh, Chad. 1979. *The Literary Legacy of C. S. Lewis.* London: Sheldon.

Ward, James, and Christine Ward. 1995. *Preaching From the Prophets.* Nashville, TN: Abingdon Press.

Ward, Ken. 1989. *Mass Communications and the Modern World.* London: Macmillan.

Ward, L. B. 1933. *Father Charles Coughlin.* Detroit, MI: Tower Publications.

Ward, Mark. 1994. *Air of Salvation: The Story of Christian Broadcasting.* Grand Rapids, MI: Baker Book House.

Ward, Richard. 1992. *Speaking from the Heart: Preaching with Passion.* Nashville, TN: Abingdon Press.

Ward, Richard. 1996. 'Beyond Televangelism: Preaching on the Pathway of Ritual Formation', in *Preaching on the Brink: The Future of Homiletics.* Martha J. Simmons, editor. Nashville, TN: Abingdon Press.

Wardlaw, Don M., editor. 1983. *Preaching Biblically.* Philadelphia, PA: Westminster.

Warnock, Mary. 1976. *Imagination.* London: Faber & Faber.

Warren, Michael. 1992. *Communications and Cultural Analysis: A Religious View.* Westport, CT: Bergin & Garvey.

Warren, Michael. 1997. *Seeing Through the Media: A Religious View of Communications and Cultural Analysis.* Harrisburg, PA: Trinity Press International.

Watson, Mary Ann. 1995. 'Seems Radio is Here to Stay', in *Radio: The Forgotten Medium.* Edward C. Pease and Everetter E. Dennis, editors. London: Transaction Publishers.

Waznak, Robert P. 1996. 'Preaching the Gospel in a Video Culture', in *Media, Culture and Catholicism.* Paul Soukup, editor. Kansas City, MO: Sheed & Ward.

Waznak, Robert P. 1998. *An Introduction to the Homily.* Collegeville, MN: Liturgical Press.

Webb, Joseph M. 1998a. *Comedy and Preaching.* St Louis, MO: Chalice Press.

Webb, Joseph M. 1998b. *Preaching and the Challenge of Pluralism.* St Louis, MO: Chalice Press.

Webb, Pauline M. 1988. 'Preaching in the Media', in *Epworth Review* 15/3, 18–21.

Weber, Derek. 1991. *Discerning Images: The Media and Theological Education.* Edinburgh: Centre for Theology and Public Issues.

Weber, Derek. 1993. 'Preaching To Be Heard in a Television Age'. Unpublished PhD Thesis, University of Edinburgh,

Wells, Samuel. 1998. *Transforming Fate into Destiny: The Theological Ethics of Stanley Hauerwas.* Carlisle: Paternoster Press.

Welsby, Paul A. editor. 1970. *Sermons and Society: An Anglican Anthology.* Harmondsworth: Penguin.

Westermann, Claus. 1984 (1974). *Genesis 1–11: A Commentary.* London: SPCK.

White, R. E. O. 1973. *A Guide to Preaching.* London: Pickering and Inglis.

White, Susan. 1998. 'A Story to Live By', in *Transmission,* Spring, 3–4.

Wiersbe, Warren W. 1994. *Preaching and Teaching With Imagination.* Wheaton, IL: Victor Books.

Wilby, Pete, and Andy Conroy. 1994. *The Radio Handbook.* London: Routledge.

Wilder, Amos. 1971 (1964). *Early Christian Rhetoric: The Language of the Gospel.* Cambridge, MA: Harvard University Press.

Wilder, Amos. 1982. *Jesus' Parables and the War of Myths: Essays on Imagination in the Scripture.* Philadelphia, PA: Fortress Press.

Williams, Raymond. 1990 (1975). *Television Technology and Cultural Forms.* Ederyn Williams, editor. London: Routledge.

Williams, W. E. 1941. 'The Critic on the Hearth' in *The Listener* 26, 11 December.

Williams, W. E. 1942. 'The Padre Again', in 'Critic on the Hearth' – Weekly Comments on BBC Programmes by Independent Critics, in *The Listener* 27, 7 May.

Willimon, William H. 1992. *Peculiar Speech: Preaching to the Baptised.* Grand Rapids, MI: Eerdmans.

Willimon, William H. 1994. *The Intrusive Word: Preaching to the Unbaptized.* Grand Rapids, MI: Eerdmans.

Wilson, A. N. 1990. *C. S. Lewis: A Biography.* London: HarperCollins.

Wilson, Paul Scott. 1988. *Imagination of the Heart: New Understandings in Preaching.* Nashville, TN: Abingdon Press.

Wilson, Paul Scott. 1992. *A Concise History of Preaching.* Nashville, TN: Abingdon Press.

Wilson, Paul Scott. 1995. *The Practice of Preaching.* Nashville, TN: Abingdon Press.

Wilson-Kastner, Patricia. 1989. *Imagery for Preaching.* Minneapolis, MN: Fortress Press.

Wimsatt Jr, W. K. 1970 (1954). *The Verbal Icon: Studies in the Meaning of Poetry.* London: Methuen.

Wink, Walter. 1992. *Engaging the Powers, Discernment and Resistance in a World of Domination.* Minneapolis, MN: Fortress Press.

Winter, David, editor. 1988. *The Church of the Air: Celebrating 60 Years of BBC Radio's Daily Service.* London: Marshall Pickering.

Winter, David. 1995. *Seeing Through the Eye: Muggeridge, the Prophet of the Media Age.* Dedicatory Address, Wheaton College, Illinois, 18 November.

Wittgenstein, Ludwig. 1968 (1953). *Philosophical Investigations.* Third Edition. New York, NY: Macmillan.

Wittgenstein, Ludwig. 1980. *Culture and Value.* G. H. von Wright and H. Nyman, editors. Oxford: Basil Blackwell.

Wolf, Herbert M. 1987. 'When "Literal" is not accurate', in *The Making of a Contemporary Translation: New International Version.* Kenneth Baker, editor. London: Hodder & Stoughton.

Wolfe, Kenneth M. 1984. *The Churches and the British Broadcasting Corporation, 1922–1956, The Politics of Broadcast Religion.* London: SCM Press.

Wood, David, editor. 1991. *On Paul Ricoeur: Narrative and Interpretation.* London: Routledge.

Wood, John. 1987. *On Your Radio.* London: Hodder & Stoughton.

Wright, N. T. 1996. *Jesus and the Victory of God.* London: SPCK.

Wright, Ronald Selby. 1942. *The Average Man: Broadcast Addresses by the Radio Padre.* London: Longmans, Green.

Wright, Ronald Selby. 1943a. *Let's Ask the Padre: Some Broadcast Talks.* Second Edition. Edinburgh: Oliver & Boyd.

Wright, Ronald Selby. 1943b. *Greater Victory: Further Broadcast Talks.* London: Longmans, Green.

Wright, Ronald Selby. 1944. *The Padre Presents: Discussions about Life in the Forces.* Edinburgh and London: Melagan & Cumming.

Wright, Ronald Selby. 1970. *Haply I May Remember.* Edinburgh: Blackwood.

Wright, Ronald Selby. 1980. *Another Home.* Edinburgh: Blackwood.

Wuthnow, Robert. 1992. *Rediscovering the Sacred: Perspectives on Religion in Contemporary Society.* Grand Rapids, MI: Eerdmans.

Wuthnow, Robert, and Matthew P. Lawson. 1994. 'Sources of Christian Fundamentalism in the United States', in *Accounting for Fundamentalisms: The Dynamic Character of Movements.*

Martin E. Marty and R. Scott Appleby, editors. Chicago, IL: University of Chicago Press.

Yoder, John Howard. 1984. *The Priestly Kingdom.* Notre Dame, IN: University of Notre Dame Press.

Young, La Monte. 1993. 'Ruminations on Radio', in *Radiotext(e).* Neil Strauss, editor. New York, NY: Semiotext(e).

Zibaini, Mahmoud. 1993. *The Icon: Its Meaning and History.* Collegeville, MN: Liturgical Press.

Private Recorded Interviews (cited) (with Jolyon Mitchell, unless stated)

Rabbi Lionel Blue in Edinburgh, 31 October 1995.

Professor David Buttrick, Vanderbelt Divinity School, Nashville, TN, 29 March 1994.

David Coomes at Broadcasting House, London, 19 December 1996.

Professor Fred Craddock in Atlanta, GA, 1 April 1994.

Pastor Irving Gallimore at WMHV in Hillsville, VA, 24 March 1994.

Rt Revd James Jones in Oxford, 15 June 1997.

J. B. Lineberry at WHHV in Hillsville, VA, 21 March 1994.

Professor Tom Long in Princeton, NJ, 20 March 1994.

George McClintock at WNQM in Nashville, TN, 28 March 1994.

Revd John Newbury in Mexico City, Mexico, 12 October 1995.

Toby Powers at WGMI, Bremen, GA, 5 April 1995.

Craig E. Soaries at WAEC, Atlanta, GA, 6 April 1994.

Curtis Stoops at Max Meadows, VA, 24 March 1994.

Rt Revd Don Taylor in Edinburgh, 20 August 1995.

Dr Gregg Thomas in New Orleans, LA, 9 April 1994.

Angela Tilby in St Albans, 16 July 1996.

Fred Westenberger at WVOG in Metaire, LA, near New Orleans, 10 April 1994.

Revd Canon David Winter at Christchurch College in Oxford, 14 September 1995.

Revd R. S. Wright with Rev. David G. Coulter, in Edinburgh, 28 October 1993.

Rev. R. S. Wright interviewed by member of the Imperial War Museum staff, date unknown.

Newspaper and Magazine Articles (Chronological Order)

W. E. Williams, in 'Critic on the Hearth – Weekly Comments on BBC Programmes by Independent Critics', in *The Listener* 26, 11 December 1941.

J. W. Welch, 'A Day of Challenge', in *The Listener* 27, 8 January 1942. no. 678.

W. E. Williams, in 'Critic on the Hearth – Weekly Comments on BBC Programmes by Independent Critics', in *The Listener* 27, 7 May 1942.

Henry R. Luce, editor, 'Don–Devil' Cover Story in *Time,* 8 September 1947, 27–9.

Jim Pennington, 'Christian Radio: Breaking Out of the Gospel Ghetto', in *Christianity Today,* 29 June 1979.

Mark Noll, in *Christianity Today,* 1987, 22–3.

Gayle White, 'The Protestant Hour – Long-running radio ministry broadcast nears 50th anniversary' in the *Atlanta Journal/Atlanta Constitution,* 1993, E8.

Stephen Ward, 'Preachers decide time is right to cut back on tradition', in *The Independent,* 3 May 1994.

John Kennedy, 'Mixing Politics and Piety', in *Christianity Today* 38/9, 15 August 1994.

Maggie Brown, 'Warning: your wireless is exploding', in *The Independent,* 19 January 1995.

Andrew Grimes, 'Radio News', in the *Manchester Evening News,* 11 February 1995.

James Fenton, 'Thought for the day: dispense with bishops', in *The Independent,* 13 March 1995.

Alexandra Faith, 'Radio 4 "God slot" to keep the faith', in *The Times,* 14 April 1995. In Brief Section: 'BBC keeps faith with listeners', in the *Daily Telegraph,* 14 April 1995.

Andrew Culf, 'Radio slot closed to atheists', in *The Guardian*, 14 April 1995.

Adam Luck, 'Radio God Slot ban on atheists', in the *Daily Express*, 15 April 1995.

Polly Toynbee, 'From Where I Stand', in *The Independent*, Section 2. 25 July 1995.

Tom Gardiner, on 'Songs in Space' in the *Church Times*' radio review, 29 September 1995.

Diana Pulson,' "God Slot" Rabbi's Revelation', in the *Liverpool Echo*, 7 October 1995. 'Radio Four's Thought for the Day was under attack yesterday for handing a platform to the Hare Krishna religious sect', in the *Daily Mail*, 12 June 1996.

Paul Donovan, 'No more holy than thou', *The Times* Radio Waves Column, 14 July 1996.

David Hughes, 'Thought for the Day: Don't let Lefties lecture', in the *Daily Mail*, 28 August 1996.

Polly Toynbee, 'Give us hellfire, not opiate, in the God slot', in *The Independent*, 14 October 1996.

Patricia Williams cited by Anne Karpf in 'Fighting Talk', in *The Guardian*, G2 5, 23 January 1997.

Anne Karpf, 'Spoonface stirs it up', in *The Guardian*, G2, 19 February 1997.

Mark Tran, 'Loneliness of Virtual Living', in *The Guardian*, 31 August 1998.

Radio Programmes, Scripts and Talking Books

Buse, Mellie, producer. *The Diary of a Young Girl: Anne Frank.* The Definitive Edition Read by Sophie Thompson. Harmondsworth: Penguin, 1997.

Blue, Lionel. *Thought for the Day.* BBC Radio 4, 14 September 1987, 30 January 1989, 6 March 1989. (See also cassette produced by J. Newbury cited below.)

Cooke, Alistair. 1996. 'Now Here is the Nightly News', in *Letter From America 2.* London: BBC Worldwide. Heather MacLean, producer.

Coomes, David, producer. *The Moral Maze.* Chaired by Michael Buerk. BBC Radio 4, 1 May 1997.

Corwin, Norman. 1939. 'Seems Radio is Here to Stay'. CBS.

Garner, Winnifred. Recorded sermon for WGMI, Bremen, Georgia, 1994.

Grant, Tony, producer. *Fergal Keane: Letter to Daniel – Despatches from the Heart.* London: BBC, 1997.

Handy, Charles. 1998. *Thoughts for Today.* London: Random House, Audio Books.

Jones, James. *Thought for the Day.* BBC Radio 4, 16, 22, 29 August, 1996; 29 November, 6, 13, 20 December 1996; 17, 24 February, 3 March, 1997.

Lewis, C. S. *Right or Wrong: A Clue to the Meaning of the Universe: Materialism or Religion?* BBC Archives, Caversham, 921/Lewis Scripts, 20 August 1941.

Lewis, C. S. *Four Talks on Love: Storge, Philia, Eros, Agape.* First Edition. The Parish of the Air, The Episcopal Radio-TV Foundation, Atlanta, Georgia, 1970.

McLean, Heather, producer. *Alistair Cooke: Letter from America 2. The Middle Years: The 1970s.* London: BBC Worldwide, 1996.

McGee, J. Vernon. *Thru the Bible.* Isaiah 1:4–18, broadcast on WBGW, 24 March 1994.

McKay, Johnston, producer. *The Radio Padre.* Presented by Stewart Lamont. BBC Radio 4, Remembrance Sunday 1993.

Mitchell, Jolyon, producer. *Garrison Keillor's Radio Preachers.* Presented by Garrison Keillor. BBC Radio 4, 10 August 1994.

Murrow, Edward R. *News Talk: Buchenwald.* BBC Archives, Caversham, 15 April 1945. See also: Edward R. Murrow, 'Broadcast from Buchenwald', in *Radiotext(e).* Neill Strauss, editor. New York, NY: Semiotext(e), 1993, 152–4.

Newbury, John, producer. *Rabbi Lionel Blue: 50 Thoughts for the Day.* London: BBC Radio Collection, 1990.

Rowland, Kate, producer. *Spoonface Steinberg.* Written by Lee Hall, BBC Radio 4, 27 January 1997.

Soaries, Craig E. 'Political Incorrectness', a radio message for Love WAEC AM 86, Atlanta, Georgia, 3 April 1994.

Starkey, David. *Moral Maze.* BBC Radio 4, 1 May 1997.

Stoops, Curtis. Untitled sermon, recorded Max Meadows, Virginia, 9 December 1993.

Tilby, Angela. *Thought for the Day.* BBC Radio 4, 18 September 1995, 4 March 1996, 13, 20, 27 May 1996, 1, 9, 16 July 1996.

Thomas, Gregg. 'Jesus will use you to bring forth miracles', sermon used for broadcast on WSHO, on tape from the Christian Faith Temple Family Worship Centre, New Orleans, 20 February 1994.

Winter, Norman, producer. *The Jesus Diary.* Written and presented by Angela Tilby. Radio 3, 2–6 December 1996.

Winter, David. *Thought for the Day.* BBC Radio 4, 4 March 1995, 6 April 1996, 12 August 1995, 13 April 1996, 21, 28 May 1996, 3 June 1996.

Welles, Orson. *The War of the Worlds.* The Mercury Theatre on the Air, 30 October 1938.

Films, Videos, CDs and TV Programmes

Allen, Woody, director. *Radio Days.* Orion Pictures. 1987.

Allen, Woody, director. *Bullets Over Broadway.* Miramax Films. 1994.

American Bible Society. *A Father and Two Sons.* 1995.

BFI. *Early Cinema, Primitives and Pioneers.* London: British Film Institute, Volumes I and II, 1895–1906.

The Buggles. *Video Killed the Radio Star.* New York: Island Records. 1981.

Cameron, James, director. *Titanic.* 20th Century Fox and Paramount Pictures. 1997.

Duvall, Robert, director. *The Apostle.* Butchers Run Films. 1997.

Gibson, Mel, director. *Braveheart.* 20th Century Fox and Paramount Pictures. 1995.

Graham-Dixon, Andrew, presenter and writer, *The History of British Art.* BBC 2. 19 May 1996.

Higham, Nick, presenter. *The Technophobe's Guide to the Future.* London: BBC 2. 7 May 1996.

Kennedy, Ludovic. *Richard Dimbleby: Voice of the Nation.* London: BBC Videos. 1990.

Lucas, George, director. *Star Wars: Episode 1 – The Phantom Menace.* Lucasfilm Ltd and 20th Century Fox. 1999.

Lumiere Brothers. *La Sortie des Ouvriers de l'Usine Lumière.* 1895.

Madonna. *Papa Don't Preach,* from *The Immaculate Collection.* Music Video, Warner Music Vision. 1990.

Madonna. *Swim*, from *Ray of Light*. CD, Warner Bros Records Inc. 1998.

Mann, Chris, producer. *Heart of the Matter*. London: BBC 1. 8 April 1996. Presented by Joan Bakewell.

Roberts, Michael, producer. *Everyman: Vote, Vote, Vote for the Almighty*. London: BBC 1. 27 October 1996.

Spielberg, Steven, director. *Jurassic Park*. Universal Pictures. 1993.

Stern, Howard, director. *Private Parts*. Paramount Pictures. 1997.

Tilby, Angela, series producer. *Lives of Jesus*. Presented by Mark Tully. BBC 1, 4 Sundays in December 1996.

Wachowski, Andy and Wachowski, Larry, directors. *The Matrix*. Warner Brothers. 1999.

Weir, Peter, director. 1998. *The Truman Show*. Paramount Pictures.

Zinnemann, Fred, director. *High Noon*. United Artists. 1952.

Unpublished Reports, Diaries, Letters and Lectures

Central Religious Advisory Committee (CRAC), *Religious Broadcasting: History and Current Practice, 1943*. Unpublished report held at BBC Archives, Caversham, R34/814/2 – Religious Broadcasting in Wartime 1941–44, File, 1a, n. 73.

Fenn, Eric. Letter to Professor C. S. Lewis, 29 December 1943, BBC Archives, Caversham, 910/Talks File 1a, 1941–43.

Harries, Richard. Letter to Jolyon Mitchell, 18 August 1998.

Morris, Colin. Letter to Jolyon Mitchell, 25 August 1998.

Reynolds, Gillian. 'Opportunities and Responsibilities'. Lecture at the Local Broadcasting Conference, Swanwick, 20–22 June 1994.

Tilby, Angela. Letter to Jolyon Mitchell, 10 April 1997.

Wright, Ronald Selby. *The Radio Padre, 1941–1943, Report*. Unpublished document from BBC Archives, Caversham, Talks File/G, from RCONT/1B 1943–49.

Wright, Ronald Selby. *Personal Journal/Diary*. National Library, Edinburgh: Unpublished, 1942, from R. S. Wright Archives.

Index